Growth and Change in the Future City Region

GROWTH AND CHANGE IN THE FUTURE CITY REGION

edited by
TOM HANCOCK

Contributors
John Boynton
Maurice Ash
Gordon E. Cherry
John Davoll
Marcial Echenique
Tony Eddison
David Eversley
Tom Hancock
David Lock
W.F. Luttrell
Peter Self
Murray Stewart
Ronald White

Leonard Hill

Published by Leonard Hill a division of International Textbook Company Limited
450 Edgware Road, London W2 1EG
a member of the Blackie Group

© International Textbook Company Limited 1976

First published 1976
ISBN 249 44148 9

Printed in Great Britain by
Robert MacLehose and Company Limited, Printers to the University of Glasgow

Photo Typesetting by Print Origination, Merseyside L20 6NS

Foreword

Lord Esher

I have been fortunate enough in my work on urban problems to visit many countries and meet colleagues struggling to understand and master the urban explosion. The crisis is of course worldwide, and there has never been a greater need for the exchange of ideas and techniques. It seemed to me that planners in every country ought to make their experience freely available—their failures as well as their successes. So I was delighted when the British Council decided last year to organise an international symposium for this purpose. The papers given form the basis of this important book. One theme runs through them all: that we move from 'systems' intellectually conceived to human need established by genuine participation—an infinitely more arduous exercise in which we are all of us mere beginners, but the only firm foundation on which to build.

Acknowledgements

To The British Council which organized the original course and in particular Pat Lighthill, Ken Monro, Helen Meixner, Jean Wheeler, Audrey Gennens and Yvette Billingham in London and Bill Charlton and John Allen in Bristol; to John Haddon, Newton Park College, Bath who so kindly showed that city to our visitors; to the Director of the Royal Institution of Great Britain and his staff; to the Director, Secretary and staff, of the School for Advanced Urban Studies, University of Bristol, my thanks. I am grateful to Lord Esher; he first suggested the symposium and gave inestimable help in the formulation of the content of it.

My own staff took over from me much of my normal work so that I could undertake the tasks of directing the symposium and, later, editing this book. To them, and in particular Liza Girling and Mary Rossetti, my thanks.

Tom Hancock

The publishers would like to thank Peterborough Development Corporation for permission to use the photographs on pages 16, 160, 192, and Jim Doveton on page 74.

CONTENTS

BIOGRAPHICAL NOTES

MAURICE ASH is the Chairman of the Executive Committee of the
Town and Country Planning Association; Chairman of the
Dartington Hall Trust; former member of the Economic Planning Council for the South-West Region; author of several
books on planning and a contributor to various journals on
planning, education and international relations.

JOHN BOYNTON is now the Chief Executive of Cheshire County
Council, after a continuous career in Local Government. He is
Senior Vice President of the Royal Town Planning Institute
and a member of the Planning Law Committee of the Law
Society. He was, until 1975, a member of the Economic Plan-
ning Council for the North West, and is a member of the
Council of the Centre for Studies in Social Policy, and of the
Industrial Society.

GORDON CHERRY is Professor of Urban and Regional Planning at the
Centre for Urban and Regional Studies (where he is Deputy
Director) at the University of Birmingham. Previously he was
Research Officer at Newcastle upon Tyne and has spent several
years with other Local Planning Authorities. He is the author
of several well known planning books.

JOHN DAVOLL is the Director of the Conservation Society, and previously a founder-member and Chairman. Early in his career he was at the Sloan-Kettering Institute for Cancer Research in New York and then in the Chemical Research Department of Parke, Davis & Co.

MARCIAL ECHENIQUE is presently Director of the Martin Centre for Architectural and Urban Studies at the University of Cambridge. He worked in practices in Spain, Chile and the U.K. before being appointed Senior Research Officer in 1967 at the Centre for Land Use and Built Form Studies at the University of Cambridge. He has contributed articles to many publications both in the U.K. and abroad.

TONY EDDISON is Professor of Urban Policy Studies and Director of the School for Advanced Urban Studies at the University of Bristol. Previously he was Senior Lecturer and Assistant Director of the Institute of Local Government Studies, University of Birmingham. He has written extensively for planning journals, and is the author of several books on corporate planning.

DAVID EVERSLEY is a teacher and research worker at the Centre for Environmental Studies, London. He was previously Chief Strategic Planner of the Greater London Council. He is Chairman of the Regional Studies Association. He has written extensively in journals on history, demography and planning and is the author of several books on these subjects.

TOM HANCOCK is an architect and consultant planner. He is on the Executive Committee of the Town and Country Planning Association. He was planning adviser to Shelter and a member of the City Poverty Committee. His projects include proposals for the New Town in Mid-Wales and the plan for Greater Peterborough New Town. He is Consultant to the Dartington Trust. He has designed many housing neighbourhoods and clusters.

DAVID LOCK is the Planning Aid Officer of the Town and Country Planning Association. He is a Council member of the Royal Town Planning Institute. He writes extensively on planning theory and practice both in the journals and books.

BILL LUTTRELL is an economist and planning consultant. He is on the Executive of the Town and Country Planning Association and of the Regional Studies Association. Previously he worked for Central Government as a research officer. He was the economic adviser for the Strategic Plan for South-East England. He is the author of many papers and articles on industrial and regional development.

PETER SELF is Professor of Public Administration at the London School of Economics. For several years he was on the editorial staff of the *Economist*. He is a member of the Regional Economic Planning Council for the South East and Vice Chairman of the Executive of the Town and Country Planning Association. He has written extensively on administration, politics and planning.

MURRAY STEWART is Professor of Urban Government and Deputy Director at the School for Advanced Urban Studies at the University of Bristol. Previously he was lecturer in Interdisciplinary Studies at the Centre for Research in the Social Sciences at the University of Kent. He is a former member of the South East Economic Planning Council and was specialist adviser to the House of Commons Expenditure Committee (Environment Sub-Committee) from 1973 to 1975. He has written extensively for journals on planning and economics and is editor of a book on city planning problems.

RONALD WHITE is Assistant Chief Planner at the Department of the Environment. He was a researcher with the Ministry of Town and Country Planning and later was seconded to the Local Government Commission for England. He was responsible for the preparation of the South East Study.

Preface

Urban Growth

The great urban regions of the World are in constant growth and change. Their spreading patterns show remarkable similarities. The initial powerful implosion to the city from the rural hinterlands is followed by the outward thrust of tentacular suburbs and the growth of peripheral towns. Then sprawling random growth infills the web, leaving the protrusions of hills and the meanders of river valleys and estuaries. The concentric rings of growth naturally tend to decay from the centre outwards. Yet it is the centre which still retains the essential metropolitan functions, government, finance and exchange, law, specialized shopping and entertainment. The major transportation routes focus on this centre passing through the inner areas of dereliction, redevelopment schemes, and overcrowded obsolescent housing. But the view from the radial roads and railways is often misleading—beyond the ribbons which grew alongside them are still found elegant city quarters of the more wealthy. The inner city is a collection of precincts each with its own milieu, lived in by particular groups of people. Each has its local economy and culture, as evident in the transient areas as in old-established slow changing quarters. The wider city beyond is not as clearly precinctualized, yet to the inhabitants each sprawling suburb is recognizably distinct. The lesions between the quarters, precincts, areas and suburbs are the old routes, river and stream valleys, woodlands and tracks. The many old villages which have been engulfed by sprawl are still the local foci.

Like speeded up films of plant life the unfolding patterns of the cities are similar. And so are the social and environmental problems within the city regions. There are gross inequities in housing, in transportation, in the proximity and use of green open spaces for leisure and recreation. The poor are found in the decaying areas and experience the worst of the pollution which the intense activity of the urban regions produces. These are problems which governments face everywhere. To them are added the concern to enhance the efficiency and productivity of the region; greater growth can, it is assumed be used to solve the primary problems of poverty and deprivation. Yet it is now clear that in solving the latter—providing new motorways, industrial estates and mass housing—the primary problems are intensified.

As the magnetism of the city is increased the housing shortages get worse and traffic congestion increases. Further clearance and redevelopment at higher densities and new major roads are built with further destruction of many communities in the precincts and quarters of the city. The already deprived are made homeless or retreat to the already overcrowded poor districts which are still left standing. Each attempt to solve the urban problem within the city sends a destructive wave through it.

The magnetism of the growing city region is most intense in the poorest countries, or those with the greatest inequalities of income and status. These are the countries where drastically reduced infant mortality and increased life expectancy has lead to an exploding population. Where the cultural traditions are unassailable, and birth control is unlikely to affect this growth for several generations. By the turn of the century a further 1500 million people will be living in the urban areas of the World, the vast majority in the major city regions.

In the cities of Latin America, Africa and Asia, a large fraction of the people are living as squatters in the favelas, bustees and barong-barongs. Their districts are the derelict lands, the steep hillsides or flood areas left undeveloped. Some become transformed within a generation to permanent respectable settlements of taxpayers, but most will remain at the 'initial stage' of disease and squalor, unless broad policies are strenuously applied to the root problems of rural depopulation and chaotic urban growth. Land reform measures, combined with the encouragement of rural industries and scientifically-based intensive small scale agriculture, are essential. The urban region must be extended so that numerous planned growth points, preferably at the small settlement scale, can be established in a widening network around the parent city. The form of 'social city' will vary from region to region but the concept of it is emerging as a practical necessity rather than a utopian vision; a constellation of towns, new and old, each tending to have a special function. Each in turn structured to readily accept a contiguous web of precincts. The *community cluster* can then grow to take up a particular social structure within these precincts; it may be regarded as the basic module of the social city region.

Community Cluster

Black Road, Macclesfield in England, is a typical long street of obsolete terraced housing, part of a large area undergoing the process of clearance and rebuilding as new mass housing. One small precinct in this street has been completely rehabilitated by the owners and tenants, led by a neighbourhood architect. Using existing housing legislation, and winning the cooperation of Local Government, they created in one year 1973/74 their community cluster; the concept of this basic module is as valid in the old urban areas as in new settlements.

The same principle is applied in the proposals which I made in 1974 for local growth in the rural area of Dartington in Devon; part of the Torquay city region. A group of community clusters is related within walking distance of the parent village, linked by small roads and footpaths, the network defined by lines and thickets of trees. Thus over the present pattern of the landscape, will be constructed a new 'social' landscape; small clusters of houses, self-determined in design by the occupants; each to have a community workshop, craft workshops and an extensive border of gardens for horticulture, sheltered by tree belts. The growth pattern is a natural evolution from the villages of the region (which have experienced so much infill of their open lands and sprawling extensions during the past twenty years).

Expression of this very local scale is found in different parts of the World despite the contrasting cultural backgrounds. In India the small village is still the natural scale of the basic unit of the sprawling cities—'home' refers to a community cluster of close kith and kin. This too is the pattern of the older urbanized areas in Europe where similar strong ties have grown up within a street scale. Even in the places where strenuous individualism and competition underpins the culture, as diverse as the Levittowns of the USA and the favelas of Brazil, the immediate locality is of critical importance. Community and cooperation are born of the proximity of people of similar aspirations. If there are strong cultural or religious distinctions then the community cluster is much less able to crystalize. Adaptation used to follow by the definition of castes or classes. But the placing of such invidious stresses on minorities is no longer tenable as education and social awareness spreads.

In most urban regions social policies and housing programmes are rarely coordinated. The latter is crudely conceived of in terms of product and numbers rather than as a primary means of creating communities and harmony. Such notions as tenants or owners being enabled to design their house or apartment in cooperation with professionals, whilst commonplace for centuries among the wealthy, is still thought of as a radical innovation; and the idea of people deciding their own local, social, planned environment is still anathema to the majority of professional planners.

If such modest ideas, which are so relevant to the historic changes now taking place in the world, do not succeed then the larger organizations of government, industry and finance can continue without hindrance. The large scale organization is geared to cost effectiveness and profit optimization, it is a continuation of exploitive capitalism rather than representative of post-industrial civilization. These organizations increasingly rely on power politics, and in the last analysis, militarism. Their actions are destructive of communities and nature. Much of the structure of the present city region stems from the nature of the technological and technocratic economy.

The people of the future post-industrial civilization will have to be naturally courageous in character and cooperative in enterprise, widely read in natural philosophy and science, applying these to matters of everyday life, able in crafts and the skills needed for survival. The polynucleated city region, composed of numberless community clusters may be the form of city that their ways of life will create. It will be a form of city because the highest levels of education and culture must be attained for reasons of survival.

The present events of the World are demonstrating these opposed directions, but the trends are towards the kind of society I have touched on. The changes in the attitudes to nature and fellow men, the nurturing of community in balance with the ecosphere will lead to consequent changes in the structure of the city region.

It is certain that lateral scientific thought about non-exploitive and community goals can bring about new forms of habitat and cluster, with immense personal and cultural gains.

The opposed direction of technical giantism has provided for a relative few extraordinary levels of personal comfort, but with considerable losses of personal and psychic attainment. The realization of the brutal cost of this limited achievement is spreading and with it a determination to find some more beneficent way of applying science to the predicaments of the World.

The links between the economic structures of nation states, their relative exploitation of natural resources and people, and their urban cultures are so close as to make such apocalyptic reasoning necessary if unusual in a book of this kind.

The emphasis in much of the recent literature on the exploding urban regions of the world is on planned intervention (or amelioration through policies) rather than on social invention and experiment based on keen historical perceptions. To these cautious intervenors the tenuous connections which I have drawn between Black Road and the future of the world's cities will be unreal. It is comical to think of the dour people of Macclesfield in the forefront of present cultural change. But remember how unrespectable it was 10 years ago to suggest that the vast squatter communities of the Third World might be a pattern for the majority of future mankind, whereas now they are the 'spontaneous' communities of 'self-help', which hold lessons for the most technically advanced cities.

Those working in planning and policy-making have a heavy responsibility to the future which can best be discharged by ensuring that the social and physical structure of the city region is open, easily accepting pluralisms; that new patterns relating home and work in small communities are encouraged.

The various contributions to this book, made by practising consultants and planners, academics and government officials, build up a composite model of evolution of the social city region. Many aspects are discussed but in the space of the discussion many left unexplored.

The aim has been to study the subject from the people end rather than in the more usual way of studying their support services and urban needs as elements; housing; traffic and transportation; open space; conservation and so on. That these elements are generally absent from this text signals a changed response to the urban problem.

It is encouraging that my colleagues are unanimous in their efforts to relate their particular area of study (or practice) to the lives of the people of the city region. In composite form the book presents an overview of the social structure and the economic geographhy, which together are the cultural as well as the spatial determinates.

The view of the processes of government and policy making points towards the need for a reversal of the governmental trends of the recent past; a much greater representation of the local people in the making of policy. An active acceptance of spontaneous innovation and self help is a necessary part of our further growth as individuals and communities.

The symposium on which this book is based was held under the auspices of The British Council in the late spring of 1975. The previous year Lord Esher had discussed with me the setting up of a forum where international discussion and exchange of ideas on the city region could take place. This in turn led to the series of lectures and discussions which I directed being held in London and Bristol. These were attended by senior administrators and planners from many countries in several regions of the world; Africa, Asia, Latin America, Australasia, South East Asia and Europe. My aim was to give a balanced presentation of present theory and practice in Britain. In this I was greatly helped by Lord Esher who kindly acted as consultant. The lectures were given by distinguished speakers from academic and official backgrounds—they are, in the main, the authors of the chapters of this book. I would like, however, to thank those who contributed to the original symposium but were not able, because of other commitments, to contribute to the book. They have been generous in allowing their contributions to be freely available to the other authors and to myself as the editor. Murray Stewart undertook to write Chapter 6: *The People of the City Region,* drawing freely on Ray Pahl's symposium contribution. Similarly I have used the contribution of Peter Hall in preparing Chapter 1: *The City Region and the Changing Basis of Planning* and of George Clark and Chris Holmes in Chapters 7: *The Inner City* and 8: *An Urban Programme.* This book is about the British experience of city regions and their planning from the diverse standpoints of the contributors. There are advantages in relating our specific experience to a wider context. The advantages firstly are to widen the debate about the relevance of our highly advanced planning legislation to conditions in other World regions; secondly to study parallels in city regional patterns at different stages of development; and thirdly to examine the possible application of the British endeavours in analytical method.

The book can be divided into four parts. After the introductory Chapter it continues in Part One with an outline by Ronald White of current trends and a historical review of the population distribution in Great Britain, examining the social and economic reasons for migration. The discussion of urban growth and dispersal including the role of planned dispersal leads to Chapter 2 where Peter Self reasons that improved structuring of the large and growing urban regions is necessary to provide a better way of life for all their citizens. In Chapter 4 Gordon Cherry examines the post-war planning policies and the management of urban change, reviewing the results and highlighting the plight of the inner city.

Having set the background of the city regional structure Part Two concentrates on the people and the social structure. The need to change attitudes to the various problems—not least in articulating responses to environmental change is discussed. In Chapter 5 Murray Stewart describes the various broad groups and their interaction, relating their changing life styles. In Chapter 6 I outline the way in which the dispersal of the city creates relative deprivation in the old centre, and how this is often worsened rather than improved by planning strategies. I go on in Chapter 7 to examine how these deep residual problems are being approached by the social and meagre fiscal policies of the Urban Programme rather than by relieving the pressures caused by the structural changes of the past 30 years. The conclusion that the micro-scale structure is an essential political component in planning is naturally followed by Chapter 8 where Tony Eddison looks at the developments in British Local Authorities since the end of the Second World War, including the recent reform of Local Government. He then studies the new approaches to urban governance and discusses the latest ideas on policy formulation with their implications for inter-governmental relations. In the last chapter of Part Two the evolution of Local Government is described by John Boynton. He then extends the study into some examples of city regional and regional authorities in Britain and in other countries. Finally he evaluates the achievements of the reorganized local government and discusses the possibility of regional authorities.

Part Three, the shortest part of the book, consists of two chapters. The first is an analysis of industrial location in the city region by William Luttrell. In it he considers the types of industry; services as well as manufacturing and the scales of city regions from 15 million population in size (London) to 250,000 (Cambridge, Norwich). Current trends are examined drawing on British evidence and these are explained in terms of the natural preferences for location and as affected by government policies including planning controls and transportation investment. The social advantages and disadvantages of these current trends are outlined.

In Chapter 12 Marcial Echenique describes, through a basic Lowry type model, the changes in form which result from changes in the economic base of the city region. The resulting picture, frame by frame, clearly shows the dynamic patterns of initial implosion to the centre followed by outward sprawl. The effects of planning controls to guide development and the likely urban patterns which result are discussed.

Part Four is a compilation of views of the future patterns of life and activity in the city regions. It commences with an essay by David Lock on the continued relevance of the social city concept of Ebenezer Howard, in which a future New Towns programme in the old central city as well as in the new growth areas is put forward.

Chapter 13 is in the form of two divergent views of the future. Maurice Ash approaches the city region in a philosophical vein and concludes that personal and local attitudes will largely determine our future way of life. John Davoll studies 'futurism' itself commenting that narrowly based projections of current trends generate complacency—the root problems of pollution and misuse of resources are forgotten.

In contrast the final Chapter by David Eversley describes the evolution of the planning profession. He sets out the important changes of recent years including the regional scale, the essential involvement of citizen groups and the involvement of land use/transportation planning with social and economic problems. The unforeseen role of the planner as a principal allocator of scarce resources is discussed. The book ends with the need for planning education to be towards corporate management concerned with social policy rather than with technical solutions to existing problems of city structure.

Tom Hancock
1976

CHAPTER ONE

The City Region and the Changing Basis of Planning

Tom Hancock

The City Region concept

The concepts of city which are commonly held are geographical and historical in origin. The notion that a 'city' is any place with a cathedral still persists among children. We still refer to 'the walled city' and in the case of the English capital to 'the City of London'— the old walled district containing the Tower of London and St. Paul's Cathedral; an area which is now largely the uninhabited central financial district of the metropolis.

Commonly, however, the confusion persists because of the way in which we think of places as being made specific by their very names. The image of the old centre symbolizes the name. Thus, among English cities, the smaller market centres like Worcester, Chester, Cambridge and Salisbury are more obviously cities in the common mind than the larger, more amorphous industrial centres which are still just recognizably isolated cities, for example Leicester, Nottingham and Leeds.

The most powerful image of the city is of the regional service centre or *capital*; such as Exeter, Bristol or Norwich. These cities are thought of as *thriving*, as centres of *culture*, and each has a memorable historic centre. Each has the old professional services— solicitors, banking, agents and brokers—which are linked to the rural wealth of its hinterland. They have a discreet order and steadiness supporting a culture which is *in imagery* very widely admired. Much of the symbolism of consumer advertising, for instance, reflects the assumed life-style of these cities. They are the larger jewels on the tourist routes; the places where the big hotels are and where some city life can be experienced. Thus days spent in the Cotswolds are ended in Bristol and after the Bronte country in York.

Commonly too the geographers' early idea of city region is exemplified by these regional capitals. Though each has spreading suburbs these have defined limits. Beyond those limits is the green countryside, the matrix in which this city of the imagination is placed. And the notion persists that it is the landed gentry and the farming communities of this agricultural (and super cultural) hinterland who create the central activities, the exchanges and markets, the shopping centres and universities of these idealized cities.

Now it is clear that such a view is perhaps entirely wrong. The regional capitals do retain much of their regional marketing functions but the major changes of the past 30 years are in the very economy of these places. In Norwich, perhaps *the* exemplar of the regional capital, much new office employment has located precisely *because* of the unique image of the city. The process of expansion there has emphasized other changes which are occurring—the enormous spread of car-borne commuters to the surrounding villages and small towns of the sub-region and the massive increase in car traffic which this entails for the old centre. The old centre, having changed itself to an office employment area rather than a purely professional and residential one, is now, like many of the regional capitals, no longer the dominant place of residence for the influential and wealthy.

The other hidden aspect is shopping. The multiples and superstores required larger shops with mass parking provision, and space for delivery services from large articulated vehicles. The orthodoxies of post-war planning insisted that in the interests of the *life* of these cities this new shopping pattern should be carved out in their old, medieval centres. Further traffic chaos has resulted with consequent destruction of much of the old structure. In some cities, notably Norwich, pedestrian shopping streets have proved to be a great success, but only after traffic congestion had become ludicrous, with giant vehicles attempting to negotiate medieval lanes.

The central identity of these regional cities has entirely changed. A bird's eye view will now show a major ring road completely surrounding the centre, with carparks on cleared land

and on the old cattle market. Within the ring road are major areas of redevelopment with multiple stores, large supermarkets and office buildings contrasting with the ancient streets and alleys of the remaining old city. Here and there are the green spaces of the old churchyards. To one side is the great cathedral and its precincts. Beyond, after the inner ring of poorer housing now sliced through by the road system, begin the suburbs—avenues and schools' playing fields which fade into the Green Belt. But then there is a 'hidden city' beyond, in the green hinterland.

This was revealed to me some years ago when I successfully led an appeal against Berkshire's refusal to allow the development of a community within the village of Blewbury, just in the northern lee of the Downs. (This community consists of a group of small houses for old, and some young, people and is centred on Dibleys, a nice yeoman house in the village.) It was adduced by Berkshire that not only was my design out of character but that the social and employment structure of the old village still consisted of a balance of rural skills and trades which would be disturbed by this project. From the survey which was carried out to find out if this latter were true (the former being a matter of opinion rather than fact) it emerged that a high percentage of the 'villagers' were employed in Oxford or Reading and in occupations far removed from the smithy or the mill. Since the 1960s these changes in the hinterland have been almost total. The pattern of life in the countryside, even among the relatively small proportion of farm workers, is no longer centred on village trades. These people use the regional shopping centres which the old capitals now represent. The traditional social organization of the villages, the pub, the WI and the cricket teams, now include quantity surveyors, young business and industrial executives and their wives.

In a sense, too, the overlap of images of these regional capitals has created a greater impetus to continued growth. The traditions, the apparent peaceableness, the good solid quality of the place, and its rural matrix are highly attractive. The opportunity to find a desirable residence, good suburban schools and the possibility of meeting similar people while enjoying similar leisure pastimes have been among the reasons why 'younger' industries, particularly in the 'quarternary sector' have moved into these 'honeypot' cities. Cambridge has its constellation of new electronic and scientific plants. Around Oxford are found major research institutions: Harwell, Culham and Wallingford.

But the process is seen at its most dynamic at Southampton/Portsmouth. On this littoral, looking over the Solent and backed by the New Forest many new industries and research companies have located. In doing so over the last 20 years the contained solid structure of two major cities of the sub-region has been completely changed. The highly mobile and affluent people of the outer area are enjoying a small, many-centred 'city region', a place of many foci. These are not necessarily urban. However the Forest and the marinas of the Hamble, the hypermarkets and small town centres, and the hotels and motels of the area do add up to a new urban structure.

Thus it is of some historical interest to look at the Buchanan Plan of 1966 (1.1) for the urbanizing littoral; a plan which attempted to place this sporadic growth within a directional grid of roads, based on a clear hierarchy of routes. The concept was based on the theories which had been evolved shortly before in the U.S.A. by Foley, Webber and others (1.2). The notion was that urban activities will naturally locate according to access/cost balance, and in so doing will create a balanced plan; balanced in the sense of achieving optimization of accessibility to the served populations.

The particular qualities of the villages and towns within this city region was apparently unrecognized—they are desirable because of their individual identities. The people of these old places, now converted into new residential districts, and employment areas, could not accept an abstract 'grid'.

The Buchanan Plan for Solent City was not adopted. Following the 1968 Town and County Planning Act the County Council started to prepare a Structure Plan for South Hampshire. This plan accepts further growth on the basis of the existing pattern of the sub-region. The economic reality and the social facts of life both indicate that the whole area is now a polynucleated city region. But the Structure Plan shows that this form of great urban complexity need not change the physical pattern out of recognition. Whether the Plan can cope with the multiplicity of cross country journeys by car which will result from the attempt to retain the present pattern virtually intact remains to be seen.

The industrial conurbation

Places which, from the historical viewpoint, are much more difficult to recognize as cities are the great industrial conurbations of the nineteenth century. It is clear that, speaking of Leeds and Manchester, the condensed cluster of towns forming the conurbation is intended. 'Manchester' includes places as distinct as Salford, Stockport and Oldham. However to the inhabitants of these each is still understood as a distinct town. This is particularly so in the Potteries where the famous 'Five Towns' (Tunstall, Burslem, Hanley, Fenton and Longton) are places of specific identiy. Yet to the stranger each is identical in structure and appearance and indistinguishable from the whole urban area which makes up the Potteries.

If we consider the total area which is involved in the economy and social structure of Manchester it clearly extends beyond the conurbation. The city region of Manchester in these terms overlaps with that of Liverpool on the Wigan/Warrington/Crewe axis. Though defined to the east by the great spine of the Pennines, the building of the M62 motorway link to the Leeds city region has already weakened this easterly isolation and is leading to growing economic linkages and thus to a greater conjunction of the three city regions which together make up the west/east axis: Liverpool, Manchester and Leeds.

To apply the earlier description of the *idealized* isolate city region to this cluster requires the inclusion of the recreational hinterlands which are readily available for day and weekend use to the millions of people in their urban areas. Four great National Parks would be included: at the very doorstep of Manchester the Peak District; to the west of Liverpool the Snowdonia National Park; To the north the Yorkshire Dales and the Lake District beyond.

The higher income, more mobile group from Manchester have for a very long time (certainly since the 1920s and the use of reliable motor cars) opted to live beyond the built-up areas. Initially in isolates and villages, toward the major recreational areas, but increasingly since the 1950s they have located in the great plain of Cheshire and northwards along the littoral of the Fylde peninsula, in the small towns and villages around Preston and on the western fringe of the Forest of Bowland. This has been partially due to the total constraint on development in areas of great natural beauty (including, of course, the National Parks) which have been carefully guarded by the respective County Planning Authorities. Additionally, however, there has been a distinct effort for people to locate their residence where a balance is achieved of three related factors: promixity of good shopping and education; easy access to the regional road and rail networks; and surroundings which are 'rural' and green.

The operation of the planning system has enabled very large numbers of people who are only relatively affluent—including many blue collar workers—to move out of the old urban areas into these new exurban and small town environments. But in doing so they have not left the Manchester city region; their economy and society are very much part of it. Therefore the definition, as in the smaller Southampton/Ports mouth example, must be extended to include the greater part of Lancashire and the whole of northern Cheshire. Stretching the net to include the west-east city regional cluster described earlier the scale becomes that of megalopolis (1.3). However the roots of this word, as the earlier 'conurbation', refer to coalescent urban fabric and are perjorative.

This huge scale poses several dilemmas. The first is the boundaries of governance. The Local Government reform which came out of the Redcliffe-Maud Commission changed the boundaries, but did not tackle the problem of city regional scale (1.4). From 1974 six 'Metropolitan Counties' (somewhat on the pattern of the 1965 Greater London Council) were established which, whilst incorporating the conurbations of Liverpool (Merseyside) Manchester (South East Lancashire and North-East Cheshire), Birmingham (the West Midlands), Leeds (West Yorkshire) Sheffield (South Yorkshire) and Newcastle (Tyne and Wear), by no means reflected the city regions as defined above. Elsewhere modifications and some amalgamations were made to County boundaries and the great number of Rural and Urban District Authorities was reduced from 1397 to 456 (see Chapter 9). The possibility of relating the reforms to the city region reality was missed.

Since that time the regionalist faction, which has growing political support, has been joined by many of those who wish to see regional government approximating to the city region clusters; it will be the nearest equivalent to defined city region government that we are likely to see in this century.

A further dilemma is the appropriate scale of local governance. It is commonly held now that the Districts which compose the Counties or Metropolitan Counties are too large to meet the growing needs for grass roots contact, yet not large enough to provide with economy the level of services which are demanded. Although the numerical size is much greater (in some cases 25,000 people) than in the previous rural and urban districts there is already a new vigour in Local Government at this level (see Chapter 6).

But a lower level of representation is becoming a necessity. This is proxied at the present time by the hundreds of local civic and amenity societies and the action groups which have sprung up all over the country. Usually they are middle class in origin, bent on preserving their local environment. However, in many cases they are concerned with the inequities which are resulting from changes in the older urban areas—the plight of the homeless and the poor. At the very local (or grass roots) level people are becoming more aware and politicized. The myriad endeavours in community action are discernibly changing policies at District and County level. It is essential that the Neighbourhood Council is brought into being soon so that there is a representative elected body at this level. These Councils should be largely voluntary. Their professionals, acting at the levels of the general practitioner in medicine, could be of great benefit to most neighbourhoods, particularly in the social services, in education and in urban change (including in this housing policies, and traffic management). It is the grass roots reaction which has stopped so much of the old style plans and policies of Government, and it is the same source which can enable a better social and urban environment to be created, and at least cost.

The evident need for detailed knowledge of the many neighbourhoods which make up a district could readily be met by the annual Community Review. This has been discussed since the Sunderland study was published (1.5). The authors of that study envisaged the District itself undertaking this overview of its problems, but how much better it would be if each Neighbourhood Council had the responsibility for making its own Community Review and for communicating the results to the District in an agreed form. Given this lower level of governance the new Districts can be highly successful.

It is at the higher level of County and Metropolitan County that there are graver doubts. Their planning powers are diminished. The Districts, as the *planning control* authorities, have now taken over the realities of planning which, as this book will help to demonstrate, lies in the many thousands of small decisions which are taken as much as in the great *strategic* decisions about New Towns, motorways and so on. And the role of Districts will be further strengthened by their necessary cooperation with County Councils in the operation of the Community Land Act.

The County Councils are unlikely to be changed again for some considerable time. If they were dissolved city regional government would be needed to replace them. There would have to be an elected council which would decide with Central Government the larger problems of the region—water supply, economic growth and the conservation of the countryside. The dozens of districts which make up the city regions would need a focus for debate and decision making. Each city region would need an executive and a highly skilled cadre of professionals. The city regional government which would result would be *de facto* the best basic unit of regional government, guarding the interests of the vast majority of us who live in the urban areas, and *at the same time* having a careful regard to the rural hinterland which will continue to supply our water and much of our food.

A third dilemma is that of inter-regional relationships. City regional government would naturally overcome many of the conflicts which occurred prior to the Royal Commission. These arise as we have seen because the scale of the society and economy of the city region has overtaken the old and new boundaries. And it is for Central Government to hold the arena so far as conflicting demands for resource allocation between the city regions (and the rural regions) is concerned.

The changing basis of planning

It is some 15 years since urban activity systems have been subjected to any deep analysis. And only in the past 10 years has there been a widespread consciousness of the social and economic results of urban growth and change.

The great plans made during the 1939-45 war were premised on essentially simple ideas which derive from an unlikely combination of utopian vision and sanitary preoccupations. This is not a reference to the broad political realism of Barlow (1.6) and Uthwatt (1.7) concerning the need to achieve a more equitable division of resources between the growth areas and the old, suffering industrial conurbations of the North and Wales, or the achievement of a system which could levy the financial gains given to land owners as a result of actions by the community in constraining or encouraging urban growth and change. The ideas referred to here are those concerning the nature of planning. Thus we find the Greater London Plan of 1944, premised on a declining regional population without majority car ownership, is based upon the decentralization of the central urban area (so that urban renewal could take place) and the voluntary direction of the resultant overspill to a ring of satellite New Towns beyond a Green Belt (which would, and has, effectively contained any further growth of pre-war London).

Thus a great *pattern* was defined rather in the manner of an architect devising a balanced plan to be executed over a finite period. Planning as pattern making was embodied in the 1947 Act which required each county to prepare a Development Plan. These Plans, on an accurate Ordnance Survey map base, were to indicate by notation exactly what was to happen to all land within the area and up to the early sixties the Development Plans were followed closely or loosely, but by then it was pragmatically clear that the pressures for development were so great that the Plans were no longer being followed. A whole series of *ad hoc* patterns were produced as policy guides. These often took the form of envelope designations of towns and villages allowing a great deal of 'infill' to take place in the areas which had been generally unannotated—White Land. And it was clear enough by the mid-sixties that the results of myriad decisions (for what were generally small scale residential developments) had eroded the meaning of the Development Plans. It was clear too that the results of 'planning' on communities and individuals had been largely unforeseen. Rural villages and towns had burgeoned with new housing estates full of city people from beyond the Green Belt. Traffic had enormously increased to flood the old roads and the major radials and had made the physical environment hideous. And the first results of comprehensive redevelopment in the old cities were being greeted with considerable alarm from some quarters; with prescience the Town and Country Planning Association deplored the high-density, high rise flats which are beginning to appear. F. J. Osborn, in his correspondence with Lewis Mumford, records the doubts which the author of the Greater London Plan 1944, Sir Patrick Abercrombie, retained until the end of his life, about his recommendations on housing densities (1.8).

The scale and complexity of urban growth were beginning to emerge so differently to the expected results of those neatly planned *patterns*. It gradually dawned that planning was a process which involves many aspects of urban activity.

The first discovery, around 1954, was that land-use, its intensity (measured density) and its location determines traffic volumes and direction (1.9). This discovery led directly to the land use/traffic studies of the mid-sixties including the London Traffic Study. These studies were based on traffic models which could be accurately correlated provided that a full origin/destination survey (backed by a household interview surveys and vehicle counts) was carried out. In effect the models and zones, all interconnected; calculated the flows in and out of each zone depending on the

9

relative industrial, office, shopping and residential pattern in it; counted the resulting flows between all zones and *assigned* these to the existing network (hence the need for careful survey to correlate the model), and any hypothetical network which the planner or traffic engineer might suggest. Hence they were often called *assignment models*. The more advanced could calculate the relative costs of various networks. The simpler just produced the numerical flows which could be expected.

It was not long before the mistakes of a model which referred to *one point in time* began to be seen in traffic analysis. As the first urban roads were built (usually on the basis of the 1940s pattern plans rather than any result of the traffic planning era) the traffic behaved unpredictably because the very construction of a new road did not so much *channelize traffic* as create wholly different land use patterns (and therefore land values) in wide areas related to the feeder system of roads leading to it. Moreover urban road building had unforeseen social results. It was assumed that, if a preliminary survey was made of the age and condition of the urban fabric, the areas which showed up badly were the potential routes for new roads. After all, the pace of urban renewal was expected to increase with each year and those slums could not be expected to remain long. Old established neighbourhoods were axed through by the roads; communities were divided. High density and essential housing stock was lost by the very people who would have the most difficulty in finding any other place in the city region. Hardly had the urban roads programme begun in London that it was under attack from the socially conscious. Elsewhere, as already mentioned, the urban ring roads have been ruthlessly completed with consequent devastation of the inner environment of the city.

The destruction was virtually completed by the additional massive clearances required for comprehensive redevelopment between 1950-1974. These reached the proportion of catastrophe in the older urban cities like Liverpool. Advised by the National Building Agency this city undertook to clear nearly 80,000 houses within 10 years.

By the mid-sixties studies such as *Explorations into Urban Structure* were being published. In this book Foley discussed the relationships of the activities in the city region spatially and in terms of organization, and Webber put forward the concept of 'Urban place and the non place urban realm'. He set out the shortcomings of land use/density concepts, calling for "a way of viewing the city as a dynamic system in action... The problem calls for something akin to a musical score—a recordable language capable of expressing action"; and "I am here searching for a holistic conception of the city that can analytically identify process-relations and form-relations. . . and thus facilitate our understanding of the relationships among the physical patterns, the spatial activity patterns, and the spatial interaction patterns that are the expression of economic and social behaviour" (1.10).

From this critical point onwards in the evolution of urban theory the realization has steadily grown that 'planning' is involved in the essential areas of our lives and our polity; that it can, and has, resulted in crude changes to our social structure. What is only guessed at is how far it has affected our city regional economies and what might have been the case if planning had not intervened in such a deliberate fashion. In 1964 the Planning Advisory Group was set up by Central Government, chaired by the Minister of Housing and Local Government, Richard Crossman. The resulting report of 1965 emphasized the need for flexibility in plan making, to be responsive to changes in social and economic trends (1.11). The 1968 Town and Country Planning Act which followed was to change plan making from the *patterns* of the old 1947 Act Development Plans to Structure Plans and Local Plans. Structure Plans are intended to be statements of general planning policy in the written context of social and economic forces. They are 'broad brush' plans only. Local Plans on the other hand are detailed proposals for small areas. They are the responsibility of the Local Authorities, and unlike the Structure Plans, do not need the approval of the Secretary of State. County authorities have subsequently had great difficulty in preparing Structure Plans and most are not likely to have them ready by the end of the 1970s. The basic reason for this dilatoriness lies in the expected content of a Structure Plan. Most counties simply do not have the resources to prepare a full economic/social analysis related to physical patterns of land use/transportation. And there is no generally accepted field theory which can inter-relate these matters.

In addition the clouded planning relationships of the reformed Counties and Districts has hindered the preparation of agreed Structure Plans. It is a difficult enough to agree an acceptable land use pattern, but the views of Counties and Districts on economic and social change are sometimes irreconcilable. Although the 1968 legislation was very close to the most advanced thinking in the urban field, it might now be said that the reason for its relative failure lies in the nature of the pattern making which was still required of it. Andrew Thorburn, County Planning Officer, East Sussex, recently described his concept of the Structure Plan as being in the nature of a review, rather than a plan, collated quinquennially, but updated on a year by year basis. Such a concept is very close to the Community Review referred to earlier, and shows how the urgent need for *amelioration* of the worst of our social and urban problems is overcoming the desire for dramatic plans.

The evolution of planning theory meanwhile is proceeding on many fronts. Where it perhaps most closely relates to present practice in the UK is in the field of corporate planning (1.12) (see Chapter 8). The realization that all the departments of Local Authorities are instrumental in 'planning' so as to alleviate the many faceted problems of the city has led to a new format and style of cooperative policy making. The town clerk became the Chief Executive and the management methods which had been evolved by industrial organizations were translated into the public sector. In the field of urban physics the insights of Foley, Webber and Dykman led to a greater interest by the early 1970s in *urban modelling*. The land use/transportation types described earlier evolved into much more sophisticated urban systems evaluative models. The classic demonstration of a 'gravity model' where (as in the Copernican universe) each urban area has a certain gravitational attraction, the whole city region being viewed as a balanced universe, was that of Lowry published in 1964 (after the Economic Study of the Pittsburgh Region of 1962) (see Chapter 11).

The incorporation of this model and its many variations into the heart of official planning practice was a result of the work carried out by J. Brian McLoughlin and others. McLoughlin was responsible for the Leicester and Leicestershire Sub-Regional Planning Study, and in his subsequent book (1.13) he extended his net to include cost-benefit analysis. He was primarily concerned with achieving an overview of the city region as an evolving dynamic set of interrelated systems. By the mid-1970s the numeracy and knowledge of urban physics which this approach required has become the hall mark of the succesful urban plan makers in consultancy and Government and of the most sought-after teachers in the planning schools.

This quite small group, well known to each other, have achieved a considerable breakthrough in the application of theoretical knowledge and made the link between systems analysis (the simulation of urban activities) and corporate planning (the coordinated execution of policies in the social and economic fields sometimes through planning strategy and policy) a real possibility.

The style of the group is in direct contract with the alternative social planning stream which grew out of the consequential failure of the Development Plans and comprehensive development era. There was, however, no theory of social planning equivalent to the Lowry model in urban physics, which could help evaluate *in social terms* the likely results of land-use changes imposed by 'planning' policies. True, there were many writings on the subject but these were in the territory of sociology or anthropology (or protest literature).

Thee was, however, a great deal that could be adduced from the planning events of the previous 20 years. This book shows how planning was often undertaken in a simplistic way, with dire and unexpected social results. Plans which were to create a better environment for all have instead created a worse environment for sizeable minorities. The alienation and confusion which a swift transition of a society creates has not been entirely ameliorated by the planning system (1.14). There is a temptation, therefore, to abjure planning. A case can be made to show that as planning increased in effectiveness (in the carrying out of plans) society also suffered increasingly in the dislocation of community. A reduction of the manifold pluralisms which are found in 'normal growth' cities and in the opportunities of work, leisure and culture can be attributed to planning. However, this negative attitude should be countered by the prevailing need to retain and enhance the qualities of the myriad communities and their environments in our city regions, a need which can be met by a conjunction of corporate planning and reformed city regional government. These two, informed by the understanding of urban systems in both 'social planning' and 'model building' terms can certainly make a balanced and mended society in the city region possible.

Without this conjunction the forces of greed which regard the urban fabric as a jungle to be exploited will again come into the ascendancy. At present there is an uneasy lull. Exploitive development is held back by the economic climate combined with the extremely powerful community concern about development. But if the climate changes the community will have a hard battle to withstand another decade of massive central development and exurban sprawl. We are now culturally conscious, too, of the side effects urban growth and change has on nature—the ecological balance is delicate. We do not want further erosive change but this will occur without the right machinery of representative government at city regional level.

References

1.1   *South Hampshire Study*, HMSO, 1966.
1.2   WEBBER, M., DYCKMAN, J., FOLEY, D.L., GUTTENBERG, A.Z., WHEATON, W.L.C. and WURSTER, G.B., *Explorations into Urban Structure*. University of Pennsylvania Press, 1966.
1.3   HALL, P., CRACEY, H., DREWETT, R., THOMAS, R., *et al.*, *The Containment of Rural England*, Vols. 1 and 2, (P.E.P.), Allen and Unwin, 1973.
1.4   SENIOR, D., (Ed.), *The Regional City*, Longmans, 1966.
1.5   *The Sunderland Study*, Vols. I and II, HMSO, 1973.
1.6   *Report of the Royal Commission on the Distribution of Industrial Population*,(Barlow Report), Cmnd. 6153, HMSO, 1940.
1.7   *Final Report: Expert Committee on Compensation and Betterment*, (Uthwatt Report), Cmnd. 6386, HMSO, 1942.
1.8   *The Letters of Lewis Mumford and Fredric J. Osborn*, Adams and Dart, 1971.
1.9   For instance: MITCHELL, R.B. and RAPKIN, C., *Urban Traffic: a Function of Land Use*, Columbia University Press, 1954.
1.10   WEBBER, M., *et al., op. cit.*
1.11   *The Future of Development* Plans, HMSO, 1965.
1.12   EDDISON, T., *Local Government: Management and Corporate Planning*, 2nd Ed., Leonard Hill.
1.13   McLOUGHLIN, J.B., *Urban and Regional Planning: a Systems Approach*, Faber & Faber, 1969.
Systems Approach, Faber & Faber, 1969.
1.14   BERRY, B.J.L., *The Human Consequences of Urbanization*, Macmillan, 1973.

PART ONE

CHAPTER TWO

Population Shifts and Movements

Ronald T. White

Introduction

Whilst the terms *shifts* and *movements* might be regarded as more or less synonymous, for demographic purposes it is useful to draw some distinction between them. Changes in the total population of the country or of any constituent part of it are brought about as a result of the balance struck both between the numbers of births and deaths, i.e. natural change of population, and between the number of persons moving into and out of it, i.e. net migration. 'Movements' in the present context clearly refer to migration. Within the country, variations in the rate of total population change arising from differential rates of natural change and of migration can in the course of time bring about significant changes in the national pattern of population distribution, i.e. marked 'shifts' in the regional proportions of the national population total. In the context of this book it is the changes in the distribution of population, in particular the role played by migration, that is important.

Of the 56 million people currently living in the United Kingdom, a little over 97% are contained within Great Britain—about 9% in Scotland, 5% in Wales and 83% in England. For the present purpose attention is concentrated primarily on the changes which have taken place within Great Britain. Further, the viewpoint is that of the planner rather than of the demographer, the main objective being to present a general picture of the salient characteristics of population shifts and movements as a background to the study of growth and change in the future city region.

The salient characteristic of demographic trends during this century has been the rapid and accelerating rate of growth of the World's population: on current trends the global population will double in size within only 35 years to produce a total of 6.5 billion by the year 2000. The environmental, social and economic implications of a growth of such magnitude are formidable and it was in order to focus attention on these problems that the United Nations Population Commission convened the World Population Conference in Bucharest in August, 1974. The alarming rate of current World population growth is the direct result of accelerating growth rates in the less developed countries. Great Britain, however, was one of the first countries to experience this relatively modern demographic trend.

For many centuries the population of Great Britain was relatively stable at a level well below that of the present population of Greater London (7.2 million). Relatively high birth rates were matched by relatively high death rates, life expectancy was by modern standards short, and the total size of the population was restricted to what the developable resources of the time could support.

The gradual change-over from this long established state of demographic equilibrium to progressive growth took place during the latter half of the eighteenth century and was closely associated with the agricultural and industrial revolutions. The specific effects of the new agricultural and industrial developments upon fertility, marriage and mortality rates among the component classes of the population were highly complex; however, in general, the increase in food supply, including a more balanced winter diet, arising from agricultural improvements, and the growing employment opportunities in the industrial towns, provided the basic economic support for a growing population. The advancements in scientific knowledge, and more particularly in medicine and public hygiene, following from the industrial revolution, progressively lengthened life expectancy during the nineteenth century. In brief, all these associated advances combined to reduce mortality rates—a growing proportion of children survived to produce families of their own—and to develop the resources capable fo sustaining an ever growing population.

The subsequent history of population growth can be traced in more precise quantitative terms from the first population census of

1801 onwards. By that date the population of Great Britain had already reached 10.5 million. During the next half century the population almost doubled, increasing by 10.3 million, or 98.2%, to 20.8 million in 1851. By 1901 the population rose by a further 16.2 million, or 77.7%, to 37.0 million. The exceptionally high rates of growth, however, fell sharply after the first decade of the present century so that, although the total population increased by 11.9 million to reach 48.9 million by 1951, the percentage increase over this period had fallen to 32.0% and one-third of this absolute growth had already taken place by 1911.

Over the next 20 years up to the last census held in 1971, the total population grew by 5.1 million, or 10.5%, to 54.0 million. Growth rates during this period were somewhat erratic, a disproportionate amount occurring between the mid-1950s and mid-1960s when fertility rates rose temporarily for reasons which are not yet fully understood. Since then fertility rates have re-assumed a declining trend, and although the latest population projections envisage a very modest growth for Great Britain of about three million during the remainder of this century, it is reasonable to conclude that this country's contribution to the World's growth trends lies in the past rather than the future.

Whereas the great population expansion starting in the mid-eighteenth century was brought about mainly by a progressive reduction in mortality rates rather than a rise in fertility rates, the return during this century to the present little or no growth situation has resulted from a fall in fertility rates. A complex of social and economic factors has contributed to this marked reduction of the population growth rate, primarily through the current ability of the vast majority of the population to control the size of their families. We may be returning to a new period of relative population stability such as existed before the mid-eighteenth century, and it is evident that whilst that earlier state of equilibrium resulted from high death rates offsetting high birth rates, the present situation arises from low birth rates matching low death rates, and birth control has now replaced disease and famine as the prime restraint on population growth.

Patterns of distribution

The marked changes in population size which occurred as a result of the agricultural and industrial revolutions were accompanied by radical changes in the national pattern of population distribution.

In pre-industrial Britain, the population was only about one-tenth of its present size; the overall population density was low. Society was overwhelmingly rural, only about one-tenth lived in towns of any size, and was by no means evenly distributed over the whole country. The pattern was a relatively stable one. For the most part people concentrated where the soils and climate favoured the then dominant agricultural economy based on the production of cereals, wool and hides—in the main 'Lowland Britain' of the Midlands and the South. A line from the estuary of the river Tees in North-East England to that of the Exe in Devonshire, divides this area from 'Upland Britain' to the North and West. From the mid-eighteenth century onwards for about 150 years, with the rapid growth of industrialization, the areas of major economic activity shifted North-westwards to Upland Britain. Here the coal-fields, often associated with iron ore deposits, provided the source of industrial power and the basis for the development of the iron, steel, heavy engineering and textile industries. The difficulties of road transport meant that ready access to local raw materials combined with the convenient esturial posts determined the locations of the new economic and population growth. But London, located in Lowland Britain, the capital, main commercial centre and premier port, shared as always in the national economic growth.

Two principle features characterized the major change in the national pattern of population distribution from the mid-eighteenth century onwards. First, there was a growing movement of population from the countryside to the newly developing industrial towns. This migration was primarily a response to the 'pull' factor of growing employment opportunities in the new factories and mines, but it was aided by the 'push' factor in the rural areas where, as one feature of the new agricultural economy, the effect of the successive Enclosure Acts was to deprive increasingly by large numbers of the rural population of their former livelihood on the land. Second, this migration from the countryside was primarily drawn to the new urban areas on or near the coalfields and the deepwater estuaries in North-Western, or Upland, Britain.

Once established, these population shifts tended to be self-perpetuating. An ever-increasing proportion of the national population became concentrated in the new industrial and commercial areas, and a growing proportion of the now accelerating natural increase of population occurred in these urban centres.

Significant changes in population distribution had already taken place by the time of the first census in 1801. The magnitude of the continuing overall shift North-westwards during the nineteenth century is summarized in the table below.

Area	Growth Rate as Percentage of the National Rate		Percentage Share of the National Population		
	1801—51	1851—1901	1801	1851	1901
Scotland, Wales and Northern Regions of England (Upland Britain)	113	111	43.1	45.9	48.0
Midland and Southern Regions of England (Lowland Britain)	90	91	56.9	54.1	52.0
Great Britian	100	100	100	100	100

During the first half of the nineteenth century when the total national population increased by 98%, the largest regional growths took place in North-West England (186%), Yorkshire and Humberside (122%) and the South-East (104%), this last largely reflecting the growth of London itself. The West Midlands, parts of which—the Potteries and Black Country—belong geographically to Upland Britain, recorded a growth (100%) marginally above the national level, and all other major areas of Great Britain apart from Wales (98%) experienced growth below the average.

Between 1851 and 1901, with a national growth of 78%, above-average growth occurred in the Northern region of England (115%), the North-West (109%), the South-East (106%) and Yorkshire and Humberside (95%). As a further indication of the very wide variations in regional population growth rates during the nineteenth century, the lowest percentage growths were located in two regions of Lowland Britain, East Anglia and the South-West of England. Here population increased respectively by 68% and 67% between 1801 and 1851 and by only 8% and 14% between 1851 and 1901.

The growing railway network during the latter part of the nineteenth century, facilitating the bulk transport of coal and other raw materials, began gradually to loosen the close ties of industrial growth to the coalfields of Upland Britain. The railways were responsible for the first stage in the erosion of the firm boundaries that marked the earlier sudden transition from the low-density scatter of the agricultural population of the countryside to the high-density concentration of the urban populations where travel by foot or horse-drawn transport had severely limited the distance between residence and workplace. Towards the end of the last century a small but steadily rising proportion of the urban population took advantage of quicker rail transport to move their homes to and beyond the rural periphery of towns and began the development of suburbia, a dominant characteristic of twentieth century urban evolution.

The exploitation of oil as an alternative source of energy and the consequent development of motorized road transport since the beginning of this century has radically reduced industrial ties with the coalfields and established ports. With accelerating technological advances, a growing range of new industries have arisen which is largely independent of the location of raw materials. The vehicle manufacturing industry, for example, developed in the Midlands and the aircraft and electronics industries mainly in the South of England.

This growth of modern industry and new sources of power resulted in a decline in the demand for coal and indeed for many of the products of the nineteenth century factories of Upland Britain. High levels of unemployment arising from the major decline in the older primary industries there have been matched by growing employment opportunities in the more modern industrial centres developing in Lowland Britain. There has been major growth during this century in the non-manufacturing or 'service', industries. The rising employment in basic services such as transport, health, welfare and education, are closely related to population distribution and have been widespread throughout the country. The growth of other service industries has taken place mainly in the major centres of more recent economic growth and the expansion of insurance, banking and finance has been particularly concentrated in Greater London.

These developments have been reflected in corresponding shifts in the areas of main population growth amounting to a general reversal of the trends experienced during the previous 150 years. Whilst the national rate of population growth has decelerated, and the rates of growth in the regions of Upland Britain have fallen still lower, above-average rates of growth are now concentrated in Lowland Britain.

The extent of this reversal of the earlier pattern of growth is summarized in the following table:

Area	Growth Rate as Percentage of the National Rate		Percentage Share of the National Population		
	1901—51	1951—71	1901	1951	1971
Scotland, Wales and Northern Regions of England (Upland Britain)	71	45	48.0	44.6	42.2
Midland and Southern Regions of England (Lowland Britain)	127	145	52.0	55.4	57.8
Great Britain	100	100	100	100	100

Thus, the shift of population back to Lowland Britain during the present century had by 1971 more than offset the opposite nineteenth century trend so that it now supports 57.8% of the national total as against 56.9% in 1801. Between 1901 and 1951 when the national population increased by 32% the only regions experiencing above-average growth were the West Midlands (48.1%), the South-East (43.7%) and the East Midlands (43.6%), all lying within Lowland Britain, with the smallest percentage growth occurring in Scotland (14.0%). During the later period 1951-71, with an overall national population growth of 10.5%, the contrast between Upland and Lowland Britain has become even more marked: all the regions of Lowland Britain experienced above-average population growth ranging from 20.9% in East Anglia to 13.9% in the South-East of England whilst below-average growth occurred in all the regions of Upland Britain, ranging from 6.6% in Yorkshire and Humberside to only 2.6% in Scotland.

This twentieth century shift in the main areas of growth back to the Midlands and Southern Regions of England which had contained the greater part of the pre-industrial population came about as a result of persistent migration flows from the slower growing, or declining, economies of the older industrial areas based on the coalfields to the newer expanding industrial and commercial centres in Lowland Britain. Furthermore, those who chose to migrate in search of employment were largely made up of the younger, more enterprising elements of the population, i.e. those either still single or in the early stages of married life. So this migration tended to diminish birth rates in the older industrial areas and increase them in the Midlands and South. Net gains by migration and high rates of natural growth thus combined to accentuate population growth differentials between Upland and Lowland Britain.

As an indication of the magnitude of these movements in the more recent post-war period, between 1951 and 1961 the estimated net loss by migration, including moves to and from overseas, from Scotland, Wales and all three Northern regions of England amounted to a little over 630,000, ranging in size from 282,000 from Scotland to 49,000 from Wales, whilst estimated net gains to all five regions of Lowland Britain totalled 650,000, of which the South-East region of England accounted for 438,000. In the next decade ending 1971 (when there was an estimated overall net emigration from Great Britain of about 250,000) the net losses from Scotland, Wales and the Northern regions still exceeded 620,000, while the loss from Wales was reduced to negligible proportions, and the overall net gain to Lowland Britain amounted to well over 360,000, but with small net losses now occurring in the West Midlands and South-East.

It is important to note that the general migratory drift of population to the Midland and Southern regions of England, particularly since the last war, would have assumed much greater proportions had it not been for growing Government intervention by means of developing regional economic planning policies designed both to assist new industrial development in the less prosperous regions of the north and west and to restrain industrial expansion in the more prosperous regions of Lowland Britain.

Migration motivation

In contrast to the relative stability of population distribution in pre-industrial Britain, migration has played an important role in bringing about the ever changing patterns of population distribution throughout the last 200 years. With the more recent declines in the birth rate, migration has, indeed, now become the dominant element in population change over most parts of Great Britain. Its growing significance has been reflected in the Government's decision, with effect from 1961, to include questions on migration in the periodic Censuses of Population, so that it has become possible to monitor the changing magnitude, pattern and socio-economic characteristics of migration flows within the country.

Census data reveal, for example, that 10% or more of the total population change their place of residence during the course of a single year (5.9 million, or 10.9% of the population of Great Britain in the year 1970-71). The volume of movement, however, falls sharply as the distance moved increases. Rather more than half of the annual moves (3.0 million in 1970-71) were essentially local, confined within the local authority area of original residence, about one-third (2.0 million in 1970-71) moved from one local authority area to another but remained within their regions of origin, and only one-seventh (830,000 in 1970-71, or 1.5% of the total population), moved from one region to another.

The Census constitutes an objective count of population and its characteristics, including migration, but does not include questions relating to migration motivation. There are a great variety of factors associated with family relationships; the size, cost and tenure of dwellings; the nature of the physical and social environment; accessibility to employment, to educational, shopping, recreational facilities, etc., which play a part, either singly or in come combination, in a decision to move. Some influence local migration, whilst others tend to operate irrespective of the distance involved.

The challenging complexity of migration motivation has been attracting increasing research attention in recent years. Some motivational factors, however, can be inferred from the known characteristics of migration flows. The close association between the changing patterns of distribution of population and economic activity during the last two hundred years indicate the importance of economic motivation—moves made to secure employment or better employment opportunities.

Census data relating to longer distance inter-regional migration provides some supporting evidence. The propensity to migrate is greatest among those aged 15-24 years, i.e. those leaving full-time education for employment; and the net gains of migrants in this age group are confined exclusively to the more prosperous regions. Further, whereas the censuses since 1961 indicate that the gross flows of migrants into and out of all regions are very much greater than the resultant net balances, the socio-economic characteristics of the gross flows differ to a significant degree, revealing that the more prosperous regions tend to experience net gains particularly among the better qualified professional and 'white collar' groups of the economically active population.

Certain areas, especially in the South-West of England and East Anglia, provide attractive climatic and physical environments to which increasing numbers of older people move to live on retirement. However, migration for retirement purposes also takes place

25

on a considerable scale over much shorter distances within all regions of Great Britain.

Changes in urban population distribution in the present century

Apart from the changing broad shifts in the national distribution of the population between Upland and Lowland Britain, the one dominant feature prevailing throughout the industrial era to date has been the progressive urbanization of the population. With continuing rises in agricultral productivity associated with modern mechanized farming, this shift from the countryside into urban settlements has persisted right up to the present day, although it has now been reduced to very modest proportions. The extent of the transformation from a rural to an essentially urbanized society is such that, whereas in pre-industrial Britain only about one-tenth of the population lived in urban environments, now almost nine-tenths do so.

During this continuous evolution of a predominantly urban pattern of population distribution, however, important changes have taken place in the nature of urbanization, dating mainly from the early years of this century. It is with such changes that the migration flows at intra-regional and intra-local authority levels are closely associated, responding to a more complex and wider range of migration motivations than at the inter-regional level.

Until about the first decade of this century, the very rapidly growing urban population was mainly accommodated at high residential densities experiencing increasing urban congestion and overcrowding of dwellings. Although towns necessarily grew in physical size, the division between 'town' and 'country' was sharply defined. Up to this time, the phenomenon of urban growth may be aptly described as an urban implosion.

One of the major factors which now began to radically change the character of urbanization was the progressive increase in personal mobility. The earliest indication of this development has already been noted—the advantage taken of the spreading railway network by a small minority to commute to work from residences outside the towns—but it was the development of the motor car and modern public road transport which has permitted an ever-increasing proportion of the urban population to break the former very close ties bwtween workplace and residence and to choose more attractive local environments from which to travel to their places of urban employment.

A second factor of major importance has been the marked rise in the standard of living of the mass of the population. In personal terms this has been expressed, for example, in a major transfer of residence from high-density rented accommodation to low density home-ownership on or beyond the urban peripheries and in the dramatic rise in car ownership, thereby facilitating longer journeys to work. In more general urban terms, rising wealth has been reflected in rising spatial standards of provision for all forms of urban development—roads, factories, shops, schools, etc. as well as dwellings. Thus, as the outworn fabric of the older, inner urban areas has been progressively redeveloped at much higher modern standards of provision; their residential capacity has been markedly reduced, creating an 'overspill' of population requiring re-accommodation beyond the existing limits of the built-up areas.

These developments led to a rapid spatial expansion of the built-up areas. The rising tide of peripheral suburban growth often resulted in the coalesence of formerly physically separate urban settlements; and in those major old industrial areas with an already close grouping of towns, their combined expansion led to the emergence of large complex urban conurbations, centred on Glasgow in West Central Scotland, Newcastle in the North region of England, Liverpool and Manchester in the North-West, Birmingham in the West Midlands, to a lesser extent among the towns of West Yorkshire, and to the greatest extent of all centred on London in the South-East. Despite the major displacement of population which has also taken place, consequent upon urban redevelopment, from these urban masses to reception areas well beyond their limits, the six conurbations within England together still contain almost 16 million people, or 32.1% of the national total.

This shift of population away from the inner urban areas is an almost universal feature of urban evolution throughout the country: all but the most recently established urban settlements reveal a common trend—population declines in their inner areas and population increases on their outer fringes. The outward spread of towns associated with urban redevelopment at rising standards of provision means that urban development during this century has been disproportionately greater than the growth of population. As an example of the magnitude of this trend, while the population of

England and Wales increased from 32.5 million to almost 49.0 million, i.e. a little over 50%, between 1901 and 1971, the estimated total area of urban development grew from 0.8 to almost 1.8 million hectares—an increase of 120%: thus during this period the overall urban land provision per 1000 population rose from 24.9 to 36.4 hectares.

A third significant factor influencing urban growth patterns, particularly since the Second World War, has been the development under the Town and Country Planning legislation of physical planning policies governing the use of land. Green Belts have been established round Greater London and other major urban concentrations which have effectively limited their periperal expansion. The New Towns Act of 1946 enabled the Government directly to assist in the planned decongestion, first of Greater London, and later of other large urban areas. New Towns were established to relieve the urban overcrowding and the pressure on peripheral land for development by the transfer of both population and employment to new settlements in the surrounding countryside at some considerable distance from the conurbations. The New Towns programme which began with the setting up of eight New Towns in the Greater London hinterland has subsequently been extended, to deal with similar problems in other older urban areas and twenty-eight New Towns have now been designated in Great Britain, five in Scotland, two in Wales and twenty-one in England. New housing has already been provided within them for well over 800,000 incoming people and on current programmes they will provide accommodation for over a further one million by the end of the century.

The Town Development Act of 1952 served to supplement the Government's New Town programme by providing the machinery, with central government financial aid, for the joint financing of population transfers between congested 'exporting' cities and the 'receiving' local authorities, usually small towns. Sixty-nine such town expansion schemes have been arranged, forty of which are currently in operation, contributing to the decongestion principally of Greater London, but also of Birmingham, Liverpool, Manchester and Newcastle on Tyne.

Whilst the New and Expanded Towns are playing an integral part in the redistribution of the congested urban populations, the whole of the outward movement from most large towns, and the large majority of movements from the conurbations benefiting from the New Expanded Towns programme, is of a private nature. For example, during the 1960s when net outward migration from

London amounted to just under 100,000 persons per annum, the gross migration to the planned growth towns related to London was running at only some 15-20,000 persons per annum.

Thus, urban evolution during much of the present century has been characterized by a massive outward movement of population from the older urban areas with a resultant lowering of urban residential densities, a rapid spread of suburban development often extending into the countryside well beyond the urban local administrative area boundaries. Where planning policies have increasingly controlled the physical extent of urban expansion, the outward drift of urban population has moved still further afield either to planned New and Expanded Towns to which mobile employment has also been attracted, or to other existing smaller urban settlements which serve as dormitories from which the economically active immigrants commute for work. The nineteenth century urban implosion has been transformed into a twentieth century urban explosion.

The size hierarchy of urban settlements

Because published population statistics necessarily relate to the administrative local authority areas, but the built-up areas themselves often extend well beyond these boundaries, such data provide only a rough indication of the population size structure of urban settlements. Indeed, they form an unreliable basis on which to determine whether individual built-up areas are changing in population size. An unpublished study carried out within the Department of the Environment—De Facto Urban Areas in England and Wales, 1966—was designed to determine the population size of physically separate urban settlements at that date.

This study reveals that there were then 1333 *de facto* urban areas in England and Wales with populations for the most part in excess of 3000 persons which together contained 41.6 million people, or 88.3% of the total national population. The table on page 30 summarizes the population size structure of these urban settlements.

It is of interest to note that the three largest urban areas on this basis were centred on Greater London (8.3 million population), Birmingham (2.4 million) and Manchester (2.2 million). Unfortunately, until such an analysis is repeated at a subsequent date, it is not possible to measure the population change trends of these *de facto* urban areas.

Population Size (thousands)	Number of De Facto Urban Areas	Total Population (millions)
Over 1000	3	13.0
500—1000	5	4.1
250—500	11	3.8
100—250	38	5.7
45—100	60	4.0
10—45	337	6.9
Under 10	879	4.0

Conclusion

A comparison between the population patterns of pre-industrial and modern Britain reveal both stark contrasts and interesting similarities. A small, low density rural population has been transformed into a more than seven times larger, relatively high-density and essentially urban one to-day. At the same time, however, the early economically motivated northward drift to the areas of earliest industrial development has been replaced more recently by a return drift to the more favoured environments of the Midlands and South; and the great surge of population growth has now passed so that births and deaths are again, at least temporarily, more or less in balance as they were in pre-industrial times. Perhaps most interesting and significant of all, the centripetal nature which characterized urbanization until the early part of this century has been replaced by a centrifugal tendency—a mass movement of people away from the older high density urban areas to spreading suburban development and growing smaller settlements in closer association with the countryside from which their forbears originally moved. An increasing number of those who still remain within a short distance of the major urban employment centres are taking the opportunity on retirement to move away to the attractive, smaller settlements in the countryside or on the coasts.

Finally, one major feature of the present urbanized society stands out in marked contrast to the situation which prevailed both in pre-industrial times and subsequently in the towns and cities of urbanized Britain until the early decades of this century. Then the vast bulk of the population satisfied all their needs within very short distances of their homes. To-day, with the development of modern public and private means of transport, the population enjoys a very much greater degree of mobility. Personal needs are no longer satisfied within the limited confines of the hamlet, village or even the compact nineteenth century town. Members of families living in one urban community may well travel daily to another for employment, another for education and yet another for shopping purposes and meet their recreational needs in the surrounding countryside. The orbit within which the population move for all purposes, apart from vacations and highly exceptional visits, has during the course of this century expanded to encompass a whole hierarchy of inter-related settlements and the intervening countryside within the hinterland of a dominant city. The single town no longer delimits the environment within which the bulk of the urbanized population live, work, and satisfy their social and leisure needs; it has been replaced by a much wider and more diverse environment in which both 'town' and 'country' have a role to play—the city region.

CHAPTER THREE

Strategic Planning for Quality of Life

Peter Self

Characteristics of City Regions

The *structuring* of the city region represents the main focus of this book. The dynamics of urban growth are analyzed by other contributors. Certain relevant 'natural' features of this process (i.e. ignoring the intervention of planning) apply to large city regions in Britain and, to a considerable degree, in other Western societies.

(a) The basic process is one of pull-push, that is concentration of population and activity around a major centre followed by its progressive spread and dispersal over a broad area.

(b) Population densities thin out towards the periphery, with the richer citizens (except for a specialized minority occupying central locations, particularly in World capitals like London) moving towards the more distant locations as they display their preference for space and social exclusiveness over proximity to work—suburbs are succeeded by 'exurbs'.

(c) Nucleated centres occur within this diffused population spread where (i) a major transport node arises or (ii) an existing free-standing town is engulfed. However these secondary centres, though numerous, remain for some time very small and weak in relation to the one major centre, although a more hierarchical pattern gradually emerges. (Where the city region emerges through the coalescence of industrial towns, the secondary centres naturally retain greater importance.)

(d) The transportation system powers the whole process, but with differential spatial effects. In the era of rail and mass transit the dominant pattern is radial, and new development and population movements follow sectoral patterns of access. Cross-urban movement is relatively difficult, and rapid rail services facilitate long and often relatively comfortable commuting, for those who can afford it. Motorization 'opens up' the zones between the radials and facilitates orbital travel, but reduces at least as much as it extends the outer limits of commuting. (It helps the exurbanite who 'parks and rides' but only hardy motorists will commute as far as the fast train traveller, although road competition is often sufficient to reduce the quality of train services.)

(e) Employment—first industrial and then white-collar—disperses more slowly in the wake of population, and relocates at a great variety of points. The effect is to reduce the relative, although not for a long time the absolute, importance of journeys to the centre, and to create complex commuting patterns which often depend on use of a car.

(f) There is increasing specialization of residential areas by income and by age (families with young children moving out successively further while older households stay behind). The organization of the private housing market caters for and encourages this specialization by age and income, while in practice mass public housing develops comparable patterns.

(g) Finally the dynamics of regional change are loosely correlated with rates of economic growth, so that population and employment dispersal are sluggish in a period of economic stagnation such as the present one, while the scope for both change and growth is much less (even allowing for their smaller size) in for example the city regions of Northern England than in the London region.

Against this brief descriptive background we can consider what aspects of quality of life planners have sought to conserve or promote within city regions.

Aims of British planners

British planning for the city region was much influenced by the regional plans produced during and immediately after World War II, particularly those of Sir Patrick Abercrombie. Subsequent plans for the London region such as the South East Study (1964) and Strategic Plan for the South East (1970), although on a broader scale, have been influenced by similar aims. These plans were only advisory but despite the institutional weakness of regional planning in Britain their ideas have been influential.

The result has been a macroscopic or outside-in perspective upon the city region which has concentrated upon issues of urban dispersal and upon the relationship between the city and its changing, expanding hinterland. Murray Stewart claims with some justice that the structural problems of the built-up mass of the 'old' city were hardly recognized until the long-drawn, inconclusive public hearings into the Greater London Development Plan which was issued by the Greater London Council in 1969 (3.1). Actually Abercrombie and others did have a conception of this structure, but their ideas would no longer be generally accepted as adequate. The concepts of the regional planners have come increasingly under attack, yet no new orthodoxy has emerged. Much of the current voluminous writing about city planning is concerned with either its organization and methodology, or else with the claims of the underprivileged in the inner areas for more jobs, facilities, and public investment. There is also a strong tendency to downplay physical planning in favour of either comprehensive community planning and/or more systematic and sensitive resource allocation. Agnosticism about physical planning, while an understandable reaction to the excessive faith of many architect-planners in geometric forms as purveyed (for example) in the grand but simplistic vistas for a Doxiadis, can easily be pushed too far. Whilst the physical form of development cannot of itself produce happy individuals or societies, it does affect quality of life; at a broader level the structure of the city region has considerable effects upon the availability and distribution of facilities of all kinds.

Certain ideas pervaded earlier British thinking about city regions.

(a) Green Belts and urban containment

British planners followed a long cultural tradition, somewhat tinged with anti-urbanism, in their stress upon the value of access to the countryside for recreation and enjoyment. The direct value of Green Belts has mainly been reaped by those living near them, leaving the poorer populations of inner areas dependent upon the urban parks, the best and largest of which (Hampstead Heath,

Richmond Park) are used by rich suburbanites. However the Green Belt, or parts of it, can be defended for its long-term utility to the large population which will eventually surround it (cf. the Royal Parks) and for its association with New Towns.

(b) *New Towns*

New Towns have the value of nucleating what would otherwise be diffused growth patterns, thereby replacing scattered growth with a planned urban form and facilities, and of integrating movements of population and employment which would otherwise constitute separate, uneven flows. New Towns have not avoided unbalanced age structures, although the range of occupations and income groups is more varied than in most suburbs. Styles of social life and community involvement in New Towns do not seem to differ greatly from many suburbs, which does suggest that their sponsors put too much faith in the social effects of a contained urban form. The quality of life effects of their internal designs is a fascinating and varied subject beyond the scope of this Chapter. But their planned and nucleated character, when compared with other growing settlements in the outer city region, does offer their residents a more effective set of choices between (1) a fair range of localized occupations and of public facilities and (2) access if and when required to the more specialized facilities and opportunities available in the principal city.

(c) *Urban redevelopment*

The original concept was of wholesale replacement of old 'obsolescent' housing by new public housing at lower densities, supported by improved facilities and open space. It was assumed that a substantial reduction of population was necessary to and compatible with a higher quality of life for those who remained. This has turned out to be only a half-truth. These areas have been left with higher ratios of old, sick, dependent, and poor people, because of the exodus of young skilled workers and (usually) the more prosperous local industries to overspill areas. Additional problems have been created by the unnecessary introduction of tall blocks of flats into the new housing projects. In the end the reduced densities and modern public housing have proved much less significant for 'quality of life' than the loss of community networks and social vitality. But there existed no obvious way of retaining the potential migrants seeking a 'better environment' save through better housing at lower densities. The poor design and high cost of new housing led, in the 1960s, to a switch of public policy in favour of the rehabilitation of old dwellings, although private landlords lack incentives for this task and local authorities are taking it over very slowly. In areas of falling population and relatively low incomes it is hard to attract or to justify much public investment (other than the large investment in public housing which is politically impelled). The rehabilitation of once attractive neighbourhoods by a small middle-class influx does at least secure the necessary investment and improve social mix, even though it stirs the politics of deprivation.

(d) *Conservation*

Finally a brief reference must be made to the British planner's role as conservationist. As disillusion with not only the design but the social purpose of much new development has grown, so the conservation of existing townscapes, landscapes and 'amenities' has become increasingly popular. Much of this preservation is of the natural or built environment, but some has social connotations— for example the current efforts to protect the Covent Garden area whose varied mixture of land uses and activities represents the sort of ideal inner area sketched by Jane Jacobs (3.2), although such areas are not so widespread or ideal as she supposes. The planners will usually embrace conservationism where it has political support, almost invariably from the middle classes, but waver if there are opposing commercial or administrative opponents, such as the public cost-benefit analysts who 'prove' the need for a highway project. Thus the planners originally sponsored the redevelopment of Covent Garden for new offices and shops, because of the City's financial interest, and they—or rather the politicians—had to be persuaded otherwise by a persistent pressure group. Planning policies for the central area of London seem only to have won support when they have been conservationist, for example when trying to protect theatres or the residential areas of Mayfair and Bloomsbury against office take-overs.

Prospects for British planning

Strategic physical planning cannot itself determine the microenvironment which is so crucial for quality of life at home and work; but it can conserve and utilize good micro-environments where these exist, and help to establish the conditions under which they can develop.

In the structuring of city-regions, strategic planning must be primarily concerned with housing, employment and transportation, and the dynamic relations between these elements. It cannot directly deal with employment policy, educational policy, or social welfare policy, because these embrace different zones of political action and discourse, even though the physical planner should be 'reaching out' to understand and should be more concerned with general societal goals. But utopianism—whether of a physical design form or of a comprehensive social planning form—has always been an occupational disease of planners. Utopianism can have vitality in the spheres of individual life or small-scale experiment, but easily becomes impotent in complex institutional contexts.

In the critical fields of housing and transportation British planning has been virtually impotent although for quite different reasons. Housing presents the paradox that, while the occupancy rate in housing has generally improved, and dramatically so in London where population has fallen by almost one million in little more than a decade, yet housing shortages appear as serious a social problem as ever—in some respects more so because those literally homeless (and hence an immediate charge upon local government resources) have grown in numbers. The explanation lies in the politics of the housing market, which has remorselessly squeezed the rented sector while enabling both owner-occupiers and council tenants to enjoy rising standards of housing space (that is, on the average—there are also serious distortions within each sector). The urgent need is for a very much larger pool of housing freely available for renting both in inner areas and new growth areas, much of which in the former case could be met by rehabilitation. New public housing is often very expensive in inner areas, and because of residential qualifications is an ineffective way of meeting this demand. Such housing absorbs a large share of public investment and reduces the capacity of planners to secure facilities, such as community centres, or small parks and playgrounds, which are important for the quality of life in new developments. It is a highly political subject, but the planner cannot ignore this misallocation of housing resources.

In the case of transportation strategic planners have been outflanked, not by politics, but by the elaborate techniques of a more specialized type of expert, the transportation planner. The integration of planning and transportation was the administrative nostrum of the 1960s following the Buchanan Report on 'Traffic in Towns'.

It proved a misalliance in Greater London where this integration was in theory organizationally complete. But the Greater London Development Plan suggested no clear relationship between the functioning of the proposed series of orbital motorways and concepts of urban structure. (There *was* in fact a historical relationship because these proposed motorways were largely delineated in the wartime Abercrombie Plan, where they presupposed a completely dominant central area surrounded by concentric suburban rings (3.3). It is strange that these road plans were not effectively tested against *other* concepts of London, such as a more polycentric pattern. Instead the planners apparently accepted the road experts' technical conclusion that the enormous cost and social disruption of the motorways would 'pay off' in increased mobility.

Given the limited success of the earlier planning beliefs, and the current state of disenchantment, it would be rash, and impracticable within this space, to provide a new blueprint. But certain approaches to strategic planning, involving a mix of older and new ideas, follow tentatively from this analysis. For convenience the field is restricted to the London region, inasmuch as other city regions (for reasons indicated) cannot be adequately covered by a brief statement.

(a) *Central London*

Although much anxiety has been voiced about the effect on London's prosperity and inner area workers of the continued dispersal of employment, the effects on quality of life could be highly beneficial *in the long run*. At one time office growth in the centre looked like putting very severe strains upon the transportation system, as well as threatening certain much-valued traditional functions and facilities.

The rationing of total office development gave temporary bonuses to office developers, whereas advice and exhortation in a favourable climate (cf. the work of Location of Offices Bureau), and more careful control over detailed siting would have been more effective. The future of central London should be seen in terms of increasingly specialized forms of business, administrative and professional activity, and as a unique and expanding cultural centre serving regional, national and international clienteles. This aim requires steady dispersal of the more routinized office functions.

The exodus of manufacturing industry from the inner ring has produced employment and income problems, but in the long run it offers an opportunity for relating the population of this ring much more closely to the employment opportunities of the central area, which would then achieve a better social mix. Simultaneously the office workers who move back from suburbs or exurbs to inner areas can be replaced by more industrial workers living in proximity to dispersed plants.

(b) *Secondary centres*

The concept of 'nucleation' embodied in New Towns needs to be fed back into the structure of the built-up mass (3.4). A set of substantial secondary centres for business, shopping, and culture located within the built-up mass can serve both to spread access to facilities more widely and to reduce the need for long journeys to the still overloaded centre. Some such centres are growing naturally (Croydon, Kingston), but usually within the more affluent areas and sometime (e.g. Croydon) against actual opposition from the strategic planners. The proposed urban motorway system flew in the face of this concept which requires that priority be given to cutting down the heavy mass of through traffic which clogs the high streets of existing centres, and to improving access by both public and private transport to the selected major centres. At the same time it is essential to open up the scale of these centres (which tends to be narrow and restricted) so as to provide a good micro-environment for a host of activities.

(c) *The Metropolitan Region*

Unlike the built-up area, development in the surrounding region can be planned against a Green Belt and other protected areas which could be treated with more flexibility so long as a strong conservation policy is continued.

The grouping of new development can be flexible. The new towns originally posited self-contained settlements of about 50,000 people, later changed to somewhat less self-contained units of 80,000 or more, with a district and neighbourhood structure. Possible new patterns include compact New Towns with a single centre, large New Towns structured by a road grid with facilities locating and relocating freely, groupings of New Towns or new villages around a regional centre which could be embedded in a larger town or freestanding on an open site, etc. One basic test is how far the location of facilities is allowed to respond to the special opportunities of the automobile age or is restrained in the interests of a broader public; as the movements of private and public transport become progressively differentiated, they produce a sort of duopoly of facilities and movement patterns. This result is socially divisive, inimical to the assembly of a range of good facilities in any one centre, and contrary to the case for some degree of ordered structure as an offset to the flux and restlessness of modern life. Some planners, in their reaction to the more authoritarian concepts of planning, have gone too far in endorsing the values of change and mobility, oblivious of the fact that the planner is only called in at all as a protector of more enduring social values against the rapid shifts of technology and market fashion. (If this be untrue, why not trust technology and the market?)

It is the planner's special task to organize access to facilities effeciently and equitably, whilst contributing so far as he can to the promotion of community life, so that: (i) some hierarchy of centres is still desirable, so organized as to integrate access by both public and private transport; and (ii) a good range of employment and facilities should be fairly easily accessible from most homes, and more specialized opportunities should be reachable as and if required. It is desirable that a variety of patterns should be tried, and that those who place privacy or aesthetics well above ease of access—by burying themselves deep in the countryside, for example—should be able so to act. But the case for strategic planning rests or falls upon the proposition that dykes should be built for containing and ordering the dynamics of regional growth. It is a case that could do with more successful demonstration.

The planner in the City Region

What mandate have planners to improve 'the quality of life' in the city region, and how can they do it? If one accepts the sovereignty of consumers' preferences, then the planner's function seems to be limited and arguable. Individuals can express their wants and tastes through economic markets and (according to one school of thought) through demanding those specific services from public agencies for which they are ready to pay. If the distribution of wealth be thought unfair, then political pressure can be applied to its correction through a more progressive pattern of taxation; but this is not the planners' job and, successful or not, such action need not affect the principle of 'consumers' sovereignity'.

True, within this philosophy planners can claim a certain minimal role. Thus individuals may not foresee sufficiently the consequences of their choices, and so may need planners to restrain and guide them. Mishan argues that each individual who buys a car does not realize that, as others follow suit, traffic congestion and the rundown of public transport will eventually follow (3.5). But it is not clear whether individuals would act any differently *as private consumers* if they did foresee the consequences, and planners themselves have not such a notable record for foresight, as witness the neglect of traffic problems in post-war British plans. It could be argued that the planner ought first to demonstrate his foresight to a sceptical world through persuasion, rather than control.

Planning claims to achieve economies of scale and functionally convenient patterns of development which are broadly beneficial. This is an argument of substance but it still needs to be tested at every step. If, for example, housing densities are compressed in order to reduce the cost of public utilities, one has to ask: would individuals prefer to pay the public costs entailed by lower densities? If the answer is no, then the planner is right but the answer cannot (in terms of an individual choice criterion) just be assumed. Again, when the planner separates zones of employment and residences, he may accord with most peoples' wishes but there are exceptions— many people like to live close to some kinds of jobs.

It is sometimes suggested that planners should assist the realization of a wide variety of individual aspirations and life-styles. If this *is* his job he does not seem conspicuously successful, but here he may try to turn the tables and say that it is the standardized facilities provided by the market and by many public agencies which restrict the choices available to individuals. One basic problem here is the economics of mass production, which allocate individuals between large housing estates according to age, marital status, and income, and then present them with standardized shopping and other facilities. While planners doubtless should try to assist minority tastes, they can only do so to the extent that a real demand exists which has been *unnecessarily* suppressed. In practice it is a more usual rebuke against planners that they encourage uniformity, and that for variety of life styles one goes naturally to the 'unplanned' parts of the town. This is not quite fair because these 'unplanned' areas grew up in an era of less specialization of production (hence of more diversified land uses), and it is now the planners who must be invoked to try to protect these 'unplanned' zones of diversity against large-scale or specialized new developments.

One limitation upon consumers' preference is that an individual can only choose between those alternatives that are available and known to him, and modern government plays a substantial part in influencing and changing the available alternatives. Until there were New Towns in Britain, no individual could choose whether or not to live in one, and no new town (as now understood) is the product of ordinary market enterprise; the required investment was too large and too long-term for private capital. Of course this public experiment depended upon previous pioneering done by private philanthropists, and *might* have proved unpopular, in which case there would have been little reason for its continuation.

A deeper problem is the ambivalence or complexity contained in the idea of 'individual preference'. Individuals appear to have different preference scales in market and political contexts. This is intelligible when one reflects that the former choice is concerned (quite legitimately) with tangible and often calculable individual gain and the latter choice with more flexible and intangible ideas of social advantage. The advantages in view may relate to family, class, nation, or world, and may be conceived altruistically or be aggressively selfish, but are usually concerned with a broader range of consequences than is market choice, which are differently evaluated. Moreover the 'market approach' tends to treat each want or preference seriatim whereas the planner is concerned with integrated concepts of living (3.6).

Planners cannot 'contract out' of a view of man as a social being as well as an individual consumer, because therein lies much of the rationale for their existence. Yet it is a precarious rationale, because planners have to live with social conflicts while only being able to reach viable policies on the basis of a good deal of consensus. Hence the importance of continuous education of both public and planners.

The relevance of these theories to life in the city region becomes clearer when we consider cetain fashionable theories about planning. One such is the belief that the planner's aim should be to maximize individual opportunities and facilities. The idea sounds all right but begs some questions. 'Access' is not an absolute value but has to be related to the character and environment of the facility in question, and to the importance attached by the individual to other factors such as space in and around his home; while in addition easier access for some people often produces harder access for others. And the stress upon *individual* opportunity overlooks the significance of community life.

It is true that local community has become less important, as a consequence of greater individual mobility and of the bureaucratization of service and welfare functions which once were handled by kinship or neighbourhood groups, or by small local authorities. These local ties have been partly replaced by free associations among individuals, which are less geographically restricted. At the same time the upward social mobility of married couples seeking a 'better environment' and the increase in job mobility, has contributed (along with the specialization of the housing market) to the devitalization of inner areas, rapid population turnover in many suburbs, and very unbalanced age structures in most localities.

To those concerned with individual mobility (social and geographic) these results have not mattered too much. Melvin Webber's highly influential theories of 'the non-place urban realm' portray and seemingly commend a society in which local community has become unimportant, frictions of space are presumed to have been largely overcome, and individuals choose their 'way of life' on a basis of their occupational and leisure interests (3.7). The theory is most misleading, because frictions of space remain considerable even in a very affluent society. Many people are affected by deteriorating public transport and by the location of facilities to meet the convenience of motorists, and the price of mobility is high in terms of the consumption of natural resources, traffic pollution, and time spent on travel.

The emphasis upon individual mobility and opportunity tends to be associated with the endorsement of a market system which prizes novelty and accepts rapid obsolescence. The most important people in a city region are then the 'trend-setters' who pioneer changes of fashion in the production and consumption of goods, and who themselves lead highly mobile lives at work and recreation. This is the impression left by Richard Meier's ideas about the future of the Japanese megalopolis (3.8). The benefits of economic growth and change spread from this elite to the general population, but as Meier recognizes, their ways of life become restless and unstable. The chief problem is not that change itself is necessarily bad, but that it penalizes all those who cannot make the necessary adjustments to their ways of life. They lose their traditional roles and satisfactions, without finding adequate new ones.

Physical planners are primarily concerned with locational issues and relationships, and they can no longer overlook (as they once did) social conflicts about these issues. Sometimes these conflicts are overt—as in the 'homes versus motorways' controversies in London and elsewhere—but often they are latent. It can be argued, as David Harvey does, that the growth of Western cities is associated with increasing inequality in the distribution of locational advantages. He contends that the wealthier inhabitants understand better how to manipulate their environment, both through personal choice and political action, so as to improve access to the best facilities and to escape technological 'bads' like polluted air and traffic blight. The poor are in a reverse position. If this is true, then the posited effects are incremental and widely scattered, and will only sometimes produce direct conflicts (3.9).

Harvey's thesis is plausible, although the distinction between rich and poor seems too crude. In particular transport mode is a critical factor in questions of access. New motorways speed access to distant coastlines and national parks, but a two mile journey by bus to the nearest town park gets harder. The availability of private transport is broadly but not closely correlated with wealth. Leaving aside the many complexities that a full analysis here would require, the issue for planners can be simply put: is it their task to seek greater equality of locational advantages? One does not have to be an economic egalitarian to answer yes, because the first goal (if the problem has been correctly stated) is to offset the *cumulative* inequalities which wealth and mobility produce, and this is surely desirable if planners are legitimately concerned with social justice and cohesion.

One possible reaction to the sprawl and ugliness of modern city regions is nostalgia for the traditional image of the city as a vital meeting-place and a scene of diversified activities within a confined space (3.10). But the parts of the inner city which best retain this vitality and variety are *quartiers Latin* which function as specialized components of a highly complex society. One cannot overcome the spatial scale and specialization of land uses in city regions by such simple prescriptions, although it is true enough that planning has accentuated the separation of land uses whereas more mixed activities would improve most areas.

Current disillusion with *any* morphology makes it hard to envisage the desirable form of future city regions. Such ideas as there are seem often to be impressionistic, superficial, and culturally idiosyncratic. There are reasons for this. The planner's view of the city cannot just be technical but is bound to express (consciously or not) some concepts of social order, which must be related to a complex apparatus of technology, economy and institutions. The concepts themselves are necessarily superficial unless adapted effectively to this complex apparatus, and in an uncertain and anarchic age *any* notions of social order are hard to render credible.

If there is a positive, viable theory of city regional structure, it has

44

to be expressed in terms of some balance between the values of mobility and stability, as applied both to individual opportunities and to social structure, and as realized under the specific technological and economic conditions now emergent. The dispersed city region has grown, and is still growing, under the impetus of the search for a better residential environment by increasing numbers of people. There is nothing wrong about this goal but it is dearly bought in terms of long journeys to work and to other facilities, of segregation of new residential areas by age and income, and of the devitalization of traditional communities. The goal itself has become somewhat stereotyped and given excessive weight in terms of other constituents of a good life.

The newer factors in the shape of employment dispersal and extensive motorization now propel the long-standing dispersal of population into new and more fragmented directions. The scattering of 'exurbs', places of employment, shopping centres and other facilities express the further mobility now available to those with cars. But a further price must also be paid for these opportunities, particularly by the less mobile. At the same time these newer factors present opportunities for overcoming the defects of the earlier phase of the dispersal process. Planned dispersal of employment can be correlated with that of residences, and motorization can offer wider opportunities to many people without bankrupting public transport or dominating the location of facilities.

It has been a strength of British planning to have resisted some of the trends towards a still more dispersed and mobile society. Partly this has occurred through lack of funds for road projects, and through the influence of the vested interests concerned with the protection and redevelopment of existing down-town shopping centres. Even so, and even if the planners have been over-committed to an ideology of control and restriction, a breathing-space for more balanced policies to be worked out has been given.

These policies should be based upon a distinction between localized and regional facilities. Under modern conditions a fair variety of work opportunities and social facilities should be available within 30 minutes' travel of the home of almost any resident of the city region unless (for reasons of idiosyncrasy or isolation) he prefers otherwise. The population within this sort of range can be put at between 100,000 and 500,000, although the lower end of the scale is more feasible in terms of residential tastes and the reservation of 'green zones'. Of course a pattern of this sort rests upon an efficient public transport system which can be supplemented (but

45

not replaced) by private transport. At the same time an efficient *regional* transportation system will cater for those seeking more specialized types of jobs or requiring on occasion specialized services or cultural facilities.

There is nothing very dramatic about this picture, which as already noted draws upon some aspects of new town structure which are then fed back into the structure of the city region generally, producing a polynucleated pattern of service and work centres catering for variable residential patterns and densities, related to distance from the major centre and other factors. The general 'rationale' or philosophy is easy enough to see—namely that one is seeking some balance between the values of the mobile individual and the stabilized community; between the opportunity to move around widely and the advantage of not having to do so; between the individual's privilege of a free life and some support for local community and kinship groups; between the ladder of opportunity and considerations of social justice.

Admittedly these are very general prescriptions or nostrums. They have to be worked out on the ground according to a variety of special needs and circumstances, and moreover (and this is a point of very great difficulty) they must be related to the character of a city region at its present point of transformation. And it is here that sociological and cultural issues arise which demand attention. How far is a balance of age and income groups to be sought in each part of the city region? Income groups are variously distributed according to the local mix of occupations and to the differential and cumulative attractions of quite broad zones. On the other hand age groups have been fragmented more by successive stages of the dispersal process, and by local shortages of land for second-generation families. Whilst limited improvements may be possible and desirable in the localized income mix, it would seem more important to check the involuntary separation of kinship groups which is linked with age imbalance. This aim has considerable implications for housing policies and the reservation of some land wherever possible for the needs of second and later generations. The more open framework for the city region which is now practicable means that the claustrophobic effects of a locality having no room to grow can be mitigated. Here and in other matters a balance has to be found between individual mobility and protection of the social structure, not so as to immobilize or imprison the individual but so as to guard community values against involuntary and unnecessary types of loss.

46

A still larger question is whether the 'deviant cultures' of the inner city are to remain concentrated there, or are also to be partly dispersed to the secondary centres. The phrase 'deviant culture' is not used pejoratively but refers to those groups who find in the inner city their only appropriate milieu, whether held there by a culture of poverty, of immigration, of nonconformity or rebellion. As some of these centres grow to a substantial size, they will reproduce around them to some extent the conditions to be found in the inner city, thus attracting new groups. However, the various cultures of the inner city are also related to its large resources of old housing and other properties which cannot be replicated elsewhere. For too long this resource has been thought of as mainly a liability which should be cleared and replaced. Now it is better appreciated that effective policies for the maintenance and rehabilitation of much of this property is essential for the maintenance of some activities and some ways of life which cannot easily exist elsewhere.

Many writers on planning either seem to accept the dissolution of cities altogether or cling nostalgically to a purely traditional image (3.11) but some attempts have been made to see the 'patterns of the future' (3.12), and these could be taken a good deal further.

Lessons for the Third World

It would be wrong to claim strong conclusions about the planning of city regions in Latin America, Africa or Asia on the basis of British experience. The causes and conditions or urban growth in the numerous states of these continents are, obviously, different from those in Britain, and they differ greatly among themselves as well. Only specific and detailed analysis of the situation in each country or region, carried out in an undogmatic and thorough manner, is likely to yield much worthwhile advice. All the same, and even allowing for very basic differences in the urbanization process, it is still possible to argue cautiously in favour of the following approach to policy-making.

In very general terms the process of urbanization in 'Third World' countries differs from that in Western Europe during the last two centuries, in at least three respects.

(a) Due to health control measures, population growth is even faster.

(b) The 'surplus' underemployed population on the land is often much greater.

(c) Urbanization is much less a product of industrialization.

The first two factors represent quantitative differences in the rate of urbanization, while the third represents a qualitative difference in the nature of urbanization. The growth of Manchester, England was the result of a strong demand for factory hands, for whom mass low-quality housing was then built by employers or speculators. But in Third World cities, industrialization cannot absorb and does not require the large population growth, and a high proportion of the population live, work and house themselves in a makeshift way.

Why, in these circumstances, are the largest cities growing so much faster than national population rates? There are familiar explanations of why people exchange rural poverty for big city poverty, especially if there seems to be no effective 'intermediate' alternative. Rural life usually provides a job and a bare subsistence (although these disappear if the weather fails) and the social supports of kinship and traditional custom. But rural life is often narrow and bereft of opportunities; rural societies are stratified and sometimes oppressive. Life in the city at least offers some possibility of getting a job that is well-paid by rural standards or of living with a relative who has one. City life is much less secure, even though helped by kinship links with other migrants, but its deprivations and dangers are balanced to some extent by the greater vitality, excitement, and range of opportunities.

The choice is often a stark one between contrasting deprivations. Is it better to live in an Anatolian village of mud huts and mangy goats, with no modern buildings save the schoolmaster's bungalow, no communal facilities save the school, an eroded countryside, and a long walk or weekly bus to the nearest 'services'? Or in the mushroom housing on the edge of Ankara where one can build a shack with bought frame and joists, trade in numerous markets, and jostle with the crowd for work and survival? It has to be remembered also that, with rural populations growing fast, a relatively small proportion of migrants is enough to trigger an urban population explosion if there are only one or a few destinations.

In Latin America most capital cities such as Mexico City, Bogota, Caracas have multiplied four, five or six times over within the last thirty years. Some Asian capitals such as Bangkok show the same pattern, as does Cairo. Most African capitals are growing somewhat slower from more modest base-lines. In a vast country such as India more cities are involved but the largest (Calcutta, Bombay) show equally frenetic growth rates. Conceding that rapid urbanization is to be expected one should still ask: is this growth not seriously overconcentrated in a few great centres?

Unlike (for example) cities in the North of England during the industrial revolution, growth of the Third World capital cities is attributable as much to political and cultural as economic reasons. As centres of government these cities occupy a dominant position over cultural facilities, modernized services, and transportation, thus attracting and retaining any new business or industry, especially of an international kind. As population grows, political pressure from the unemployed leads easily to the inflation of the government bureaucracy which can be used to absorb underemployment in much the same way as subsistence agriculture. Political pressure also often enables illegal squatters to achieve some security of occupation which would be impossible in smaller towns where they are fewer. Thus the great city confers certain advantages upon both its rich and its impoverished, although these may in a sense be paid for by the rest of the nation.

This is a thumbnail sketch of a particular situation—that of a highly dominant capital city—although it is a frequently found one. How far the growth of the largest Third World cities is parasitical for their nations is a hard question to answer in general, as it depends on each city's circumstances. Some economists would say that this concentration of modernized types of industry and commerce achieves economies of scale and maximizes use of the limited transportation infrastructure. As the economy grows, other cities will 'take off' economically also.

If economic growth is considered from the viewpoint of the modernized sector and its beneficiaries, this conclusion may be warranted. But if investment is to be spread so as to absorb in employment a larger share of the vast unused labour force, backed by import controls which check the conspicuous consumption of the rich in the main city and spread productive investment, a different development strategy evolves. Since at present a large urban population hangs on the coat tails of a small modernized sector, the dispersal and transformation of even a small part of this sector will have a considerable 'multiplier' effect upon the location of population.

If developing countries are to make fuller and more diffused use of their over-abundant resources of labour, then 'intermediate technology' should be favoured, and small-scale crafts and industries

49

should be encouraged and the advantages (such as they are) of large-scale concentration should be balanced by a more diffused pattern of economic activities; various consequences follow. The scarce supplies of industrial capital, imports, and infra-structure investment have to be allocated with these ends in view. Physical planning has to help with the selection and structuring of appropriate growth points, suggesting the re-deployment of economic incentives so as to achieve desired results, without thereby producing rigid *master plans*.

Modern technology is not intrinsically inimical to these possibilities, and in many ways could be helpful. While it can be mistakenly linked with high capitalization and industrial concentration, it also offers a degree of locational flexibility which was not available to Western societies in their early phase of industrialization. Electric power, road transport, and telecommunications free industry and its workforce from the degree of concentration at nodal points that occurred in the age of canals, railways, and coal. Of course this flexibility is very limited in poor countries, but it exists and will grow.

There is no iron law of development or modernization which requires vast concentrations of population to be gathered in a very few cities. Governments, if they wished, could do much to amend this trend through their economic and tax policies, and through their own very substantial role as employers. Administrative and where possible political decentralization is beneficial for the spread of economic activities, and for the avoidance of social disruption and political discontent.

The questions of how far such policies might imply (a) the boosting of second-rank cities as countermagnets to an over-inflated capital city; (b) the promotion of small industries and crafts in country towns and in the countryside itself; and (c) the restructuring of the largest city itself, cannot be entered into here. Probably a mix of all these policies is indicated. An essential need is to encourage to the utmost the willingness of new arrivals to help build their own housing and other facilities. This calls for the assembly and release of large tracts of land, reasonably located for new industrial estates and for transport facilities as these gradually develop (3.13). Such tasks, which presently defeat the best efforts of planners, would at least become more manageable if the rate of population influx was slowed down. The largest cities have enormous problems in coping with their natural rates of increase, without the burden of further large-scale immigration.

Although we are talking in each case about the control and dispersal of urban growth, the scope for any such policy in Third World countries seems very different from in Britain. In Britain planners are coping with a transformation of city regions brought about for other reasons than population growth which is negative in the built-up cores and rapid hardly anywhere save some outer parts of the London region. If one seeks a country where British planning does seem clearly relevant, and attracts some attention, it would be Japan. Japan has purchased very rapid economic growth at the expense of all those 'dis-amenities' (urban sprawl, extensive pollution, long work journeys, lack of open space) which are the concern of British planning, and Japan has now developed and modernized to the point where a restructuring of the Tokyo region into a more controlled and dispersed pattern has become feasible and very desirable.

In Third World cities the conditions and dynamic for a British-type dispersal policy do not exist in the same way. Nonetheless, modern technologies of electric power and road transport can help these cities to avoid the heavy concentration of industry associated with the rail and coal age in Britain. Indeed the conditions of modern technology make dispersal of economic growth much more feasible in principle in these countries that it once was in Britain.

Ultimately perhaps British planning has some relevance simply because it has refused to accept that 'economic forces' were a sufficient rationale for indefinite urban growth if the results appeared contrary to the welfare of the nation. This firm verdict was delivered by the Barlow Commission in 1940 in relation to the then rapid growth of London, and started a dual stream of policies, concerning both the balance *between* regions and the restructuring of cities, which have persisted since. The still faster growth of Third World cities poses precisely the same issues as did the Barlow report, and would repay examination from a similar standpoint.

References

3.1   STEWART, M., 'Introduction', in STEWART, M., *The City*, Penguin, 1972, pp. 9-63.

3.2   JACOBS, J., *The Life and Death of Great American Cities*, Penguin, 1965.

3.3   HART, D., *Strategic Planning in London*, Pergamon, 1976.

3.4   ASH, M., *Regions of Tomorrow*, Adams and Dart, 1969.

3.5   MISHAN, E., *The Costs of Economic Growth*, Penguin, 1967, pp. 233-240.

3.6   SELF, P., *Econocrats and the Policy Process*, Macmillan, 1976, Chapter 6.
3.7   WEBBER, M.M., 'Community Without Propinquity', in LOWDON, W. Jr., (Ed.), *Cities and Space*, John Hopkins Press, 1963.
3.8   MEIER, R., in BELL, G. and TYRWHITT, J., (Eds.), *Human Identity in the Urban Environment*, 1972.
3.9   HARVEY, D., in STEWART, M., (Ed.), *The City*, Penguin, 1972, pp. 269-337.
3.10 JACOBS, J., *op.cit.*
3.11 SELF, P., in BENTHALL, J., (Ed.), *Ecology in Theory and Practice*, Viking Press, 1972, pp. 81-101.
3.12 ASH, M., *Guide to the Structure of London*, Adams and Dart, 1972.
3.13 ABRAMS, C., *Housing in the Modern World*, Faber & Faber, 1964.

CHAPTER FOUR

Aspects of Urban Renewal

Gordon E. Cherry

Introduction

The future is hostage to the past, and present trends are shackled on times unborn. In considering the future city region it is imperative therefore to have a firm grasp of the factors affecting contemporary change in order to understand these particular constraints.

This Chapter looks at the processes and consequences of urban renewal in Britain since the end of World War II, and highlights a number of social and planning questions which have a bearing on the course of future development. The last 30 years has been a period of great change for British cities, during a continuous span unaffected by war and upheavals other than economic booms or depressions of relatively slight consequence: it is a good example in which to examine the working out of trends and policies without major external intervention over a long period.

During this period urban transformations occurred on a considerable scale. But the pace of development is perhaps not unique in recent urban history; there have been equally dramatic periods. At the beginning of the nineteenth century, for example, the larger Northern industrial towns grew very rapidly. In late Victorian Britain aggregation of central area commercial functions and the beginning of city decentralization through suburban expansion illustrated a qualitative as well as quantitative urban metamorphosis. Post-war Britain is therefore one of a number of pivotal periods of recent urban evolution. In this Chapter we stress the rebuilding aspect and the re-use both of urban land and the stock of buildings.

In the last 30 years vast areas of the older, central districts of British cities have been demolished and rebuilt; new layouts, new structures and new uses have replaced the old. Other areas have been saved from destruction by means of improvement in the physical condition of old plant or buildings, sometimes with conversion to a new use. Roads have been widened and new highways, some elevated, others underground, have been constructed; some roads have been obliterated, a few have taken on a new function as in the pedestrian shopping precincts. Factories and warehouses have been built to accommodate new machinery and new processes; old ones, unsatisfactory by reason of space, design or location, have been demolished. New forms of employment have produced new buildings; the processing of data is beginning to rival the processing of raw materials in its demand for labour, and the office rather than the factory has become the working environment for many. Schools, hospitals, churches, shops, other commercial premises and leisure buildings, and recreation land in the form of open space, playing fields and golf courses, have been added in great quantities.

Over Britain as a whole, the area covered by urban land use has been considerably extended; between 1945 and 1965 the average annual rate of conversion from agricultural to urban use was more than 15,000 ha (37,000 acres) in England and Wales (a figure much surpassed, however, in the 1930s when the conversion rate was more than 24,000 ha (60,000 acres) (4.1). In this phase of urban expansion millions of people have been redistributed to new homes. City regions can now be identified as far flung spheres of metropolitan influence. The tight-knit city has exploded. New neighbourhoods have been created extending the urban periphery ever outwards; old ones in the central districts are often now populated by very different community groups, perhaps of distinctive ethnic origin.

A highly complex process of economic, technological and social change, sometimes guided, sometimes constrained by public intervention, is the background to what is called urban renewal of the central districts. It is an important phase in contemporary urbanization. The city looks very different in 1976 than formerly; collectively and through a variety of institutions society has effected radical change on the urban environment. Territorial expansion of the whole built up area has been accompanied by massive redevelopment of the central core.

From this introduction the Chapter unfolds, first with an explanation of the post-war planning background. The course of urban renewal has a certain logic because there was a generally agreed view about the nature of the urban problem 30 years ago and a broad unanimity about the way in which policies might be framed to tackle that problem. Second, an overview is made of those aspects of urban renewal where social consequences are particularly apparent: housing, employment, and transportation. Third, some of the results of urban renewal are assessed, particularly the social implications for the inner city. Lastly, some of the planning lessons which should be clear from three decades of experimental public policy are reviewed. These point to some of the likely major factors in patterns of growth and change in the future city region.

The planning background

The future city does not emerge in a vacuum; its origins have a very distinct context, being forged in the crucible of technological possibilities, likely economic developments, political realities, social trends and above all a widely accepted perception of contemporary ills. The British city in the year 2000 will be shaped by trends already apparent and by the emergent shifts of opinion as to the shortcomings of our present urban environments. In the same way, the British city in 1976 has been moulded by sets of circumstances inherited from the past (4.2). At the beginning of the post-war period there was a set of strongly held views about the British city, which have been maintained with remarkable consistency.

During the 1930s conventional wisdom in planning circles was increasingly supported by protest literature and a popular political expression; it became clearly articulated during the war (4.3). This held that the large urban concentrations in Britain (largely London and the industrial conurbations, but free-standing cities were not excluded) were subject to profound social and economic disadvantages, failing to provide an acceptable setting for the majority of people. The legacy of bad housing was still overwhelming, there was congestion and lack of space for recreation, smoke and noise were environmental evils, and while an increasing number had escaped to suburbia, enforced lengthy journeys to work added to health hazards and pressures on everyday life. Redevelopment was urgently needed but was prejudiced by high land values and an absence of statutory powers for local authorities to formulate renewal schemes of their own. It was therefore necessary to develop national policies to deal with a variety of related issues: urban sprawl, the preservation of the countryside, the reservation of land for recreation, policies for the regions grievously hit by unemployment and the creation of living conditions at the local scale which offered comfort and dignity for all. This demanded an agonizing reappraisal of political wills and machineries of government; the Barlow Royal Commission (1937-40) on the Distribution of the Industrial Population helped to articulate and sharpen the national discussion when war broke out.

World War II exercised profound influences on the planning scene. In a remarkably short time the country was managed economically as never before: labour was steered, industrial production controlled, unemployment virtually eradicated, the backward regions were stimulated, agriculture was revived and the rural areas became prosperous, and our cities experienced decentralization through the evacuation of school children. Britain began to plan from the centre, and the results were remarkably effective. A consequence was a political acceptance of centralist intervention to put the country's house in order, not just during the war but after it. The blitz on London and other British cities proved of incalculable significance. Houses were destroyed and land laid to waste: there had to be urgent policies for rebuilding. Determination was added to the realization of new opportunities: the need for reconstruction, economic, physical, social and moral, led to the overwhelming desire to achieve a better Britain. The idea of planning had a receptive press and the promise of town and country planning, through which urban redevelopment and social regeneration might be promoted, was eagerly seized. The literature of the time, both technical and popular, reflected the extraordinary consensus on what needed to be done.

A new form of statutory land use planning was devised as the basis for urban and rural planning. Only a brief resume is necessary here, but the important fact to remember is that the new framework provided a context for the various aspects of urban renewal after the war. In the same way, the present day framework of statutory planning provides the first setting for renewal between now and the end of the century.

In 1943 the Ministry of Town and Country Planning was set up and legislation that year extended planning control to all land in Britain. Previously land had only been subject to planning control if it had been included in a planning scheme, and most land remained excluded, particularly in rural areas. Having rectified that omission, legislation in 1944 provided new powers for local authorities in securing reconstruction and redevelopment on blitzed and blighted land. Again, these were powers which local authorities, unless through Private Acts, did not possess. Renewal programmes to meet the long-standing criticisms of the overcrowded, badly laid out inner districts became a real possibility.

A strategic model for city-wide (indeed, region-wide) redevelopment was offered by the architect and town planner, Patrick Abercrombie. His *Greater London Plan, 1944* incorporated the grand solution of decentralization: decongestion of the inner, older areas, some peripheral expansion where permissable, but basically a restriction of continued sprawl, a Green Belt and a ring of New Towns beyond. To many it must have seemed little more than a land-use master plan, but inherent within it was a web of social policy of great imagination. The question of planning intervention in the inner areas on an unprecedented scale was a basic factor in the whole strategy, and although some early assumptions have changed substantially over the past 30 years (economic growth rather than stagnation, population expansion rather than a static, or even declining level, and an unexpected inward migration to cities, including that from overseas) it has remained so.

The Town and Country Planning Act, 1947, provided the statutory key to the future. Other legislation in 1945 (Distribution of Industry Act), 1946 (New Towns Act), 1949 (National Parks and Access to Countryside Act) and 1952 (Town Development Act) helped to frame the foundations of planning policy in specific directions. At national level this included the reversal of the flow of job opportunity to already privileged regions, the control over industrial location, the safeguarding of agricultural land and the maintenance of the vitality of rural life, and the preservation of areas of fine landscape. At regional scale there was the control of urban sprawl and the planned location of centres of population; overcrowding and high densities in the conurbations and large towns would be reduced, and decentralization promoted.

At the local level the policies were less specific and became merged in the realms of professional debate and political influences. But overall they included the orderly utilization of urban space, the promotion of amenity and convenience and the creation of good residential environments. It is important to note an important duality in the planning background, that of central government and local authority. The years immediately after 1945 were not a period solely of centralist planning; planning from the centre there was, but the agent in most aspects of town and country planning was the local authority. At this level the local council might have a very different view of planning problems and their solutions than the Ministry. There were therefore some important variations in policy and performance amongst the local planning authorities right from the start, particularly with regard to housing densities, attitudes to overspill and loss of local employment.

This then was the setting for urban renewal in post-war Britain. First there was a novel background of intervention in land use and development, with some loosely framed national and regional objectives which were prosecuted with pragmatism in the light of changing circumstances. Second, a programme of renewal was embarked upon in the central districts which set in train an unprecedented displacement of people and a wholesale demolition or improvement of dwellings. This was to be later accompanied by private commercial developmental and highway improvements, both of which led to further environment changes. The local authority became an agent of change of profound significance; its performance is central to any history of post-war British cities.

Developments, 1955-75

City renewal programmes in housing, employment, and transportation demonstrate convincingly that planning questions have both social origins and social consequences.

Housing

Britain began the post-war period with a desperate housing shortage, and it took some time before the scarcity of building materials, the need to re-equip the construction industry and the austerity of the Cripps period could be overcome. At first the assumption was that most houses would be provided by the public sector either through the New Towns programme or local authority initiatives. In fact, the restoration of the private sector commenced from the early 1950s. But the local authority has retained the mantle of redeveloper, replacement provider, and builder for those on the housing waiting lists.

The attack on slum clearance, last taken up during the 1930s was resumed in the mid-1950s. A huge backlog of unfit dwellings had long been apparent. The 1951 Census revealed that one-third of the houses in England and Wales had no bath and that more than one million houses had no flush toilet. Since then, a large number of dwellings has been cleared. In England and Wales, 1,165,000 houses were demolished or closed in the period 1955-74 (4.4). Between 1945 and 1954, 90,000 had been cleared, an average of 9000 per year, but from 1961 onwards the annual total demolished was never less than 61,000 (with the exception of 1974 when the number fell to 41,000); the years of greatest activity were 1966-72. In Scotland, a further 296,000 houses were demolished or closed in the period 1955-74. These figures imply a very high annual transference rate of people from unfit houses to alternative accommodation. In England and Wales in the period 1955-74, 3,116,000 persons were moved as a result of the clearances. In 1968, the record year for demolition, nearly 189,000 persons were moved, but throughout the 1960s and up to 1973 the annual figure was never less than 100,000 persons. With this high degree of activity, the Local Authority planner with the Medical Officer and the Public Health Inspector found himself caught up in a succession of public inquiries dealing with compulsory purchase in Clearance Areas and Comprehensive Development Areas. Never before had so much attention been devoted to the replanning of the outworn inner district.

The recent pace of slum clearance has slackened with economic crisis. But the number of identifiable unfits has also fallen and a significant movement towards house and neighbourhood improvement rather than demolition has taken place. This is a very decided change of emphasis in urban renewal programmes; perhaps the surprise is that it has taken so long to occur. Powers for house improvements have been available since 1949: local authorities were able to improve council housing and to give discretionary grants to private owners for improvement of individual properties. Incentives were increased in 1954 and this was followed by the introduction in 1959 of standard grants for the installation of basic amentities. But the rate of improvements and conversions remained disappointingly small. In the 1960s and 1970s, the policy of improvement switched from individual properties to whole areas; the 1964 Housing Act required rather cumbersome procedures, but the 1969 Housing Act, which introduced General Improvement Areas, has been taken up more widely, and Housing Action Areas can now be defined under the 1974 Act. The number of improvement grants approved in England and Wales rose sharply from 156,000 in 1970 to a record of 360,000 in 1973 (to fall again in 1974 to 231,000); in Scotland the comparable figures showing a similar pattern were 23,000 (1970), 92,000 (1973) and 68,000 (1974) (4.5).

This shift of emphasis towards improvement was accompanied by growing criticisms of wholesale demolition and comprehensive redevelopment. A policy of housing rehabilitation, social and community development and selective renewal where necessary seemed to offer greater advantages, and there seemed to be benefits too from the point of view of relative costs. But rehabilitation programmes have their difficulties. A good deal of the improvement work carried out has benefitted not the original occupant, but an incomer; a process of *gentrification*, particularly in London, has transformed large areas of working class housing into newly desirable areas for higher income households.

There are striking visual consequences of the housing renewal programmes in every British city. The urban form of central districts has been recast, and with it much of the Victorian past has been lost: the bye-law street, the tight intermixture of land uses, and the uniform housing stock. In its place we have sequences of architectural fashion: notably the low rise interlocking terraces with high rise tower blocks. The social consequences are equally dramatic. There has been a redistribution of people from the inner city to both suburban and inner city estates; disruption of community patterns and the adoption of new life styles for many. The processes of invasion and succession by one population group against another have been speeded up; some problem areas have been obliterated while other neighbourhoods have been forced into that unwelcome role.

Employment

Urban renewal affecting employment has taken place as a result of both public and private enterprise. As with housing, where a sustained shift in major tenure groups has been experienced over the last 30 years, there is a broad secular trend to observe, against which local circumstances can be seen. Subtle but profound changes in industrial structure have taken place in post-war Britain; the dominant role of manufacturing industry is being eroded by relative gains in other sectors of employment. As the total working population in manufacturing fell from 39% in 1961 to 35% in 1973, those in financial, professional and scientific services rose from 12% to 19% (4.6). City centres have experienced huge increases in employment in such service industries as insurance, banking and finance.

Against this structural background a further significant trend in job opportunity has emerged. This is not so much concerned with regional employment (the regional economic problem of the 1930s is much concealed today) but with redistribution on a city regional scale. As manufacturing industry decentralized, employment in this section fell relatively and absolutely in conurbation centres and central city districts, whereas it increased in the outer areas. Dispersal has been pronounced particularly since the 1960s; London, for example, has lost over a third of all manufacturing jobs in the last eight years (4.7). The forces of decentralization have extended to other sectors of employment too, as the recent suburban office boom in London and some provincial cities indicates.

The areas substantially at risk from these recent trends are the older central city districts, formerly the home of much manufacturing industry. But specialist areas, previously reliant on a particular trade or industry, such as the London Docklands now left upstream from the tide of new methods and requirements in shipping, have also suffered. The number and range of available jobs have declined; mechanization has done away with the need for much unskilled labour; and the small firm with its great capacity for resourcefulness and employment creation finds survival increasingly difficult.

The relatively recent rise of these new problems has been exacerbated by certain central and local planning policies (4.8). For example, there has been the policy of central government, operating through its regional offices, to persuade growing firms in the prosperous big cities to divert to areas in greater need of employment opportunities. This regional policy, operationalized through the blunt instrument of industrial development certificate (i.d.c.) control, would strive to relocate from its home base a particular establishment seeking new land for expansion. Another policy insists on improved space standards when redevelopment takes place. The number of jobs per unit area of floor space has been declining for many years as a result of new requirements of internal layout and ancillary accommodation; an additional factor is extra land for car-parking and landscape. All this has been a decisive influence in decisions to find new locations altogether—often well away from the central districts. Important too is the planner's land use control requirements of amenity and the environment. Non-conforming industry has been specifically squeezed out to alternative, better suited locations. The problems of pollution, noise, traffic considerations, nuisance, and questions of visual amenity have been responsible for both the extinction and rationalization of land use in complex, multi-purpose areas in the central districts.

What the local authority failed to do, private enterprise has often achieved. Private enterprise redevelopment schemes have contributed to urban renewal, with varying results in both employment contraction and growth. Private capital certainly fuelled the office boom and commercial redevelopment projects with consequent massive employment gains. But these have been at the expense of small backstreet industries bought out in the packaging of land ownerships or have required the relocation of some major concerns, with consequential employment losses.

Socially, a net loss of skilled jobs and a contraction of opportunity is posing severe problems for certain well defined districts. The inner city is doubly the victim of the decentralization of manufacturing industry and the central concentration of office employment.

Transportation

The sustained growth in private car ownership and road transport generally over the past quarter of a century has necessitated radical improvements to the country's highway system. Within the last 20 years the urban tramway network has disappeared, the use of public transport has considerably declined, and railway land in the heart of cities has been reclaimed for other uses, or is still derelict. Change in the period 1961-71 was certainly remarkable, and the trends continue. The number of all classes of road vehicle in Britain rose from nearly ten million to nearly 15.5 million; the number of private cars rose from nearly six million to more than 12 million. The decline of public transport in the same period is revealed by the fall in the number of passenger journeys by buses and coaches in Britain from 12.5 million to 8.6 million (4.9). Road space is now heavily utilized; traffic management schemes and localized improvements have greatly increased the capacity of existing highways, while new urban roads designed for fast flow have been built. In recent years a tiny fraction of highway space has been lost in the creation of pedestrian streets.

The full force of these changes has fallen on the central and older districts where opportunities for road building have been presented by other urban renewal schemes. Housing clearance areas have often provided the chance for major roads to be inserted in the city; the Mancunian Way in Manchester straddles an obliterated Moss Side. The results have been striking. The last great urban transport innovation was the railway, and its impact on early and mid-Victorian cities was profound through its land hunger and generation of new buildings and land activities. Great swathes cut through the urban fabric and, punctuated by elevated or sunken barriers of the tracks, these fragmented the surrounding areas, seriously interfering with general circulaton. Very much the same thing has happened with the recent phase of road building; social disruption and visual alienation in the urban scene are among the results, but on a greater scale than was ever produced by the railway.

Post-war urban renewal has typically given to the major towns and cities a superimposition of a highway net which has cut into the earlier, close knit. organic street pattern. The idea of the ring road, with radials intersected at roundabouts, received favour early in the post-war years; a geometry of town planning which has persisted a remarkably long time. The introduction of dual carriageways increased the land take but a more significantly greedy innovation was the elevated motorway with grade separated junctions. The ring road concept has continued (a typical example is at Coventry where the circle is now complete) but those cities, such as Newcastle, which began to restructure their road patterns rather later in the post-war period, proposed an inner loop road round the central district. Sometimes a national motorway approaches close to the city centre and taps into it by a spur, as at Birmingham, Leeds and Bristol.

Such examples are objectionable to many people: elevated urban expressways, once regarded as progressive new urban architecture, are now the objects of protest because they stand as symbols of unwelcome noise, pollution and alienation from the human scale, and moreover disruptive of communities. A new political wisdom has emerged. Threats to such historic towns as Bath, York and Edinburgh, and a frank reappraisal of the results of highway engineering that has already taken place in other cities, have prompted attention on alternative solutions. The continuing commercial vitality of British central areas has encouraged the success of the pedestrian shopping street. Some were originally designed as such, but an encouraging number are now being created from narrow inner roads. Contrary to former belief, the traffic which they previously accommodated, has in fact been satisfactorily absorbed in the rest of the city street network. More significantly the road building programme in urban renewal is drawing to a close, at least temporarily, and greater attention is being paid to the revival of public transport. There is no shortage of policies; the problem seems to be in the will to achieve them.

The Los Angeles highway solution is unsuited to British cities if for no other reason than limited land resources. The programme of road building over the past 20 years has created enormous environmental problems. New transportation systems such as the monorail have been investigated. But rail (underground in London, Manchester and Glasgow) and bus are the only realistic alternatives and these flexible systems are capable of improvement at costs which are relatively small compared with a motorway programme. And the social costs in land take, environmental impoverishment, and erosion of communities are reduced.

Social consequences of post-war urban renewal

A number of very distinctive trends in urban renewal, since 1945, can be identified from the examples given above. They are of major significance for the planning of the contemporary city because they reinforce the incidence of disadvantage for certain geographical areas of the city and for certain community groups. As a very broad generalization the adverse consequences of urban renewal have fallen more heavily on the unfavoured areas of the city than the favoured; on the poor rather than on the rich. It is indeed a major irony of British post-war planning that the policies which were designed to aid the disadvantaged have operated in ways which have increased rather than diminished their problems.

The many families who experienced an enforced uprooting by slum clearance, road building, or other planning projects and were subsequently rehoused (but not invariably; many became homeless) have found themselves at the difficult interface between the bureaucracy of the planning machine and the complex of community, group, family and individual interests. Although many individual benefits must have been secured through betterment in housing conditions, the results of being the victims of the bulldozer and the relocation system with all its slowness, frustrations, lack of information and sense of rejection for those affected are not acceptable. The fulminations of research workers at Newcastle and Sunderland (4.11), for example, show the lack of success which bureaucrats have enjoyed in their dealing with the public. The redevelopment areas are communities at risk which can do little to help themselves because of their economic and political powerlessness. Rapidity of change breeds fear and insecurity as the fragile stability of known environments is rudely shattered, and all with little certainty that better conditions would emerge at the end of the upheaval.

The combination of urban renewal and decentralization has not dealt only with people and their accommodation; it has also affected their work. Employment opportunities are now fewer in the central districts than formerly, and we have seen how the operation of planning has directly contributed to this. Central areas are no longer the prime employment magnets, and where new jobs have been created they are usually not suited to the relatively low skilled inhabitant of the inner city. Tourism and the hotel industry has not exactly helped either, with its tradition of low paid jobs, placing service sector workers in a dilemma of low pay and high-cost inner city living.

Inner city disadvantage has been further compounded by disparity in social service provision by local authorities. During a period when new residential areas were being built on the periphery, in New Towns and in Expanded Towns (and when in order to avoid the mistakes of the past it was deemed necessary to make these areas real communities with their own facilities), it was natural that the great weight of local authority (and development corporation) investment should have gone to them, to the relative exclusion of the old central districts. Community services, particularly in the form of new schools have gone extensively to the outskirts of cities, to private and public sector suburban estates.

The population of the inner city is unduly proportioned towards the very young or the elderly and the lower socio-economic groups. This is the area which has suffered most in the physical impact of renewal, through housing and road schemes, and for many people, housing inadequacies still remain. It has been least provided for in terms of new community and social plant: schools, hospitals, churches. The contraction in job opportunity which is now taking place means low income and a higher risk of unemployment. Urban renewal, as a vehicle of social injustice, therefore focuses attention on the inner city (4.12).

Many years of effort to eliminate slums have not solved all housing problems. The slum problem cannot be quantified in a precise way and thereafter eradicated. Not only does this particular problem remain; new problems are emerging. For example, the contraction of the private rented sector through large scale redevelopment has contributed to homelessness by reducing choices open to the people affected. Meanwhile the effects of loss of job opportunity in manufacturing industry sets in train an unwelcome set of consequences. Unemployment rises, and those requiring retraining and the unqualified school leaver are particularly vulnerable. Spending power declines. Housing choice narrows. Small shops go out of business. Environmental decay sets in. As this happens, the uncertainty felt and expressed by local authorities about the central districts becomes more pronounced. Extensive areas tend to remain derelict and blighted. The failure of local authorities to deal with physical deterioration, having helped create it, has been a frequent occurrence. The general uncertainty highlights the fundamental inability of local authorities to deal with massive socio-economic problems, the causes and manifestations of which lie beyond their control. The derelict London Docklands is an extreme case where extensive redevelopment is necessary on a scale which is far greater than the local authorities can manage from their resources.

Lessons learned

In what ways will the forces of change shape the future city? How will the nature of planning itself affect the course of development? What imperative new forces do we see emerging: is conservation, as opposed to new development, one of them? What do we say about the possibilities or limitations inherent in public sector management? From the consideration of urban renewal over the last 30 years a realistic scenario of the future city region can be glimpsed.

The urbanization of the nineteenth and twentieth centuries provided the opportunity for industrial capital to dispose of the products it created; our cities were the product of the circulation of surplus value. The internal dynamic of industrial capitalism gave some key characteristics to the emergent city: essentially the coordination of a large number of activities through market behaviour. A consequence for social structure was a stratified class society and a form of spatial organization which reflected different economic and political advantage (4.13). The contemporary city region is consequently a complex dynamic system in which spatial form and social processes are continuously interactive; a dominant spatial form has emerged with areas characterized by graduations in income, housing quality and acceptability of environmental settings. In other words, social space varies between individuals and between groups, as well as over time. This urban system has adopted an evolutionary course which is very hard to predict; there can be no assumption of equilibrium in the social process, so that spatial form is constantly in flux.

It is unlikely that these qualitative attributes of urbanism will change much over the rest of the century. Radically different assumptions for the future city region should be tempered by realism. The economic basis of capitalist society imparts a very decided characteristic to urban life and its spatial form, and we are beginning to appreciate how difficult it is to intervene as a matter of public policy in these fundamentals. The inherent complexity of the city system has so far been beyond our effective comprehension. We have failed to secure much benefit from interdisciplinary study and the planning methods we have adopted have lacked adroitness and sophistication. Consequently the results of our urban renewal programmes have frequently reinforced social disadvantage: on balance, the relocation process has improved the options for the affluent suburbanite and limited them for the low income household in a central district. The major characteristic of the modern city remains: social inequality in an uncomfortable relationship with spatial form over time.

Over the last 30 years in Britain a highly complex form of regulatory planning has been developed in a local/central government relationship. At the end of the 1940s and the beginning of the 1950s planners were confident of their ability to deal with urban, rural and regional questions, to shape cities, to meet social needs, and to create ideal communities; the war time pioneers such as Abercrombie seemed to capture the spirit of reconstruction. By the end of the 1950s and the beginning of the 1960s, frustrated by non-achievement, planners were searching for new insights. Now their confidence has been sapped, their vision reduced and their expectancy of the unquestioned benevolence of central and local bureaucracies diminished; they have turned to a participatory community for guidance and support. New directions in planning will undoubtedly emerge, but for the moment it is difficult to detect any major feature that could have radical implications for the future city.

The planner has been described thus: "a listener, a researcher, as well as a decision maker. The office of the planner is to guage trends in the economy and in society, to pinpoint shortcomings and sources of friction, and to make proposals for solving the immediate problems of the community in which he works. The grand design is at the back of his mind but in practice he is a gradualist, a social engineer capable at best of improving the immediate function and environment of this area, one section at a time, according to a scheme of priorities which he himself must help to shape" (4.14). The chief implication from this observation is that planning is becoming frankly incrementalist in nature, and only rarely can it proceed along the fixed lines of a declared plan for any length of time.

The course of urban renewal over the last 30 years has shown that there is neither political will nor a sufficient constancy of economic, demographic and other circumstances to allow a continuous prosecution of planning policy along the lines of a fixed master plan for any length of time. There are no such things as unchangable blue prints; new situations demand reassessments of policy. There can be demographic forecasts of great variation; economic conditions change abruptly; technological innovations create new opportunities and problems; social values are not constant. Single, fixed ideas about spatial form and types of urban development soon lose favour and relevance; high rise residential blocks were architecturally exciting one decade, a sociological disaster the next; the urban motorway first represented progressive technology, then an alien intrusion.

Urban renewal over the past 30 years has been carried out at a phenomenal rate. Perhaps the rate of physical change has been unnecessarily great and attention has turned to conservation of environment rather than its destruction and rebuilding. This feeling is emerging as a dominant one in Britain with implications for the future city.

The vast quantity of physical change has not been accompanied by a commensurate advance in quality. Change has not necessarily implied improvement. Protests grow about alien environments and the inhuman scale of local settings; the achievement of a new quality of life through urban renewal has become a hollow joke. This has led to the view that for a while no change at all would actually be beneficial. With regard to housing stock, rehabilitation is preferable to premature demolition and replacement; for other buildings too re-use of old stock is advantageous in order to secure continuity in the urban townscape and a scale and texture rarely achieved in modern buildings.

This contemporary mood began somewhat narrowly with architectural conservation, but a widening of concern is now reflected in environmental conservation. (4.15). The ideas implicit in the concept of conservation will require important changes of our planning system. There has to be effective management of urban traffic.

Nationally, the roaring tide of private vehicles has to be checked and held in control; the decline in public transport has to be reversed. A viable form of local traffic planning is necessary if traffic flows are to be managed in the interests of a carefully conserved environment; access to the cores of historic cities are critical aspects for control. Secondly, there has to be effective management of, and control over, the use of old buildings. This implies a measure of local authority planning control which many would be reluctant to accept. The trend in recent years has been to argue that too much detailed control was unduly paternalistic, that bureaucracy stifled initiative and that wisdom after all did not solely lie with the planner. Thirdly, there has to be careful design of new buildings. Conservation is not simply retention of the old; there has to be a constant renewal process. But once again, this requirement is somewhat contrary to present day opposition to rigorous development control.

Bound up in all these three factors is the question of planning method and the degree of management by public authority. Over the last 10 years the statutory process of conservation has grown from the protection of individual buildings through Preservation Orders to the protection of composite areas through the designation of Conservation Areas. We now contemplate the conservation of entire historic towns, such as Bath. Such statutory preservation is really a further endorsement of rigorous planning control and area management, rather as Green Belt designation was given to countryside areas around cities. It remains a moot point as to whether the institutional and technical capacities in planning are up to it. Given the inherently capitalist structure of our cities, there must be doubts as to whether our planning machine is capable of resisting the enormous forces of new development, and its implicit rejection of the old, for very long.

Environmental transformations have been effected by a variety of disjointed agencies. Government has been at two major levels, central and local, and as we have seen, local authorities have been imperfect executors of central directives. An intermediate third level, regional, has been a provincial arm from the centre. But operating in parallel, a number of *ad hoc* bodies have represented important functions such as health, New Towns, sports provision, and race relations, now recently added to by the Regional Water Authorities. Coordination within central government between various Ministries has been weak. Within local government the same fragmentation exists amongst service departments, such as Education, Health, Housing and Planning. The Development Plan (and now the

Structure Plan) has been a very inadequate document, albeit the only one, to represent a local authority's intentions regarding the *total* urban problem. The inability of these institutions to grapple with the sheer complexity of urban life has created new management structures, whereby the single service departments are replaced by integrated management teams covering the whole range of the corporate authority's work.

This search for coordination in an administrative system stems from a recognition of the interconnectivity between urban problems: education linked to job opportunity and income potential, to life style, housing, health and leisure. If problems are interlinked then so too must be solutions: hence the search for coordination in social policy. Whether we are at the point of making a breakthrough in this through improved management systems remains to be seen. The idea of corporate planning has become somewhat tarnished recently but a lengthy phase of experimentation is surely demanded. So much can be done by way of innovation; one view is that a new breed of urban administrator is required to overcome a past system of training provided firstly through over-specialist education lacking a synoptic understanding, and secondly through professionalism, purpose built to specific interests, that is now becoming outmoded.

In the meantime, the administrative plight of the big cities is getting worse. The recent threatened collapse of the financial base of New York City is seen as a portent for others, and in this country the capacity of the Greater London Council and the new Metropolitan County Councils to effectively administer their areas is a matter of some speculation. Thirty years' experience of urban renewal has shown how difficult a planned operation it is, and we seem to be getting no better at it. We talk of the failure of planning, but really it is the failure of government institutions. What confidence can we have that we could positively plan for a desirable city region of the future significantly better than the present one? At best the system can react with humanity and concern at the emergence of social problems and to implement desirable programmes of construction, houses or roads. The evolution of our cities will result from these incremental activities.

This is no novel conclusion, nor necessarily a disappointing one. What matters in city planning is our capacity to recognize the social origins of urban problems, and the social consequences of urban policies. In effect, contemporary planning is being called upon to humanize our urbanism. Post-war renewal programmes have failed to do this, and the task is before the next generation. It is one thing to pursue efficiency in our urban environment, but another to ignore the social cost in that achievement. This is the lesson of the past 30 years; it is also the hope for the future city region.

References

4.1   WHITBY, M. C., *et al.*, *Rural Resource Development*, Methuen, 1974.
4.2   For a general background, see CHERRY, G. E., *Urban Change and Planning*, G. T. Foulis, 1972.
4.3   The events are described in CHERRY, G. E., *The Evolution of British Town Planning*, Leonard Hill Books, 1974.
4.4   *Housing statistics*, H.M.S.O. Also *Housing and Construction Statistics*, H.M.S.O.
4.5   *Housing and Construction Statistics*, H.M.S.O.
4.6   *Social Trends*, 5, H.M.S.O., 1974.
4.7   DEAKIN, N., 'Some Aspects of Social Planning in London', in ROSE, R., (Ed.), *The Mangement of Urban Change in Britain and Germany*, Sage Publications, 1974.
4.8   For further reading, see SMITH, B.M.D., 'Industry and Employment', in CHERRY, G.E., (Ed.), *Urban Planning Problems*, Leonard Hill Books, 1974.
4.9   *Annual Abstract of Statistics*, H.M.S.O., 1972.
4.10   GOWER DAVIS, J., *The Evangelistic Bureaucrat*, Tavistock Publications, 1972.
4.11   DENNIS, N., *People and Planning*, Faber, 1970.
4.12   A political examination is given by FALK, N., *et.al.*, *Inner City*, Fabian Research Series 320, Fabian Society, 1975.
4.13   Essential reading for this interpretation is HARVEY, D., *Social Justice and the City*, Edward Arnold, 1973.
4.14   *Tomorrow's London*, a background to the Greater London Development Plan, Greater London Council, 1969.
4.15   For a short, but forceful, discussion, see NUTTGENS, P., 'Conservation: from Continual Change to Changing Continuity', *The Planner*, R.T.P.I. Journal, 61, 7, 1975.

PART TWO

CHAPTER FIVE

The People
of the City Region

Murray Stewart*

The nature of the City Region

Faced with accusations that the quality of the urban environment has noticeably deteriorated since 1947, that the level of provision of public services is inadequate, and that the standard of living is in real terms falling, many professionals concerned with the business of urban government express the view that somehow or other there has been an absence of concern for 'people'. Reactionary and aged bureaucrats bemoan the lack of community spirit, the decline of the family and the unwillingness of 'people' to help other 'people'. Radical young activists castigate the bureaucracy and call for power to 'the people'. Liberal bureaucrats and reactionary activists voice similar opinions. Yet this appeal for a larger popular or populist dimension to government of the city region is no more than mystification since 'the people' of the city region are as nebulous, if not more so, than the city region itself.

One assumption might be that there exists between the people of the city region a community of interest, an identity which binds them together in pursuit of common goals. There is little evidence to support such an assumption. The concept of community is one which has been extensively examined in recent years and found to be

*See note at end of Chapter

somewhat wanting in respect of its relevance to contemporary planning problems, particularly those of urban renewal, comprehensive redevelopment etc. Planned new communities—the New Towns designated by successive Ministers, the Expanded Towns established by bilateral agreement between exporting conurbations and importing towns, or the new estates developed by local authorities in response to local housing needs, have in many cases failed to provide the sense of community that the original proponents of the schemes had hoped. This is regrettable, perhaps inevitable. Even if, however, the New Towns had been more successful, even if urban renewal had been implemented with a greater awareness of the often conflicting social tensions at work, or even if peripheral housing estates had been developed with a range of community facilities and local job opportunities it is questionable whether anyone would yet have recognized 'the people of the city region'.

Webber, Meier and countless others have commented, as other Chapters of this book indicate, upon the extension of communication networks and the resultant impact upon various aspects of social behaviour—shopping, employment, leisure and recreation, education etc. The nonplace urban realm has, to an extent, replaced the locality based community. Rising car ownership, inter-urban mobility by public transport, wider job and housing opportunities have, for the young, the skilled, and the better off, raised the sights from the city region horizon, if that ever existed, to the nation-state or international horizon. The city region is not recognized in administrative terms by a tier of government; it is not perceived in a cultural or historic sense as the Kilbrandon Commission demonstrated. Cities and their surrounding areas are peopled by individuals who vary in respect of their age and sex, their socio-economic group, their occupation and their income. They vary with respect to their status at work or with their neighbours and with respect to their dwelling—its age, price and above all its tenure. The people of Govan, of Hillfields, of Toxteth, and of Deptford, have more in common with each other than the people of Deptford, Bromley and Tunbridge Wells. Equally Skelmersdale in the Merseyside region and Crawley in the London region are more similar to each other than to other towns within the same city region.

In addition to structural variations in the populations of the city region, there are also variations over time. Within Britain the pattern of inter-regional migration has altered over the decades as White demonstrates in the opening Chapter.

In the last ten years or so the regions of the South West and East

Anglia have experienced extensive population growth due in no small measure to migration inwards of retired couples, and Hancock points out in the second Chapter the decentralizing process that has occurred, and is occurring in the majority of the metropolitan areas of Great Britain.

At the onset we should note the considerable fluidity of the distribution of population. In addition to the variations in the population structures of city regions due to inter and intra-regional movement, there exists the influence of international migration. Several cities in Britain—notably London, but in addition Birmingham, Leicester, Leeds/Bradford for example—have received migrants from abroad and in the 1950s and early 1960s, the character of these city regions, in terms of population structure, certainly altered.

The 'people' of the city region, therefore, can in no sense be seen as a homogeneous mass. They age and die and they move home and job. In Britain this fluidity can be exaggerated. City regions can be characterized as much by their stability as by their dynamism. If, however, we consider the relevance of changes in the city region in England to the planning circumstances of developing countries, for example, it is clear that the changing structure of population and the opportunities and constraints that such a changing structure brings forth, are likely to be of major significance.

However stable or unstable the population of the city region, however diverse or common their concerns, however fluid the planning context, there can be no doubt that the built environment for the next decade and more is already *in situ*. Pahl has pointed out that in physical terms the city regions of the last decade of the century will look remarkably like the city regions of the 1960s, and we can be reasonably sure that the physical structures that stand at present will fulfil the majority of the needs of the next quarter of a century in terms of shelter, education, health care, economic activity, movement, etc. The people of the city region will be subject to a variety of economic, social and political pressures which are outlined below, but the built forms are, by and large, in existence. Renewal of cities represents only a low rate of replacement of fixed capital in buildings. With a declining rate of population growth, or even an absolute decline, the 'roofs over heads' priorities for new buildings will decline and we will be left with an ageing but partly rehabilitated stock of physical assets. The two aspects that I have so far identified—the relative heterogeneity of the population and the relative fixity of the built environment—paled into insignificance however beside two further sets of factors likely to affect the social patterns of the 1980s.

On the one hand there are likely to be modifications in the accepted norms of social behaviour. By and large such modifications may be marginal since the basic social institutions of the city region—the family, the school, television, etc.—are unlikely to undergo radical change and attitudes to various aspects of social behaviour—sex, drink, travel, for example—may have acquired a certain stability following the consumerist peak of the 1960s and the contrasting conservationist gloom of the early seventies. Nevertheless, we can see that social trends evolve and the city region of the future may reflect different attitudes to fertility, marriage, feminism, property ownerships, etc.

On the other hand, in addition to this incremental evolution of social patterns, there is likely to be an immediate, and possibly lasting, response to economic pressures. Income and wealth are likely to be relatively hard to come by at both ends of the scale and the two parallel resource allocating mechanisms of 1980s Britain—the free market (constrained as it is by a variety of public controls) and the public sector (constrained as it is by the necessity to maintain a viable capitalist system)—are both likely to respond to a shortage of resources by lowering the standard of real income of the people of the city region.

The labour market and public expenditure

Ray Pahl (5.1) has suggested a variety of possible trends at home and at work. Many are concerned with the role of women in the family and Pahl postulated an ambiguous future. On the one hand there may be increasing opportunities in the non-domestic labour market, wider educational facilities for women, altered attitudes to the sharing of domestic tasks and other indicators of a relative liberalization for women. On the other hand there may also be pressures towards conservatism both through a reappraisal of conventional marriage and through a trend towards 'serial monogamy'. Pahl emphasized the likely increased emphasis upon locality-based interest and suggested that in a situation where resources are scarce there may well be a movement towards a more extended family within the owned home—an economic and social asset in times of economic stringency. The practice of the uninterrupted, predictable career progression may become less common; intermittent periods of unemployment may shatter the security of the middle-classes; white-collar worker, retraining and job switching may be more prevalent, the breadwinner may be either partner in a marriage, local service cooperatives may emerge.

This is conjectural. It is quite possible, to give one example, that the pressures on the male job market, instead of encouraging female labour market participation as a complementary activity the main outcome of which would be a sustained family income, might rather lead to male retrenchment. Such jobs as did exist would be argued to be the traditional prerogative of the male. Measures to aid women workers—e.g. facilities for minding children—might be cut back and women would be forced back into the home to be supported upon a poverty wage of a low-earning but chauvinistically 'working' male.

Since so many 'social trends' are manifestations of the effects of the operation of the economic system we should look closely at the future economic environment in order to judge the most likely future characteristics and conditions of the people of the city region in 1980s. Total household incomes will probably be, in real terms, severely constrained. Real income is made up of a variety of elements—earned income from employment, unearned income from capital, unearned income in the form of supplementary state benefits of various kinds, access to services from local and central government and numerous *ad hoc* authorities (such as the Health Authorities), in combination with a set of local and national prices which determine the consumption budget chosen by the individual household. The major element within this array of real income sources remains (in most areas) earned income from employment. Considerable evidence has been available since the 1930s about the incidence of unemployment and low wages as between different parts of the country and in particular as between different regions, and for three decades regional policies have aimed to reduce the disparities between regions partly by encouraging labour mobility but predominantly through measures aimed at moving firms from the 'congested' regions to the other deprived regions (the Development Areas). These policies have not altogether eradicated regional differentials and in the last two or three years there has emerged a growing tendency to regard the problems of unemployment, low activity rates, below average earnings etc. in a regional or sub-regional context rather than in an inter-regional context. The *local* employment issue will be one of the concerns of the 1980s and the challenge to much of traditional labour market theory is to develop methods of problem analysis and policy formulation which are based on empirical evidence abut a disaggregated national labour market. Whether the appropriate level of disaggregation is that of 'the city region' is open to doubt, since at present there are numerous groups on both the demand and supply sides of the labour market whose horizons in terms of market information, job search, travel to work area, provision of training facilities etc. are less than region wide. In fact for some, the boundaries of the labour market (geographically and psychologically) will be very tight indeed and the effective area for seeking alternative job opportunities will be limited to that within a mile from home. More importantly, age, skill and industrial experience will set limits to the individual worker's competitiveness in the job market and so introduce institutional factors into the employment situation. Already the evidence of severely imbalanced local labour markets is impressive—the sign of an imperfectly working market economy to some, the inevitable consequence of an aspatial employment planning system to others. In either case the implications for the families of the city region— and perhaps for those of the old city rather more than for those of the metropolitan region—are of a diminishing real wage and of increasing uncertainties over the reliability of the second or third wage contributions to the family budget.

In many cases the worst effects will be cushioned through the mechanisms of the Welfare State. Unemployment benefits, income supplements of various kinds, rent and rate rebates, the state education and health services, local government provision and voluntary effort will all contribute to the provision of a variety of welfare services. Nevertheless the 1970s and 1980s will almost certainly see some reduction in the level of public expenditure as personal and institutional savings are sucked into the provision of industrial investment. All major political parties will find it hard to raise levels of personal taxation further and it seems more than probable that the gentle process of redistribution which has been continuing for the last quarter of a century will come to a halt or indeed be reversed. Local authorities are looking closely at the impact of constant budgets, academics are running seminars on 'zero growth'. Central government circulars have pointed the need for cutbacks in education, health, transportation, housing and planning and have canvassed the sanction of cash ceilings should local authorities not conform. To compound the problem, the traditional fall-back agencies—charities and voluntary bodies—are unable to fill the gap adequately since their sources of income are increasingly pinched in a period of inflation. Indeed the demise of a number of the non-governmental bodies in the voluntary field is likely to lead to a correspondingly large increase in the demands laid upon statutory bodies. For example, the difficulties of voluntary housing aid groups in providing temporary shelter for the homeless are manifest. If such groups are unable to continue carrying at least part of the burden of catering for the homeless, more will fall upon the appropriate local government authority (if and when the counties and districts finally decide who the appropriate authority is). Nor will expenditure cuts merely affect the voluntary agencies. Pressure on resources will force local and central government departments to concentrate primarily upon their basic objectives— family housing, roofs over heads for schools, bed spaces for hospitals, etc. The bulk of expenditure is committed to demands from these basic ends and the marginal minority needs are, again inevitably, sacrificed. The interaction between programme areas is forgotten and the impact upon people of excised and ill coordinated expenditures is ignored. At a time when in theory the consequences of multiple deprivation are at their most severe, there can be little thought for the spillover effects of social spending. The philosophy of public expenditure in the 1970s and 1980s may well have been summed up in the final sentences of a recent circular (5.2) commenting upon the interrelationship between programme areas.

"These measures (expenditure restrictions) will inevitably lead to a reduced capacity of the personal social services to meet demands made upon them by education, housing and health services and the courts."

Implications for social behaviour

What are the implications for individual and group behaviour in the 1980s within this scenario of the labour market and the public expenditure position?

(i) *Retrenchment.* There will be a general move towards making do with less, towards managing more efficiently with what resources are available and generally indulging in a 'digging in' process. This will be manifest in various ways. In the manpower field there will be redeployment of labour, retraining of professional as well as skilled and semi-skilled staff, people will be asked to undertake unaccustomed jobs; Government departments will, as noted above, have to meet unchanged or even more ambitious objectives with the same resources; there will be less incentive for innovation; there will be some strengthening of departmental or professional boundaries. In the private sector, as suggested earlier, there will be an increased regard for the owned house as a tangible asset in a period of retrenchment. To an extent this process of retrenchment may be regarded as neutral. It represents a form of managerialism, an approach to the husbanding of resources that may be unfortunate but does not significantly alter social relations. Other changes are less neutral, and the second could be beneficial in the long term.

(ii) *Cooperative effort.* The scarcity of both public and private resources and a pervading atmosphere of retrenchment will, in some cases, lead to a greater spirit of cooperation. In part this will be merely a defence mechanism—the response of those who stand to lose against the pressures of 'zero growth' in public spending and a gesture of solidarity amongst the relatively powerless. Cooperative effort will also emerge, however, as a positive response to the challenge of making do with less and as an effective means of maintaining real income standards whilst expending fewer resources of finance, manpower or materials. Cooperative effort has emerged already in a number of forms. At the workplace, for example, there have been a number of industrial cooperatives although sadly these early initiatives have tended to be established in situations offering the minimum potential, in terms of time or resources, for innovation and experiment. The Labour government is behind housing cooperatives and a number of these are now emerging, although not without their teething problems. In both these instances—the industrial and the housing cooperative—many of the real challenges to a cooperative ideology have yet to appear and will only do so when there is a real need to deal with allocative problems—the threat of redundancy, for example, or the problems of tenancy allocation in the housing field. There are other signs of emerging cooperative self-help. Numerous groups (often middle-class) operate cooperative food purchasing schemes, whilst the investment in, and shared use of, major domestic capital is increasingly under discussion. Lawn mowers, home freezers, do-it-yourself machinery, caravans, second homes are often purchased and managed on a joint basis and there is immense scope for an extension of this cooperative activity. One fundamental barrier stands in the way, of course. Since Western society is firmly wedded to private property, a major shift towards co-ownership and cooperation would require an abandonment of traditional cultural and economic norms, and it may well be unrealistic to expect this on any noticeable scale.

(iii) *Self interest.* An alternative possibility is that there will be a growing emphasis upon selfish, individualistic behaviour. With resources scarce, standards lowered, and power eroded it will be every person for him or herself, or at least every family for itself. Where the main mechanism of allocation and distribution is a market or quasi-market economy this is scarcely surprising since the major characteristic of the market is its atomistic nature. We may see, however, individual or sectional values applied to those points of society which can only function efficiently if some form of consensually based control is effective and the effect, in housing, health or education may be salutary. It is already evident that the absence of adequate housing and the ever increasing constraints that are affecting attempts to either increase the housing stock or allow more effective use of what stock there is, have led to attempts by individual people or families to gain access to housing outside the hitherto accepted machinery of allocation. Some squatting has been by groups either seeking political change or experimenting with a newer fluid life-style, but many of the squats within the conurbation cities have been by families unable to get a home by any other means. The erosion of established norms and values throughout the fifties and sixties could lead to widespread feelings of alienation, and if central and local government are increasingly unable to provide resources for services which have in the past been regarded (rightly or wrongly) as being available on demand, such feelings could find expression in a wave of self-interested, individualistic and even anarchic behaviour.

(iv) *Reaction to liberalism.* Within the city region there are a host of services, provided by a host of authorities. In Britain as elsewhere, there has been widespread criticism of the bureaucracy that provides these services and of the quality of the output of the bureaucracy. Although there is now a much wider understanding of the potential role of the local authority as a positive, policy oriented body asserting its concern for the totality of local welfare, there still remains a view that all that local government does is provide services, and that by and large it does so inefficiently. Resentment of the extent to which the public sector pre-empts its resources is therefore widespread and an inevitable consequence may be a reactionary bid to cut public services or to maintain them at a minimum level. Such bids often ignore the fact that much local expenditure is a result of central government legislation, designed to improve conditions in areas of real need—the elderly, the chronically sick, the homeless etc. In a period of severe financial stringency the Welfare State will be put to its severest test for decades and there must be some danger of a significant regressive redistribution of real income in the city region.

(v) *The emergence of conflict.* Several of the possibilities mentioned above highlight the probability that the city regions of the 1970s and 1980s will see the development of further conflict over scarce spatial and social resources. Such conflict might take the form of a sharper debate over the allocation of investment resources between different parts of the city region. In the absence of a city region level of political decision-making the existing administrative boundaries will, to some extent, determine the structure of inter-area and inter-authority conflict. In England the juxtaposition of metropolitan district, metropolitan county and shire county within whatever are loosely defined as city regions will give rise to considerable conflict over resources for housing, transport, recreation and other services. The pressures on public expenditure have already indicated that difficult enough choices have to be made between different policy objectives without having these choices further complicated by the anomalies of local government organization. Furthermore, even within authorities there are conflicts between richer and poorer areas, between housing and education programmes, between spreading whatever resources are available more widely or concentrating them on areas of highest need. Retrenchment, individualism, reactionary responses all seem likely to make the processes of resource allocation complex and bitter. The coming years may see a heightening of conflict and a struggle for power over local resources. This may result in some redistribution; alternatively there may merely be a consolidation of the existing structure of power.

Life styles in the 1980s

Speculation about future life-styles can be an idle occupation—

sociologists feeding planners with the fodder of blue-print plans without regard to process or implementation. Nevertheless, it is possible to identify in the argument presented above two contrasting strands for the future. The first emphazies conservatism, stability, the status quo, and retrenchment; the second focuses on the potentially dynamic impact of scarcity through its impact upon life styles and the labour market. In looking at the 1980s these two strands may manifest themselves as follows.

First, it may be increasingly simple to categorize individuals into broad social groupings which will become increasingly isolated from each other as movement from one to the other is subject to ever-growing constraints. On this basis it is possible to develop, as Pahl has done, a crude caricature of the social structure illustrating some possible differences between broad groupings of the population. Secondly, we may be forced to look at specific forms of consumption to see precisely how and on whom the changing economic pressures of the 1970s are likely to have an effect.

Following on his work on Strategic Planning in the South East, Pahl has elaborated his typology of classes at the regional level. He distinguished three broad categories—the Senior Salariat, the Middle-Mass and the Underclass. The Senior Salariat would be in the most privileged situation having accumulated personal investment in the fat years of the fifties and sixties in terms of education and financial stability. Their skills are likely to be highly specific, non-transferable and indeed non-acquirable by aspiring entrants to the Senior Salariat class. In addition their position is likely to be stalwartly defended by a professional institution. They may own more than one home (or indeed be even more privileged in so far as they rent an urban residence) and despite the apparent restrictions on petrol may well own three vehicles (parking for which in the cities will be in private off street facilities, permanently rented). In addition to their basic characteristics of being highly skilled and generally well-heeled, Pahl sees this group as being predominantly managerialist in function and indeed hypothesizes that such new entrants as do make it to the Senior Salariat will be managerialist /technical in terms of occupation.

Overall the Senior Salariat are perhaps unlikely to account for more than 10-15% of the population, though in particular enclaves it is not unreasonable to suppose they might form a majority surrounded only by those required to provide the service sector back-up that their consumption patterns would demand. By and large, however, the majority of the population would comprise the

Middle-Mass, characterized predominantly by their absence of wealth (other than an owned home) and by their dependence upon the market as providing access to regular income. Pahl accepts that there will be a myriad of sub-groups and classes within the Middle-Mass but suggests that there may yet be a few general 'straws in the wind affecting the patterns of urban life'—increased consciousness of the role of women; a blurring of the manual/non-manual worker distinction; a growing focus on small scale social movements based on residential locality networks and focusing on equalities of consumption rather than inequalities at the work place; and above all, the emergence of sporadic protest against the local gatekeepers.

Finally the Underclass remain much as before, if perhaps fewer in both absolute and relative terms. They are likely to be the objects rather than the subjects of urban change, affected by, yet only partially able to respond to, the conflicts that will arise over the allocation and distribution of both spatial and non-spatial resources. Here again whilst the Underclass are in a very different position from the Middle-Mass with respect to their ability to generate counter action, one of the main characteristics to emerge may be the growing dominance of local and central bureaucracy and the inability of unwillingness of such bureaucracy to influence the opportunities for social mobility.

It is indeed rarely that bureaucracy—central or local—will, in fact, ever conceive of distributional problems in terms of classes (however defined). Certainly measures such as the wealth tax or a minimum wage could have significant effects on broad groups of the population but at the city region scale, and even more evidently at the local authority or neighbourhood level where we have identified the potential for sporadic locality based social movements, the impetus is much more likely to come from particular issues of immediate policy significance than from a gradual awareness of the differential social mobility rates. It may, therefore, be necessary to look much more closely at specific forms of local consumption and to monitor changing values, attitudes, and behaviour towards these forms in order to identify, as they emerge, the changing life styles in the future city region. Two examples of the possibilities are outlined below—transportation and dogs.

Attitudes to transportation have altered radically in recent years, indeed even within a few months, but it is even more salutary to consider the changes over the past 50 years or so in order to see how rapidly a particular form of life-style can alter. Car ownership and use was, of course, increasing throughout the 1920s and 1930s but even by 1945 car ownership was a luxury confined to a minority. In the 1950s and 1960s the boom in car ownership emerged, and with a major road investment programme being undertaken to create the capacity for increased car usage, universal ownership, unrestricted use, and unlimited reliance on private transport were seen as the most desirable and most probable norms for the 1980s. In a short time there has been a radical reappraisal, the impetus for which has come from a variety of sources. First the real cost of motoring which remained absolutely and relatively low in the 1960s has begun to rise dramatically. Even if petrol is still cheaper in Britain than in other European countries, the increased cost has, without doubt, made an impact on travel patterns as is demonstrated by the fact that the mileage of road motor vehicles fell in 1974 for the first time ever. Increased fuel cost, however, is only one factor and probably not the most important. In the 1960s there was a major urban investment programme of town centre redevelopment and improvement of the road network involving inter alia extensive building of major relief roads both within and around cities. It is of course, unreasonable to evaluate the urban road programme of the 1960s without postulating what would have been the situation without it, but that is a step in the argument that is often omitted, and as a result there has been a major reaction against the scale and intensity of 'the urban motorway programme'. The loss of good housing, located in the path of the bulldozer, has aggravated popular feeling and the growth of the rehabilitation/conservation movement with respect to housing and local neighbourhoods (one example of the locality based social movement mentioned earlier) has heaped coals on the critical fires of anti-road lobbies. All of this is a somewhat crude caricature of the roads argument. There can be no doubt, however, that there has been a gut reaction to large scale physical change and the main brunt of this has been borne by the urban road programme. In addition, however, the arguments have been strengthened by a growing awareness that the case for providing for individualized travel by road was never as strong as was thought. Household car ownership will never be universal, and even in car owning household there will be several people, particularly the elderly and children, who will not have the use of a car. We are now aware of the social aspects of transport and there is growing debate about public transport in general, and fare subsidies to maintain services required on social grounds in particular. Attention is given to rural transport needs where non-availability of a car can lead to social and economic deprivation. A new system of funding transport has been introduced—the Transport Supplementary Grant which channels resources to county authorities on the basis of Transport Policies and Programmes. The system explicitly calls for the claims for road building and for public transport to be set one beside the other, a comparison which could never have been made a decade ago. Much of this is now taken for granted. The lesson for the future is not that there is a major swing away from the motor car towards public transport; it is rather that it is quite impossible to foresee more than a decade ahead what forms of personal movement will be desired and accepted.

A second example is perhaps even more interesting. For hundreds of years the dog has been regarded as man's best friend. The dog's function as companion, guard, working animal, pet, has been unquestioned and had one been preparing a scenario of the typical Middle-Mass family of 1985 it is most likely that such a family would have owned a dog. Within a few years we have begun to seriously examine our attitude to dogs and there has been a clear shift of opinion which in general can be summed up as 'anti-dog'. A private member's bill has passed through Parliament to become the Guard Dogs Act; a Committee of investigation, under Lord Houghton, has reported; the Department of the Environment has a Working Party on Dogs; more than 50 local authorities have dog wardens; the newspapers are full of articles and letters. The problem is not a simple one. There is an environmental health argument which has sparked off much of the debate as complaints of dogs fouling pavements and parks have grown. Packs of dogs are known to roam certain areas and have attacked children. Stray dogs run wild and are a frequent cause of road accidents. Guard dogs have, without warning, savaged visitors to both industrial and domestic property. On the other hand, there is some debate amongst social workers about the importance of a dog (or other pet) to the elderly for companionship and it has been suggested that provision should be made to look after dogs when a single old person is forced to go to hospital, for example. The licensing system is being re-examined since the level—37.5p—is the same as it was 100 years ago and is almost certainly less than its cost of collection. Nevertheless, it is widely accepted that the dog licence fee is the most extensively avoided charge in the country.

Clearly the question of our attitude to dogs is not central to the welfare of the whole nation. The current debate does illustrate, however, the rapidity with which a particular habit or trait of character or consumption pattern, can be subject to radical and critical questioning. It is also almost certainly true that if we can alter our views about dogs within a few years we can equally quickly alter our views about people and places. Fashions in planning can and do alter very rapidly and when we set up hypotheses about 'the people of the city region' in the 1980s we will inevitably be unclear as to whether we believe, for example, that they will be living close to the ground or ten storeys up. Catch phrases, planning fads, home truths may be caught up in a few words and translated into an urban environment of the future. At least one thought that will remain with me from my association with Colin Buchanan was his description of the essence of a good housing policy 'Don't forget the sheds', and in discussion following his talk to the British Council Conference Ray Pahl commented "my typical image of the happy average British family is that they want the chance to make a mess of their own environments on their own without anybody bothering them—creating their own little bit of shed at the back, keeping a whole heap of junk—a low key, quiet inward looking style".

There are certainly indications of an awareness within planning of the importance of the small scale. Development control is an increasingly respectable activity in planning offices in contrast to its hitherto Cinderella position; local plans are being seen as a major growth point for positive planning. Attitudes to the scale and pace of development have switched markedly in a decade. We cannot be sure of the genesis of such changes in attitude, nor of the consequences, particularly if a new view of say the local environment is based on an approach to planning which emphasizes the autonomy of the individual at the expense of the collective consensus. Extending the example of the shed for instance throws up an interesting contrast between the viewpoints of Buchanan and Pahl. The former emphasizes the shed as a recognition of the needs of men in housing policy, an expression of the chauvinist desire for domain, freedom, and the pursuit of a hobby. The shed (not literally a shed) is a means of self expression, a silent protest against the niceties of development control, a reminder of the need to evolve a housing policy that allows men (and women) to live individualistic lives. Much of this finds an echo in Dobry and other commentaries on the contemporary development control scheme but Pahl's interpretation of the shed syndrome might be different. His speculations on future life styles envisage a shared role for male and female. The shelter, the escape, the refuge of a shed has no place in the open family of the 1980s, where husband and wife interchange roles in terms of caring for house, garden, children and car. Yet Pahl recognizes the desire for personal space, the squirrel's tree hole, where acquisition and self expression are allowed full rein. Trivial as this example may be it perhaps gives some indication of the extent to which apparently small alterations in individual life styles can significantly affect the form of the built environment. For, as Buchanan has pointed out, the concept of the shed on the ground has profound implications for the design and density of residential areas. In so far as changes in the norms and aspirations of individual people in the city region impinge upon planning and housing standards, the future shape and form of the city region is far from predictable.

It is simple, however, to offer up trite generalizations about the potential impact of changed attitudes to dogs or sheds. It may be true that if there were to be a significant shift in society's view of, for example, pets, there would be a marked effect upon some aspects of environmental control, but for the particular individuals or families concerned the change would be marginal. The most important challenge to planning (defined in a wide sense) in the city region is to alter the life chances of some groups *more* than marginally. The city region has over the past quarter of a century done a good deal to accommodate the higher income groups, the young, the skilled, the mobile and to provide for them a better residential, working and leisure environment. The test of planning for people in the 1980s may be the extent to which governmental policies—the housing, educational and employment policies of central and local authorities—offer opportunities to a variety of special needs groups. I have argued that in an environment of economic constraint generated both by a shrinking job market and an inevitably cheese-paring view of public expenditure, there will be a variety of response from the community. There will be some, however, who cannot respond—the elderly, the mentally and physically handicapped, single-parent families, immigrants, ex-servicemen and a host of others whose sole characteristic in common is that they do not fall within the standard classifications of the people of the city region.

The special need groups are often found in the Inner City, tied to poorly paid jobs and physically bound by the need to live near their job. Attending to their needs demands a sensitive bureaucracy on the one hand, and an abundance of resources on the other since provision of facilities for the exceptional demand may well be in unit cost terms expensive. Many of those who make up special need groups will be in Pahl's Underclass. They will not qualify for council housing, they will have insufficient income to challenge effectively in the private rented sector. They will be unlikely to receive training for a new job and may well be in no position to take advantage of other educational opportunities. They may be starved of information about such facilities as are available and will have neither the experience nor the expertise to take advantage of what they do know about.

The challenge to the governments of the future city region is to devise a system which is at one and the same time sufficiently sensitive and sufficiently powerful to cater for the needs of particular disadvantaged individuals and groups. Sensitivity is required because there is a variety of need and one prerequisite for an effective governmental response is the ability to recognize this variety and respond differentially as the need demands. A more important prerequisite, however, is power, since in a situation of scarce resources there will be strong forces ranged against those who wish to maintain even a modicum of redistribution in favour of the disadvantaged. Economic and political power are important elements of course and the economic system will inevitably be the main medium through which resource allocation takes place. Discussion of the city region, however, implies a spatial dimension and significant redistribution will need to be channelled through the spatial system as well as through the social and economic system. A loosening of the housing and job markets on a city region basis are necessary. Physical movement—outwards—for those hitherto penned in the Inner City is essential. We may hypothesize *ad nauseam* about the life styles of the 1980s in terms of the changing demands of the affluent Middle-Mass, but the real test of planning for people in the city region will be the extent to which those whose opportunities are currently constrained are given the chance to enjoy a more stable and secure future.

References

5.1 PAHL, R., Paper presented at the British Council's Conference: Growth and Change in the Future City Region, Spring, 1975.
5.2 *Local Authority Expenditure in 1976/77, Forward Planning*, DoE Circular 88/75, September, 1975.

Note

The original paper on 'The People of the City Region' was prepared and delivered by Professor Ray Pahl, University of Kent at Canterbury.

Before writing this alternative Chapter, I was able to listen to a transcript of Professor Pahl's address and of the subsequent discussion. Although I have drawn upon this at some points, this chapter is I hope neither a paraphrase nor a plagiarism. Nevertheless, I must acknowledge the extent to which this Chapter stems from the thoughts of Ray Pahl.

CHAPTER SIX

The Inner City

Tom Hancock

The roots of Inner City problems

As the pace of change in the city regions accelerated through the sixties and early seventies so the problems of the inner city became acute.

Partially this was a matter of perception. In terms of the physical pattern the new urban motorways, the great clearances of old housing and the comprehensive development of the central areas as large scale office, shopping and service centres left exposed discrete areas of old buildings. The cleared spaces between were, and are, often left razed and derelict. Thus what had been an urban continuum—fitting in scale and concentricity the accepted idea of natural urban growth—was now a series of disparate and seemingly random areas divided by new or improved major roads with vast, complex intersections.

The older housing districts which remained, usually under threat of imminent or future clearance, were thus exposed as separate and problematical areas of deprivation. The development of new ghettoes containing the poor could be seen to be a real possibility (6.1).

The scale of change was most intense at the centre. It was the focus of the city region. The old system of radial roads and rail routes lead to it and it was natural therefore that the office development boom, utilizing this communications system, should occur at the centre.

The boom resulted from a massive change in the economic structure which was in rapid flux in this period.

Over a long period, since the 1920s, new manufacturing industry had located far out, first along the main radial roads and then the outer ring roads constructed (or pieced together) during the thirties. The new plants of the post-war period have located even further out on the fringe of the old conurbation, and increasingly beyond the Green Belt in the broadly concentric ring of greatly expanded old towns. This is the zone, too, of the New Towns where many new 'seed-bed' industries have located together with component production and new branch factories of larger industrial conglomerates. Much new industry, particularly major production and assembly plant, has been directed to the Development Areas of the country. And whether in the North East, the North West, Scotland or Wales new industry has been implanted in the outer fringe of the adopted city region.

There are several reasons. The almost complete switch from rail to road transport has made a location close to major regional and national roads advantageous. Land costs are much lower in the outer fringe. Development costs, too, are lighter and there is usually a great deal of support (in the provision of the new services and roads infrastructure) from the local authorities. Again, once a decision has been made the industrialists wish to see rapid action and the large green field sites are easier to aquire and develop than the usually fragmented sites in the old conurbations.

But there are other, deeper, reasons too. The fringe areas of city regions can provide a mobile and skilled workforce. High personal mobility means that a very large labour pool is available within a wide sector of the city region. The journey to work pattern which has evolved therefore shows that a large part of the workforce is usually travelling within the concentric layer in which the plant lies, leaving a diminishing number to reverse commute from the old city inside the Green Belt. The enormously increased choice of workforce, coupled with the lack of any old established 'community of interests', means that the propensity to industrial action on the part of workforce is lower than in the old conurbations.

The majority of working people in the new growth areas are ambitious, and in the social sense, mobile. They are prepared to move house frequently so as to achieve maximum affluence. And in their cultural values they are coming to resemble those groups which preceded them in the shift outward from the old centre—the managers, executives and professionals.

To these groups and the employees of the new industries must be added the large numbers of office employees who have also moved out to advantageous residential locations. In the growth areas of the city region the housing costs are lower and the opportunities for owner-occupation is much greater. Education, too, is likely to be of a good standard without those tensions which are increasingly experienced in the old city. Tensions which, like so many of the problems, are due to the imbalance of population structure.

The local taxes, or rates, are comparatively lower in the outer areas, with the new developments including industry, warehousing and shopping providing a good tax base. The local authorities do not have the onerous and costly problems which the inner areas have to bear. So it is unsurprising that the local authorities of the inner areas encouraged the dramatic growth of the service sector—the office boom particularly—in the effort to rapidly increase their tax revenue.

All these forces combined to reinforce the classic commuter pattern particularly in London. Places beyond the Green Belt on the radial routes grew massively as commuter towns. As has been shown only part of this growth is due to the location of new industrial employment. This often provides opportunities for wives and younger members of the family to work within a reasonable distance of home. The family economy has been boosted by these additional job opportunities and in turn the increased affluence of the family has lead to greater spending on the house, on leisure (particularly holidays abroad) and generally established a new datum in life-style expectations. The massive gain in affluence is now in vivid contrast to the condition of the inner city.

The people of the Inner City

The inevitable imbalance of population structure which the shift of these millions of families from the old centre has created has already been mentioned. The emigrants were young, energetic and, perhaps, the potential leaders in the inner communities, so that their loss tended to relatively increase the proportions of elderly and unskilled, and to leave the inner areas without those grass root energies which could have helped them to withstand the clearances of comprehensive redevelopment.

Left behind, too, were the many families and individuals who already had problems. For example the single parent family is a wide spread phenomenon and now forms a sizeable minority, but if they are living in the inner areas they have no way of moving out. Often they are at the poverty line, supported by supplementary benefits. The single parent cannot hope to find a source for a mortgage for house purchase, except from the meagre resources of the local authorities which they (like the building societies) have preferred to allocate to people with security of income and no apparent family problems. The single parent family is unlikely to make headway on the housing list of the local authority for similar reasons—and often the residence qualification (a specified period of years within that area) cannot be fulfilled; single parent families tend to be found in the 'private rented' sector of the inner city.

The large family, too, is often trapped in the inner city. Their plight has been publicized by the Child Poverty Action Group and others. Again their basic problem is one of poverty. The relatively high cost of supporting a family in the inner city has reduced the choice of housing to either the public sector or the private rented sector. Large families are often not given priority by the Local Authority and little of the new housing was built specifically for them. Their disposable income is generally so low (and reduced still further when out of work by the wage stop) that rent arrears among this group have become widespread—the large family is a problem family. The pressures of this poverty trap makes the family insecure and easily fractured. Children fall into delinquency and families break-up, and become homeless. Their problems with rent (and their frequent ignorance of rent and rates rebates) cause them to be evicted from their housing and to then be housed by the local authority in the miserable environment of hostels (or bed and breakfast hotels) where genuine family life is impossible.

The single parent and large families form, with the elderly and disabled, the majority of the indigenous residents of these inner areas. But many young small families have stayed on, buying (through a local authority mortgage) a small terraced house in areas which are not due for clearance for 15 years or so. They, too, are trapped in that they cannot earn enough to save the small capital to buy a house outside. The majority of council tenants are of this group, but again the residence qualification prevents many from obtaining a council flat. A sizeable minority end up competing in the private rented sector, or effectively homeless.

Also competing are the large minorities of immigrants to the inner city. By 1966 there were nearly one million coloured people in

England and Wales, about one-third under 15 years of age and a high proportion under five. But there were additionally over 1½ million foreign born immigrants (including 700,000 from Eire). Many of these immigrants settled in the inner areas of London and other city regions. However, since 1964 the overall flow has reversed, with more people leaving annually than have gained entry.

These large groups followed the traditional pattern of new immigrants everywhere—they tended to move to the inner city to find an initial place in the employment market and in housing. In employment they began to take over the low paid service jobs in transport, hotels and restaurants. This sector was increasing dramatically as a result of the tourist boom which really began to get under way in the 1960s and by the 1970s had become a considerable industry.

In housing they began to buy property in the run down areas (sometimes in ignorance of the future plans for clearance), frequently by banding together to provide initial capital and loan repayments. They were, like immigrants everywhere, prepared to suffer in the early years, and so the resulting overcrowding was no deterrent to them. But it was to their indigenous owner neighbours, who frequently resented their life style and culture, and attributed the fall in the value of their obsolescent housing to them. They thus established themselves in the older housing areas where the still high proportion of private rented housing is found.

This simplified composite picture illustrates the intolerable pressures on the old and new groups which the overall changes in the city regional structure created in the inner city. The resulting problems of multi-deprivation, poverty, overcrowding, insecurity, extremely poor housing, poor education and future work opportunities cannot be viewed in isolation, nor can they be solved by treating the inner areas in isolation. It is only by understanding the way in which the city region is changing, and by corporate policies at this level that solutions can be found. What might these policies be? Firstly, the reduced pressure on the inner area which has followed the end of the development boom of the 1960s must be rigorously held. As things have eased the progress of the quieter social policies in urban affairs can now be evaluated.

An instance of this is seen in the results of the Rent Act of 1974 which gave security of tenure to many furnished tenants. It has been estimated that 115,000 lettings have been withdrawn from a total of about 750,000; a much smaller number than had been feared by some. The previous rate of arbitrary eviction was intolerable, and since the Act the number of people going to SHAC (Shelter Housing Advisory Centre) with security problems—harrassment, notices to quit, or possession orders—has been halved. And tenants are now able, without fear of reprisal, to obtain other rights which might follow from a visit to the Rent Officer or Environmental Health Officer (6.2).

There is some progress on the housing front with programmes of gradual renewal—the rehabilitation of fit housing with some 'infilling' of new housing—within General Improvement Areas. Where these can be linked to aspects of the Urban programme a noticeable qualitative change is taking place in the society of the inner areas. Hopelessness is being replaced by a cautious optimism. Such areas are still in the minority but the best examples are now becoming widely known (6.3) and, given constant encouragement from Central Government and sufficient capital resources to allow rolling programmes of 'acquisition and improvement' to really become effective, 'gradual renewal' is set to entirely replace 'comprehensive redevelopment' in the inner city.

There is also a gradual change in the style of the social services. Since Local Government reorganization, and following the recommendations of the Seebohm Committee, the relationship between the deprived of the inner city and Local Government has improved. There is a more complete understanding of 'the poverty cycle' and as a result a deeper commitment by many social workers than at any time in the past.

The anxiety to increase rate revenues should be held in check. There is every reason for the inner districts and boroughs to encourage new manufacturing and service industry, but the job opportunities to be created by such new plant should be carefully evaluated and balanced against increased congestion in the transportation system and in the reduced land then available to make a genuine improvement of the environment possible. This means that the inner districts should be intent on providing really large scale open space—country parks in town as well as a great deal of new housing stock at low densities. In doing so they can attract back many families who would prefer the attractions of the city but only *if* the social and physical environment is of a high standard. This concept of a quantum leap in environmental quality must be clearly grasped by the decision-makers of the inner city.

The present classic example is the London Docklands. Whilst the Boroughs concerned wrangle to achieve the greatest revenue gains, and some jobs for the unemployed, the Government refuses to fund the proposed new spine road and underground line. But the best course is to set about creating the greatest urban park in Europe, a totally new green landscape enfolding the River. Then the Boroughs would find that they could choose carefully from the many concerns which would come forward to locate on the edge of this Eastern Park, and could draw up plans for the creation of pleasant new neighbourhoods, which could include private as well as council, cooperative and association housing. The relief to the still-congested districts of East London would be tremendous. The use of Surrey Docks for a new trade mart is exactly the wrong thing to do: many of the new jobs created will be taken by people commuting from elsewhere in the city region, and the quantum improvement to the environment which is essential to the inner city is foreclosed by a 'big shed' development surrounded by servicing and parking aprons.

Future opportunities

It is essential that a balanced way of levying local taxes across the city regions is devised. The outer areas beyond the Green Belt are not paying sufficiently for the privileges which are enjoyed there; the advantages of a large employment base in the sub-region *and* in the inner city; together with a good social, educational and physical environment. The services in Government, banking and insurance, medicine, higher education, entertainment and so on, which are found in the inner city and largely used by the outer region must be equitably supported by the whole city region.

The value of land, or rather the methods of its valuation, must be reviewed. A 'false' market can no longer be tolerated. I call it so because the result of planning controls and comprehensive development (carried out by partnerships of capital, land ownership interests and local authorities) has been to make inner city land an artificially scarce commodity. There is adequate cheap land in the city region for the development of all kinds of service and office building. At many locations the rapid development of considerable secondary urban centres, new city centres, would help the overall structure by creating a high level of services and office employment closer to the growth areas. Such a continuing purposeful policy of decentralization will enable the derelict central areas to be developed at moderate densities with parklands to provide a good environment. As already suggested, this changing environment would result in the return of many people to the city and a better balance of population with all the social advantages that would bring.

Meanwhile the perceived problems must be ameliorated. The high percentage of empty dwellings in the inner city should be made available to those in acute housing stress or homeless. They should be purchased (at sensible valuation) by the local authorities and Government must make this policy a high priority. The endemic poverty of a million or so families, the majority in the inner city, can only be relieved by a long overdue radical reform of the taxation and benefits system. There have been proposals for a form of negative income tax whereby payments are made to ensure that families do not fall below a pegged poverty line. But the vulnerability of these proposals to numerous abuses is obvious; not least in that the cash payments will usually be mis-used and need not benefit the children of the tax payer. To overcome this problem I have suggested (6.4) that certain services, of which housing is the most important example, should be paid for by a credit system.

The housing credit system would assess the relative value of the housing enjoyed, or suffered, by each person. The value would be an 'environmental' one not related to a 'false' land market evaluation. Housing payments would be made to the housing fund accordingly. (The housing fund would be, in effect, the consolidated reserves of the building societies and local authority housing accounts.) Those below the environmental threshold would receive housing credits not payable in cash but automatic credits to housing accounts established for every rentee or mortgagee whether with local authorities, private landlords, or building societies. Credits should be able to accumulate to provide working capital for house purchase as owner occupier or cooperator but for no other purpose. The abuses of the present housing finance field are well set out in the summary of evidence presented by SHELTER to the DOE review (6.5).

Alternative policies are now being pursued in the hope of bringing back industrial employment to the inner city and thus breaking the vicious circle which is caused essentially by poverty due to lack of employment or poorly paid employment (coupled with high cost, low quality housing). It is certain that new industrial plant will not of its nature readily locate in the inner city. The sheer scale and areal requirements are so big that land is not readily available. Even London's Docklands will be ruled out because of the transportation

100

problems and by the highly politicized potential work force which has been left behind since the decline of the docks.

If industry is coerced to locate there the impact on the problems could be regressive. The skilled work force will probably commute inwards leaving the lower paid jobs for the inner city dwellers. The pressures on land for development, far from being relieved by the use of docklands for low density housing and parks, will be greatly intensified as the concommitants of industrial employment grow: an increased service sector with its own divergently paid workforce will seek to establish itself in the inner area. As we have seen the problems are caused by the 'false' land market which makes the derelict land between the clumps of old housing a valuable asset. In seeking to promote new industrial growth the expectation value of this land can only be increased. If the necessary levels of new investment in transportation were available then the possibilities would be much greater. But it must be realized how much further destruction would then be wreaked upon the inner city; further old housing stock in the already reduced private sector would be demolished. The policies must be drawn up in the light of what is possible and the attempted reversal of the trends of the past 30 years will, if pursued, be an extremely expensive method of increasing the problems of poverty and poor environment in the centre of the city regions.

References

6.1 PALMER, J.A.D., Introduction to the British Edition of Goodman, R., *After the Planners*, Penguin, 1972.

6.2 ASH, M., HOLMES, C. and WADDINGTON, P., Joint SHELTER/TCPA Seminar on Inner Areas, Discussion Papers, April, 1976.

6.3 Another Chance for Cities, SNAP 69/72, Published by the Liverpool Shelter Neighbourhood Action Project.

6.4 HANCOCK, T., 'The Hidden Homeless', *The Observer*, 6 May 1973.

6.5 HOMES, C., FLETCHER, J., KILROY, B., WILLIS, J. HAWGOOD, C. and WARD, M., *Housing Finance*, A summary of the evidence presented by Shelter to the Department of the Environment review on housing finance.

CHAPTER SEVEN

An Urban Programme

Tom Hancock

Government action

As the problems of poverty were re-discovered in the 1960s, (7.1) policies were devised to treat them within the urban communities where they were most pronounced. There was the significant example of the American Poverty Programme (which had followed upon the riots in the USA) on which to build. But rarely has the discussion (or the policies which followed) been involved in the nature of the structural changes in the city region—changes already described which have stemmed from a massive 'natural' decentralization of the old inner city and from the planned investment of new roads and comprehensive redevelopment.

As the various problems were discovered Government Committees investigated their cases and made policy recommendations. The Milner Holland Committee was convened in 1963 and reported in 1965 (7.2). London's housing problems were discussed in considerable depth and the problems of insecurity and conflict were outlined. The genesis of the Committee's report lay in the Notting Hill race riots and widely reported scandals of Rachmanism: the 'winkling' out of tenants by gangster methods so that houses could be relet or sold into multi-occupation or gentrification.

In education the Plowden Committee report of 1967 called for educational priority areas (EPA's) in the deprived neighbourhoods where policies of 'positive discrimination' should be applied.

The Town and Country Planning Act 1968 (the radical legislation which swept away the old-style Development Plans replacing these with the broad brush Structure Plans and detailed local plans) introduced the 'action area' to define places where immediate redevelopment is necessary. And the same Act required that a process of public participation should be followed in preparing this hierarchy of plans. So the following year the Skeffington Committee proposed that 'community fora' should be set up, served by 'community development officers', as the focus for the formulation of plans for each locality.

Then the 1969 Housing Act introduced 'general improvement areas' (GIAs), where Local Government could undertake comprehensive renewal and even rehabilitation with the support and involvement of the residents, whether owners or tenants, giving extra powers for the acquisition of property with larger subsidies and grants for house and area improvement.

The Seebohm Committee reported in the following year (1970) with recommendations that 'multi-disciplinary' teams should focus the work of the reformed social services departments of Local Government into the deprived localities. This idea has since been extended (usually by community action groups) to become the neighbourhood centre where legal aid and advice, planning and housing expertise and the multi-disciplinary team may be located; the many local voluntary organizations can then (theoretically) be in direct touch with Local Government. In 1969 the Home Office, the department responsible for internal security and peace, fearing the polarizing of the inner city, further race riots and perhaps sporadic insurrection launched its own Poverty Programme. (It must be remembered that the events of 1968 in Germany, France and the USA had echoes in Britain. The trend to violence as the repression of new political ideas and petty regionalism increased seemed evident. It was a mistake requiring considerable sleight of mind to confuse the problems of the inner city with this nascent conflict.) This took the form of Community Development Projects (CDPs), which were set up in deprived areas. The teams were to identify, with the help of the local people, the priority needs of the neighbourhood and to demand the new resources to meet these. At the same time Government grants were offered through 'the Urban Programme' to reinforce the work of the local authorities and of the voluntary organizations in these areas.

This series of swift initiatives, amounting to a UK Poverty

Programme, came about as the extent of poverty and deprivation was exposed to a concerned nation. The underlying apprehension was that the inner cities could explode into violence, engendered by the entrapment of the deprived in permanent ghettoes of squalor, overcrowding and poverty.

The Urban Programme was announced by the Prime Minister in May 1968 one month after the notorious 'River of blood' speech by Enoch Powell. The first circular invited 34 local authorities (all of whom had concentrations of immigrants) to put forward projects for "areas of special need where existing services are under strain".

About £25 million was available for the first 4 years of the Programme and £40 million for the succeeding 4 years up to 1976, when a major review was to be undertaken. These funds were to be a charge on the Rates Support Grant (the mechanism by which central government 'tops up' the expenditures of the poorer local authorities) and therefore represented a redirection of existing funds to areas of multi-deprivation. The allocation was much too small to ever do more than alleviate the really acute cases—if these could be identified by official teams on the ground.

In any case the very ethos of the Programme was and is that the poor *can* help themselves if they have organization and direction; a thesis which has appealed to Government, Opposition and the voluntary movements alike. An Under-Secretary of State of the Home Office has coordinating responsibility for the involved Departments—Education and Science, Health and Social Security, Environment (which is of course responsible for housing and planning), the Welsh Office and the Scottish Office. By 1974 11 invitations (or phases) were circularized to local authorities and voluntary organizations inviting their applications for funds. But four of these 'phases' were solely for holiday projects. The bids which were received for each phase far outstripped the available funds—in the last five the ratio was seven to ten times. (£44m was bid for an available £4m in one phase.)

Of the approved bids 45% has gone to nursery schools, classes or nurseries—and a further 10% to 'other child care'. The large proportion of funds (77%) have gone to local authorities rather than voluntary organizations (In the early phases their share varied from 1% (phase 2) to 7% (phase 5).) But it is not known what the order of demand was from the voluntary organizations—a rather substantial number failed in the bidding procedures.

Two 'total approach' neighbourhood schemes were started, one in Liverpool, the other on Teeside which were given a special allocation of £150,000 each. These evolved an integrated action programme by the local authorities and lead to the Comprehensive Community Programmes of August 1974, which seek to identify the "range of economic, social and environmental problems" within 5 years.

There were suspicions that the launching of so many projects which had similar objectives and methods indicated departmental rivalry rather than a coordinated programme. But this is mainly due to the unspecific terms of the Urban Programme, "The purpose is to supplement the Government's other social and legislative measures to ensure as far as we can that our citizens have an equal opportunity" (7.3). The nature of the programme has thus been pragmatic. The listed groups—large families, overcrowded households, the unemployed, immigrants, delinquents—offered no view of priorities nor did it reveal how the structural problems of the city region have created multi-deprivation.

The expenditure of £70m over 8 years, even if accurately directed to priority needs, was unlikely to begin to fill the gaps left by the existing local authority services, bearing in mind that the massive resources of Government which are annually expended on these very services have not solved the problems of the inner city.

Voluntary organizations

There was an extensive rise in the voluntary movement as the extent of poverty and deprivation became public knowledge during the early sixties. New organizations were added to the list of long established charities and associations concerned with specific disabilities and problems.

In 1965 The Child Poverty Action Group emerged. Through its magazine *Poverty* and by direct publicity the existence and plight of the poor became widely known. Many people were previously unaware of the extent of old-standard unrelieved poverty—half a million children with over a third of a million parents.

The Disablement Income Group, also formed in 1965, has drawn attention, with growing success, to the conditions of the disabled.

Shelter, styled the 'National Campaign for the Homeless', emerged at the end of 1966. In May 1967 the first Director, Des Wilson, was appointed and by January 1969 (9 months ahead of expectations), the first £1 million had been raised in the cause of the homeless. The

Reverend Bruce Kenrick said at its opening that a "rescue operation" was to be mounted "in the nations housing black spots". The collected funds were directed through existing housing associations to the major problem areas of the inner cities in Liverpool, Glasgow, Birmingham and London. Although it was claimed that each collected pound was multiplied sixfold by grants and subsidies the results in numerical terms of rehabilitated and new dwellings could hardly touch the magnitude of the housing problem; homelessness has continued to increase (7.4).

The obscurity of the problem and the difficulties of discerning that a root cause of it lay in massive clearance and redevelopment programmes are illustrated by the attitude of Shelter in its first 5 years—its demand was that local authorities should *increase* their programmes of slum clearance, and at the same time look to the disintegration of the older areas, particularly the 'black spots'.

By 1967 there were 100 local Shelter groups, and 200 by August 1968. It was a campaign based on a passionate concern with the plight of ordinary people caught in the pitfalls of the housing problem; people like Cathy in the famous TV film *Cathy Come Home* which graphically described the remorseless spiral to homelessness and family disintegration, it was a remarkable educational effort which interwove the social changes of the time with the inner urban problems; it described 'the poverty cycle'.

This 'documentary' was the emotional launching pad for the success of Shelter. The first report *Back to School from a Holiday in the Slums* had the same emotional appeal, but the next report the following year, 1968, *Notice to Quit* began to examine through harrowing case studies the mechanisms of eviction and attention to the tenants rights, such as they then were. *Face the Facts* was published in 1970 and reiterated the scale of things: 3 million families in slums, near slums, or in grossly overcrowded conditions and 18,689 officially homeless, it pointed out that the real number of Britain's homeless was nearer 1 million if the condition is defined thus: " any family is actually homeless if it is split up because the home is too small, or it is living in housing conditions so unfit or overcrowded that *it cannot lead a civilised life*. Inherent in this definition is the belief that where the effects of the home environment on the family are totally negative, they cancel out its existence". In doing so it gave a good enough definition of the condition.

By this year the attitude of Shelter had begun to change. It had made a major initiative in 1969. The Shelter Neighbourhood Action

106

Project (SNAP) was given 3 years in one of the most deprived areas of Liverpool (7.5), "to experience problems, provide assistance, demonstrate improvement and promote more effective policies for the future". In doing so it became involved with the comprehensive approach which, as we have seen, was beginning to take shape as a result of Central Government policies. SNAP was, of course, primarily concerned with housing and the physical condition—it was to be an "immediate advocacy programme" for Liverpool 8. But in the Preface to the Report, J.D. McConaghy the Director, says: "In 1969 we were directed to an immediate advocacy programme for the physical improvement of part of Liverpool 8. It had seemed to many that the proposed housing Act (1969) and the new planning legislation (1968) provided an excellent opportunity to combine the energies of the mass of the people with those of their local authority. But to spend one week in such a 'real-life' situation is to realise that much of our legislation has a terrifying irrelevance for the urban poor. One month is to appreciate the inevitable conflicts between the deprived and bureaucracies. In one year we had realised that any total process of improvement lay outside the fiscal and management competence of the beleaguered cities. By the end of three years it was evident that national government needed a completely new orientation to urban problems; a new urban programme." He goes on "SNAP has been criticised by some pundits of community action for not depending entirely on the efforts of underprivileged groups to better their situation. Perhaps this criticism is justified and certainly I would be the last to denigrate workers who will continue to achieve local successes with the urban deprived. But to depend entirely on local action seemed romantic. In no conceivable way can our inner city areas be considered in isolation. Their difficulties are direct consequences of city, city-regional, national and market trends. We must conceive action which is relevant at each one of these levels."

The SNAP report thus extends to discuss the general nature, in a social and economic sense, of multiple deprivation. It was a valuable initiative, demonstrating that, in the face of a fairly intransigent city authority, a General Improvement Area could be established by voluntary effort. It was splendid proof of the benefits of gradual renewal of the older housing stock; and it was one of several projects which have harnessed the energies and skills of the people of the locality to a point where the impetus is created for the project to successfully continue after the 'team' has gone.

Following the setting up of the shelter Housing Aid Centre (SHAC) in London, it now has centres in Edinburgh, Glasgow,

Birmingham and Manchester. These centres advise on housing opportunities (and pitfalls) and are now concentrating more on *community rights*. The National Housing Aid Trust has been established so that the Housing Aid Centres can be assured of a permanent existence.

Shelter's well researched evidence to the Housing Finance Review set up by The Secretary of State for the Environment, skilfully commenting at a detailed level on the economics of housing (7.6). In Shelter a new national voluntary organization has evolved as an influential force for change.

The impact of its campaign can be seen in other aspects of social and housing policy. Thus the new Housing Corporation, which sieves, funds and encourages the housing associations, was established after Shelter had begun that same process. And an increase in rented housing stock which is not directly controlled by the local authority is following. Still a small proportion of the new or improved housing, this stock has prospects of becoming part of a very important sector as the drive to cooperative housing and housing associations gathers force.

Shelter's work in setting up advisory centres and the further Neighbourhood Action Projects with which it is involved has paralleled and strengthened the application of new legislation and government programmes to the inner city.

Community action

Thus the 10 years since 1965 has seen the emergence of a governmental and voluntary programme of apparently wide dimensions. The sheer magnitude of the inner city problems makes progress hard to define and there is a lack of coherence in the overall programme. During the same period there has been a notable resurgence of 'community action' (7.7). Many groups have emerged as local representative cells of national organizations, like the Shelter example described above. Thousands of groups have arisen from the wide range of local conflicts which the rapid changes in the structure of the city regions have caused. Their roles and attitudes are widely divergent, and a short history of 'community action' will illustrate how the priorities and style have changed as a wider consciousness of urban problems and their root causes spread during this period.

In the late 1950s there was growing concern with the neglect and decay of our beautiful old towns and the inner precincts of the cities. The Civic Trust was initiated in 1957 by the then Minister of Housing and Local Government, Duncan Sandys. The original nucleus of amenity societies was formed of the still active 60 or so registered with the Central Council of Civic Societies (1938-1962). Some of these were well established and influential, the Heath and Old Hampstead Society for instance. There has followed a steady increase in membership since the dramatic growth of the early conservation and planning movement. By 1975 there were 1250 local societies registered with The Civic Trust. Since the formulation of Structure Plans started in the late 1960s (following the 1968 Town and Country Planning Act) and particularly since the Local Government reorganization of 1974, federations of these local societies have been formed so as to bring greater leverage and expertise to bear on the planning system. This arm of community action has had a quite dramatic effect on planning. It has been effective in changing, or putting a stop to, plans for the comprehensive redevelopment of old urban centres. Major roads and motorway proposals have been thwarted or changed. And the conservation movement has created a positive awareness of the value of our urban townscapes and of their extreme fragility. It is now involved (usually through the federations) with Structure Plans, Regional and Strategic Plans and Transportation Planning. Within this short time official planning has thus become a dialogue which directly involves local conservation and amenity interests. The Civic Trust, as broadly representing this arm, helped to bring into law the Civic Amenities Act, 1967 which placed a duty on local planning authorities to identify whole areas of special interest and to designate them as conservation areas, and indeed the mandatory requirement of public participation in planning which followed from the 1968 Act.

The amenity movement is not wholly middle-class and not only in the outer reaches of city regions. The Civic Trust has societies registered from Tower Hamlets, Bermondsey, Lambeth and Vauxhall, all in central London. There are many other inner city areas which are represented by amenity groups of one kind. But the basic concern of these societies is with the conservation and enhancement of the existing urban fabric (including in this small towns and particular precincts). A recent survey by the Trust shows that this basic concern shades into the area of social planning and housing problems.

The amenity societies registered with The Civic Trust are only a part of the broad Community Action movement. There are unknown numbers of groups of bewildering diversity which affect planning throughout the city region which have arisen from the impact of change on local communities and from the social aspirations of people; these are concentrated in the inner city. In the London Borough of Islington alone there are over 400 such groups. Many are inactive, having fought against the proposed clearance of a street, or even a particular building. Others are play groups. Many have responded to traffic management schemes, opposing closure of shopping streets, the removal of street parking or the rerouting of heavy traffic along selected residential streets as part of an environmental area plan.

But in total the effect of this broad movement has been to swing planning in the inner city towards conservation and rehabilitation; to put a brake on the pace of urban change. For example, the London Motorway Box of the G.L.D.P. was shelved as a result of coordinated attacks from a broad grass roots consensus. The Labour Party pledged to abandon this inner urban motorway during the election of 1973 and fulfilled this pledge after being successfully elected.

By the mid 1970s it is virtually certain that no development, large or small, can take place without the involvement of the community action movement. The response of official planning in the inner city has been to fight a hopeless rearguard action to retain the sweeping powers which invested it in the 1950-70 period. The relationship of planner to planned has changed totally, and without a clear recognition of this fact expensive and useless plans will continue to be drawn up. But there are signs of a slow change in the offical attitude.

The planning organizations and, belatedly, the profession are moving to a new position which reinforces the diverse grass roots movement. Take the example of the influential Town and County Planning Association. This voluntary organization set up an Environmental Education Unit in April 1971, issuing the first monthly *Bulletin of Environmental Education (BEE)* in May. *BEE* has had a very warm welcome in education, particularly in teacher training; by the end of January 1972 there were 1061 subscribers. The concerns of the Unit cover a wide field, but are primarily in the understanding of urban processes. Thus the problems of the inner city are often included. There is, tacitly, an acceptance that the changing social environment is of critical importance, and that local groups educated in this understanding can play an essential part in decision making.

In January 1973 the TCPA's Planning Aid Service was instituted in response to the demands from residents' and tenants' associations. Although the main aim of the service has been to provide the advice that community groups need on planning issues, this overlaps particularly with housing and social welfare. There has recently been support from DOE for this service and there is a possibility that further planning advisory centres may now be set up (7.8). At least this was one recommendation of the Report. Again an initiative from the voluntary organizations is being closely followed by Central Government.

The Council for Urban Studies Centres (CUSC), formed in March 1973, is a further TCPA initiative. Since that time several centres have been established and there are many more in preparation. Some, in the inner city, will be able to give direct insights into the problems; the Notting Dale centre is already operating. The Council represents a great number of interests in education, planning and Government, and the intended outcome of their work is likely to be that our main urban areas will each have a study centre within a short period (7.9).

The TCPA even had links with the short-lived City Poverty Committee, which was concerned with the problems of multi-deprivation in the city and was established to form a focus for the burgeoning community action groups. The Inter City Conference, held in 1973, whilst it did not succeed in the primary aim of creating a coordinated front against poverty, was attended by representatives of grass roots groups from every major city in Britain. The collapse of the Committee in 1975 seemed an ominous sign of an impasse, although the particular neighbourhood projects which the City Poverty Committee had fostered have survived.

The impasse came about not (as the former Director, George Clark, supposed) from lack of will, but because the attempt to put together a field of action based on a coherent view of the problems of poverty in the inner city was too ambitious for the resources of the Committee. Constituent strands were the politicization of local community; the formation of active and informed neighbourhood councils; the harnessing in specific priorities of the official urban programme. Paralleled by a dialogue to explore the structural causes of multi-deprivation this programme was a tall order. Support for neighbourhood projects came from grant making bodies, but the rather distant links with radical groups were a cause for official suspicion and the attempts to construct a field theory were met with incomprehension; the reaction was that if it could be done it should be done by the proper professionals, academics and researchers, and anyway if it were possible it would have been done already.

The 'movement of sustained agitation' to change the conditions of the inner city poor which was called for in the reports by John Bennington and others associated with the Home Office Community Development Projects has not come into being and yet the inner city since 1974 has settled into a quieter state. The intensity of community action in the 1960s related to the extent of change caused by comprehensive development and social conflicts caused by planning policies (in these must be included the housing policies, particularly Improvement programmes). With the dramatic slackening of the pace since the fateful winter of 1973 a chapter of inner city affairs was apparently ended.

But the history of the previous 10 years has finally changed the nature of planning, and the relationship of the people of the inner city to government. There is growing political support for the setting up of neighbourhood councils. A scatter of neighbourhood centres is becoming firmly established. Many officials and professionals are working on successful General Improvement Areas. The Urban Programme is being consolidated by much endeavour at the local level, and society is now permeated with the idea that emancipation and equity can best be achieved by the action of people in their own neighbourhood.

The structural causes of poverty in the inner city are still not widely understood, and there is not yet any sign of central policies being devised to ameliorate deprivation by the kind of measures which I have touched on in this chapter. Until they are, gross inequities will remain with us. Meanwhile, the post-war era being over, the inner city is enjoying an interval of relative peace. It is to be hoped that we are learning from this interval that quiet gradual change in the city is less destructive of people and communities.

References

7.1   HOLMAN, R., (Ed.), *Socially Deprived Families in Britain*, The Bedford Square Press of the National Council of Social Service, 1970.
7.2   *Report of the Committee on Housing in Greater London*,
7.3   The Right Hon. James Callaghan, Home Secretary, *Hansard*, 23 July, 1968.
7.4   *Shelter Progress Report*, 1974.
7.5   HOLMES, C., FLETCHER, J., KILROY, B., WILLIS, J., HAWGOOD, C. and WARD, M., *Housing Finance*, A summary of the evidence presented by Shelter to the Department of the Environment review of housing finance.

7.6   *ibid.*
7.7   HAIN, P., *Radical Regeneration,* Quartet Books, 1975.
7.8   *Review of the Development Control System,* HMSO, 1975.
7.9   Town and Country Planning Association, *Annual Reports,* 1972, 1973, 1974, 1975/1976.

CHAPTER EIGHT

Corporate Planning

Tony Eddison

Before corporate planning

This Chapter is concerned with the response of Government to the problems which change and growth in the future city bring. It is concerned with the manner of intervention employed by government, how government approaches the shaping of policy for this intervention, whether at national, state, regional, local or community level. The experience drawn upon is almost entirely from the United Kingdom but the principles underlying the ideas and approaches, and indeed most of the diagnosis, are almost universally applicable.

Many studies have been written comparing structures of government in different countries and at different levels in those countries. Structures are far less important than the processes of policy formulation which lie behind them. There are limitations to the value of comparative studies of governmental structures, notably the failure to recognize the importance of cultural and political influences, the consideration of which is fundamental to the understanding of the significance of any structure of government.

Before discussing current developments in policy making in local government in the U.K. it is interesting, not to examine the structure of local government (although there is almost unanimous condemnation of the new structure operating since 1974 in England and

Wales and somewhat less criticism of the new system in Scotland since 1975) but very briefly to give an account of the movements which preceded the current interest in policy making innovation and development.

Up to the late 1950's it is fair to say that local government in the U.K. was dominated by law and administration. There began to develop about that time a concern for *efficiency*—namely a concern for administrative efficiency. Organization and methods studies began to grow and the efficiency movement gave rise to the setting up of two committees—Mallaby (8.1) (on staffing in local government) and Maud (8.2) (on the Management of Local Government). The latter had much more impact in that it resulted in many changes to the internal management structures of local authorities both at the elected member level (where the greatest changes took place) and also in departmental structures. Essentially, however, both these reports and the subsequent response by local authorities were preoccupied with administration and its internal efficiency.

The ink was barely dry on the Maud report when its Chairman was appointed Chairman of the Royal Commission on Local Government in England (8.3) which reported in 1970. Although, in some respects this report could be said to be concerned with administration and the structure of local government (as indeed it was) the underlying concern was about local government's capacity to produce and implement a set of coherent policies and related programmes of action to meet the needs of the end of the twentieth century. Quoting:

"But planning is not concerned only with land-use choices or questions of development. It is an instrument for satisfying people's personal and social needs. Because of their interaction on each other, the social environment and the physical environment in which people lead their lives must be planned together. The Seebohm Committee stressed that the social services must be involved in the preparation and execution of schemes that change people's physical environment, whether thes schemes take the form of entirely new developments, whose effect will be that people have to move into strange surroundings, or the radical alteration of old-established areas with which they have long been familiar (8.4). The Cullingworth Committee on the needs of new communities emphasised that social and physical planning should be parts of one process. It was particularly critical of the view 'that "the social" is a separate sphere which can be considered independently of physical planning and development'; and added that 'social planning must be an integral part of the whole planning and development process' (8.5). The Plowden and Newsom reports showed the relationship between policies and priorities in education and policies for dealing with the general environment. We endorse all these views on the interconnection between planning and the personal services. It is most desirable that these two major aspects of local government work should be more and more closely related to each other in future."

The pattern of reorganization recommended by the Royal Commission is dealt with in Chapter 10. A parallel report and reorganization was produced for Scotland. (8.6))

Thus in 1970 we had seen a noticeable but slight move away from administration (in the bureaucratic sense) to government (in the sense of positive policy intervention for the achievement of certain explicit objectives). The movement accelerated from this point to the present and was marked by the publication of two further reports, Bains (8.7) for England and Paterson (8.8) for Scotland. It is fair to say also that partly because Paterson had the benefit of Bains (it was published about a year later) it develops the movement from administration to government even further. The following extract clearly illustrates, by the very language used and the ideas to which is gives expression, the marked shift:

"The ultimate objective of corporate management is to achieve a situation where the needs of a community are viewed comprehensively and the activities of the local authority are planned, directed and controlled in a unified manner to satisfy those needs to the maximum extent consistent with available resources. The main steps in the process can be summarised as follows:

* to identify and as far as possible measure and analyse existing needs and new (and changing) problems within the community served by the authority;

* to specify the desired objectives for the provision of services to meet those needs and to quantify them;

* to consider the various alternative means of achieving these objectives;

* to evaluate the various means and in the light of the assessment of resources required and benefits expected to decide on the best means;

* in so doing to examine the inter-relationships and inter-actions of the different departments of the authority;

116

* to produce action programmes covering several years ahead to achieve the stated objectives;

* to implement the action programmes;

* to carry out a systematic and continuous review of the programmes in the light of progress made and of changing circumstances, and

* to measure real achievement in relation to the stated objectives.

An essential characteristic of the process is its continuous cyclical nature."

In a ten year period, therefore, local government has undergone a major change both in the sense that it has been restructured (as has been said in most people's view, very badly) but more importantly, in that the concern is much more about the *policy output,* the *impact* of what local government is trying to achieve. This concern has substantially found expression in the movement towards *corporate planning.*

The corporate planning approach

Corporate planning is a way of approaching policy making in government at whatever level. As will be seen, its central concern is to make policy relevant and effective to meet the needs of the situation. That objective might seem either grandiose or oversimple. In either case it has to be contrasted with a crude analysis of what actually happens in practice, whether in this country or indeed in most others. Government is more often than not viewed as administration, and governments all over the world tend to respond in administrative ways to the problems which confront them. It is true that there is a lot of talk about policies for a wide range of problems but beneath the surface the most significant manifestation is of some administrative or organizational machinery, which is set up to relate to problems. New departments, new units of administration, new divisions of organizations, are the general response of governments to problems. Indeed if most of us were asked to describe how our government worked, we would find it difficult not to rely on an organizational diagram, a chart illustrating the structure of government. We are confined to them in structural terms and not process terms. Diagrams and descriptions of structures tell very little about how policy is made in government. Corporate planning, therefore, is concerned with the way policy is invented, the processes which are best suited to invention and subsequently implementing the policies which are likely to meet the needs of the situation in our cities and their hinterlands.

One of the fundamental weaknesses of the structural approach is that each element within the structure, that is to say each unit or department, develops its own links with and its own perceptions of the environment in which it operates, its own set of skills, its own territory of operation and, most important of all, its own budget. In short, it develops a lifestyle of its own and devotes a good deal of its energy to preserving, and indeed enhancing that lifestyle. The same pattern is frequently repeated, often within departmental units. For example, a study of the recently produced transport policies and programmes of the county councils in England and Wales shows that the policies produced bear a close relationship with the organizational structure from which they derive. Transportation departments traditionally have sections dealing with major works, road improvements, road maintenance and public transport and each of these mini-units, like the parent department, develops a lifestyle of its own and fights to secure at least as great a part of the departmental budget as in previous years. In all cases the overall effect is that the policies resulting are dictated much more by organizational considerations rather than the more objective considerations of the problems involved. Departments develop their own inward obligations—at the expense of a responsiveness to external policy needs.

The case is not for the abolition of Departments or other elements in our organizational structures. They undoubtedly have their strengths. Two, in particular are important. The first is the specialism or the professionalism they bring to a particular policy area. Social workers, engineers, architects, accountants, planners, public health officers, police officers, all have their specialisms which give strength to government's capacity to tackle many of the ever-continuing flow of problems which it is its responsibility to deal with. The second important justification for a structure of departments or some equivalent set of divisions in an administration is for the purposes of *policy implementation*. Whatever policies government decides to adopt there has to be some machinery to ensure the implementation of those policies whether that involves capital works, providing services, exercising control or licensing functions or exerting influence in some way or other. Implementation

118

requires organization and that almost invariably means a departmental structure.

The case, therefore, is rather for making a distinction between the *machinery of policy implementation* and the *processes of policy invention*. Corporate planning has as its central core, a concern for the creation of processes of policy invention which are unfettered by trappings of administration and which strike at the heart of the role of government, namely the establishment of a problem/policy/action relationship. What we are looking for is a way in which a local authority can exercise real influence on the quality of life in its area—not in a piecemeal fashion by building a swimming pool, a new road, a few schools, a children's home, and so many new houses, but by a set of coherent policies, which by their continual renewal can be seen slowly but surely to be improving life across the board.

Few people would dissent from this search for coherence, this corporate approach and later some ways of making it work in practice are explored.- Before that, however, it is perhaps necessary to stress a point made by Patterson (quoted above)—namely the importance of seeing policy planning as a continuous process. Nothing in this Chapter should be taken as implying the need for a comprehensive plan. It will be apparent from other contributions to Britain that the notion of a master plan, of which this country has had plenty, has fallen into disrepute. The emphasis, quite rightly, has shifted to a concern for the planning process and the need for monitoring.

Our legislation, our professional town planners, our structure of government, the internal organizations of local authorities, are all geared to producing plans. Moreover, these plans are expected to be right. They are more often than not prepared in the belief that they will work, and even if they do not work 100%, no effort will be spared to make them come as close as possible to this state. But plans do not work. Any planning system is likely to be much improved by building into it this well established truth. Plans have three sources of obsolescence:

1. They are based on faulty forecasts.

2. They do not take into account changing aspirations.

3. They do not take into account the unexpected (especially in politics and finance).

These are not faults in a plan. They are realities of life. We do not have 'complete' information about the present, let alone the future.

A plan prepared today will be inferior to one prepared tomorrow because our information will be more complete by then. The lesson is obvious. We have a plan today based on today's data. Tomorrow we have a different plan, based on tomorrow's data and so on. We cannot ignore new information. If our plan is thereby shown to be weak, it must be changed. The practical man will immediately raise obvious difficulties in taking such a weathervane approach. The situation is perplexing. At one end of the scale there is the 'prepare a plan and implement it, come what may' approach and at the other, the hand-to-mouth existence. But the realities remain. What is required is a process of planning which seeks to set in motion a decision-making machinery affecting the future based on changing information about both present and future. Time is crucial. Information is crucial. Decisions in time are crucial. But the plan is not inherently crucial. A plan should be conceived at the outset as something which will change, which should change. It is about adaptation. It is a continuing process during which events will take place, objectives will be realized, projects will be complete but the process continues. The rest are by-products from this process. This does not deny the need for a direction, a sense of purpose. These are vital but do not make a plan as presently conceived. The commitment needs to be to the process—in terms of approach, of thinking as well as in the variety of modes of expression for policies and plans.

The objective-setting fetish

Having stressed the importance of the planning process as distinct from the production of plans it is equally important to warn against the dangers of becoming obsessed with the process as a theoretical, rational model of decision making. Local government, indeed any government, operates in a political environment and has to be robust enough in its policy making processes to cope with day to day eventualities, pressures, changes in fortune and unexpected events.

A great deal of attention has been directed in local authorities in the last two or three years to the setting of objectives. This has developed almost to a fetish. It is vital, however, that a distinction is drawn between the *ritual* of setting objectives and deriving some actual *benefit* from the activity. There has not been much evidence of the latter. True, a good number of authorities have worked out their objectives for different committees. That is only significant, however, if those same authorities are acutely conscious of what those objectives mean in practical terms. So often one hears of particular committees approving their objectives because they are so general as to be meaningless and there would be no point in *not* approving them. There *has* to be a connection between what a local authority sees as its objective and the action or policy it proposes to proceed with. Sunderland, for example, has in its 1974/75 Achievement Budget not only the expression of general and more specific objectives but, much more important, it has set itself targets to achieve in the year and beyond, which show just how the objectives have some meaning. In effect the Sunderland Achievement Budget (8.9) is the base from which they can begin the business of reviewing their performance. Having established in quite specific terms what they *want* to achieve in the next year, they can ask themselves when the time is up, 'What *have* we achieved?' 'Where did we fall short?' 'Was it the right thing to do anyway?'—in other words 'Is our policy or action having the effect we wanted?'

Let us look at just one of the Sunderland objectives and targets— in this case in the housing field:

Objectives and Targets	Departments Principally Involved
Objective HS1 To formulate an integrated housing policy for the district, based upon a review of the existing housing stock in relation to the needs of the people.	
Targets	
1. Investigate and report on the present policies of the various areas in the Borough in terms of: rent collection, terms of tenancy, maintenance, purchase of houses, rents and rebates, revitalisation and improvement, clearance, environmental improvement and special housing, and to advise on the implementation of uniform policies for the new Authority.	Housing & Estates Architects Engineers Planning Programme Planning Public Health Social Services
2. Institute regular meetings between interested officers to discuss mutual problems regarding housing matters.	Housing & Estates +

	Architects
	Education
	Engineers
	Planning
	Programme
	Planning
	Public
	Health
	Social
	Services
	Solicitors
	Treasurers
3. Produce a planning statement on special housing (sheltered housing) in the Borough.	Housing & Estates Planning Programme Planning Social Services
4. To review the existing housing stock by October 1974.	Architects Housing & Estates Planning Programme Planning Public Health
5. To investigate and report on the need for house building by December 1974.	Architects Housing & Estates Planning Programme Planning

Community review

That approach by Sunderland is one example of relating problem/policy/action and review. Another approach, oddly enough, also developed in Sunderland by a study group set up by the Department of the Environment (one of 3 such studies) (8.10). The main element in the Sunderland Study is the idea of the community review process. The basic notion consists of three stages:

1. *Taking stock* of community problems.

2. Setting *priorities* (because we can't do everything).

3. Annual report and review.

The 'taking stock' idea has much more potential than the Sunderland Study allows. It is described essentially as:

"The core of the Problem Survey should be a short but comprehensive register or catalogue of possible problems, drawn from several sources within the authority: (1) the ideas and questions of members, particularly after public meetings and ward 'surgeries'; (2) suggestions, complaints and expressions of opinion from the public, as revealed by regular sampling of incoming correspondence; (3) articles, editorials and letters in the local press; (4) the local and structure planning process; (5) the plans, proposals and current activities of similar authorities (a useful 'early warning' source); and (6) items that come up at chief officers' group meetings, and in the course of officers' work."

Whilst it is difficult to deny the importance of these elements there are others of much greater significance.

The starting point perhaps should be a fairly simple account of what the local authority is doing at present. It has come to be known as the *'position statement'*. Knowing what present policies are is critical. This is where objectives begin to bite. It is not enough to know what a programme is—*all* elected members and officers should have a fairly clear idea of the reasons why that programme exists—what its purpose is and the substantiation for it. In parallel with this the local authority, through its department, could usefully begin to build up a profile of its area against which councillors, officers and the public could begin to judge some of the policies and their impact. Lambeth London Borough has begun to do just this in its 'Community Profile'. It contains well presented data on population, employment, leisure, housing, transport, and the economic environment.

Given some clear statement of what the local authority is doing, what impact it is having, against a background knowledge of the changing state of the area generally, there begins to fall into place the start of some idea of what the local authority should be doing next, what *new* policies it should go for, what old ones it should change or abandon. This is not to say that a local authority can do everything or all it would like to—it clearly cannot. The fact that it cannot is all the more reason why it should put itself in a strong position to judge what it can do, and that it reflects priorities as the elected members see them. There is not much doubt that in the next few years local authorities will have to put themselves in stronger positions to choose priorities and make better use of their resources.

One of the purposes of the move towards corporate planning is to put local authorities in a position to get *better value for probably less money.* The break-in point to reaching that position is to build in the local authority the *questioning* approach at officer and member level not just at the top, but throughout all levels. The 'taking stock' approach in a critical fashion, with a willingness to look radically at what an authority is doing and questioning whether it is still as important as when it was started, offers the starting point for change and improvement in the service provided. It follows, therefore, that the 'taking stock' approach should be continual effort. It needs to be a general theme in the authority but it requires strengthening in specific ways.

Policy analysis

A local authority cannot change everything at once even assuming it wanted to. The 'taking stock' approach offers a general, gentle move towards opening up some possibilities for change. Authorities will need to take specific problems and look at them in more detail. Several authorities e.g. The London Boroughs of Islington and Lambeth, have started developing methodical ways of doing detailed (but not too complicated) analyses of problems and the Sunderland Study gives some examples. In Scotland a more recent and more detailed study has been carried out (8.11) for the new Lothian Regional Council. This study develops the basic approaches of the Paterson (8.12), report but stresses in particular the dangers of too complex an approach at least in the initial development stages. This point is extremely important and insufficiently recognized in the introduction of many new systems. The danger is especially acute in developing countries where systems are often imported wholesale from other alien cultures. Every organization, let alone country, has its own culture and the implantation of new complex systems more often than not suffers the rejection phenomena common in biological organ transplants. Compatability with the existing organization, personnel skills and aptitudes is of fundamental importance yet so frequently overlooked.

There are some particular points which need emphasizing. The first is to stress that the whole point of policy analysis is (a) to present as clear a picture as is possible in a limited time of the problems and needs experienced in the community relative to the particular subject concerned, and (b) to open up imaginative possibilities as to how these can be met. The initial emphasis should be to open up these things not to constrain them. Elected members can, on the whole, only respond to the information and ideas presented to them. That is why, in the beginning, the 'opening up' process is vital.

What is possible and practical obviously should be a guiding factor, but it would be wrong to put too restricted a view on this in the first instance. The world is full of people who are ready to say what *can't* be done. What local authority members want are people who can tell them what *can* be done, preferably as cheaply and effectively as possible, but it *is* action they are seeking. For that reason any analysis should list the constraints put on a local authority: legal; financial; labour; time; other people; central government; whatever it is which is preventing a local authority from moving in to a problem immediately should be listed. Alongside that there clearly has to be a list of ways of overcoming those constraints. Members and officers combined are capable of finding ways around constraints. These are the important elements in policy analysis:

(i)   knowing what the problem is—how it arises—its causes—its extent and rate of change over time;

(ii)   understand the problem's position in the institutional and behavioural context—the forces, in this sense, at play on it—who does or can influence it;

(iii)   establishing appropriate methods and techniques to build up practical ideas for meeting it drawing on as wide a range of resources in the community as is practical;

(iv)   articulating the constraints;

(v)   assessing the changing impact of the problem and the likely impacts of different intervention strategies (8.13).

Sensitivity of corporate planning

There are two major areas in which the centralized systems of policy planning can very easily become insensitive and indeed very often do. The first is an insensitivity to the changing requirements, and the range of perceptions, of need in the community for which policies are intended. The second is an insensitivity to the instruments of policy implementation and feedback. The first is perhaps more important and is amply demonstrated in the *final report* of the Coventry Community Development Project (8.14) which amounts in part to a condemnation of the management approach to urban problems.

"Over the past five years, CDP has been given generous access to the corporate planning and management system in Coventry. This has confirmed for us that it is an effective and sophisticated system for co-ordinating long range plans and controlling the local authority's budget. However, it has also led us to question why it has not been equally effective as an instrument for tackling the Hillfields problem. In the early stages of the Project we saw the problem largely as one of organisation and managerial procedure. We criticised the corporate management system for being entirely a 'top-down' process which weighted decision-making over heavily towards the long-term, the large-scale and the broad-grain (8.15). However, recent developments in Coventry and elsewhere (8.16) have begun to counter-balance this with a 'bottom-up' process which builds up a perspective on the needs of small geographical areas. However, our personal experience of being involved in the management system and of trying to work within it to deal with some of the issues raised for us in Hillfields, began to suggest that the problem was not simply about managerial re-arrangements, but more fundamentally about the basic assumptions and values being acted upon within local government, in relation to urban inequality.

My comments may seem critical of Coventry. However, I do not believe that the problems are in any way peculiar to Coventry (8.17). Coventry is probably as efficient and impressive in its approach to decision-making as any local authority. However, corporate management is a wider phenomenon. It is an approach to decision-making which is being promoted not only in local and central government but also by a new and rapidly growing breed of technocrats in industry and commerce throughout the West. It has recently become popular within parts of central government's poverty programme and is being widely recommended to local authorities as a tool for tackling urban problems (8.18). Our experience prompts us to raise questions about the kinds of analysis and the kinds of solutions which corporate management can be expected to provide; and about the relevance of these for tackling urban inequality."

Clearly this position cannot be lightly brushed aside. The main issue is whether the corporate planning or any derivative of it is capable of being operated in a manner which is at once responsive and fully understanding of community needs (in the fullest sense) or whether by definition it is bound to exacerbate the already inequitable distribution of access to opportunity in cities. The Coventry report raises some serious issues to which this chapter cannot be a response. What can be stated, however, is that in so far as a distinction can be made between the principles of the corporate policy approach and current practices, the principles have much to be explored in the wake of the perspective articulated in the × Coventry study. Clearly, conventional approaches to public participation do not penetrate the problem very far and indeed can be argued to buttress the centralizing tendencies of the corporate planning movement.

The second area of insensitivity is an internal one which is a well known organizational phenomenon which has been referred to already. Centrally placed policy units run the risk of being highly active but politically impotent. In sar far as they are seen to be a threat to the units of policy implementation (in local government, the service departments) their work is frequently frustrated, even sabotaged and frequently ignored either explicitly or in more clandestine ways. There is no need to elaborate here on this common characteristic. Clearly much depends on the degree of involvement of the whole organization in the development of policy. Some central *activity* is almost certainly required. This is quite a different proposition from creative central organization (at least of any size). The emphasis has to be on creating a central *activity* of policy invention drawing on the service departments particularly for manpower resources to generate the activity.

One of the dangers in the emergence of any new approaches to public policy making is that there can quickly develop a kind of organizational or technocratic self indulgence. A recognition of this ever-present danger is an essential prerequisite of establishing a programme of policy development.

Policy study—its analysis and development is in its infancy in the U.K. Much will happen in the next decade. Ironically enough the pace of developments is likely to quicken since resources are scarce and the vexed questions surrounding policy choice will require these developments. In this Chapter it has been possibly only to describe the beginnings of a movement and some of its strengths and weaknesses.

References

8.1   Committee on the Staffing of Local Government Report, HMSO, 1967.

8.2   Committee on the Management of Local Government Report, HMSO, 1967.

8.3   Royal Commission on Local Government in England, Report, HMSO, 1969.

8.4   Cmnd 3703, paragraphs 426 and 482, HMSO, 1968.

8.5   'The Needs of New Communities: a Report on Social Provision in New and Expanding Communities', A Report by a Sub-committee of the Central Housing Advisory Committee, paragraph 8, HMSO, 1967.

8.6   Royal Commission on Local Government in Scotland Report, HMSO, 1967.

8.7   The New Local Authorities: Management and Structures, HMSO, 1969.

8.9   The New Scottish Local Authorities: Management and Structures, HMSO, 1972.

8.9   BOROUGH OF SUNDERLAND, Achievement Budget, 1974/75.

8.10   The Sunderland Study, HMSO, 1973.

8.11   'Introducing Policy on Corporate Planning into Local Government' , P.&A. Consultants study for Lothian Regional Council.

8.12   The New Scottish Local Authorities: Management and Structures, *op. cit.*

8.13   The subject of policy analysis is receiving a good deal of attention and already the number of references is extensive. Of particular interest are:

DROR, Y., *Public Policy Making Re-examined*, Leonard Hill, 1973.

SOLESBURY, W., *Policy in Urban Planning*, Pergamon, 1974, chapters 4, 5 and 10.

SKITT, *Practical Corporate Planning*, Leonard Hill, 1975.

8.14   Coventry Community Development Project—Final Report, The Home Office and City of Coventry, 1975.

8.15   BENINGTON, J. and SKELTON, P., 'Public Participation in Decision-Making by Governments in *Government and Programme Budgeting*, Institute for Municipal Treasurers and Accountants, 1973.

8.16   For examples see reports of the Area Management Workshops run by the School for Advanced Urban Studies, Bristol University, in 1974 and 1975.

8.17   Coventry CDP's association with the Institute for Local Government Studies Birmingham University has given us access to a wide range of literature on corporate management, and personal contacts with its practioners in many local authorities.

8.18   For example, The Sunderland Study, Vol.2, Tackling Urban Problems: A Working Guide by McKinsey and Co. for the Department of the Environment, 1973.

CHAPTER NINE

Governance of the City Region

John Boynton

Historical introduction

One of the great problems facing local government of any country is the relative difficulty of making changes to it. Society changes. Ideas change. Patterns of life and work change. But the governmental format which should respond to these changes is itself usually unresponsive to the need to change.

In the United Kingdom, the legislature has not interfered in the structure of local government more than once in every 50/75 years or thereabouts. Looking back into the last century we find the great reforming Act the Municipal Corporations Act passed in 1835. This was introduced as the result of a Royal Commission which travelled the country investigating the affairs of the existing corporations. The commission found ample evidence of corruption, nepotism and the use of corporate funds for political ends.In Leicester for example:

> In political matters, the Magistrates put their own party in power using influence as Landlord, Trustees, Charities:

"From the Mayor to the humblest servant of the Corporation every office has been filled by persons of the Corporation or so called Tory Party to the total exclusion of all who entertained different opinions." (9.1)

The Act of 1835 introduced the concept that corporate property was to be applied for the common good and that councillors were trustees for their inhabitants. It abandoned the doctrine propounded by such eminent jurists as Lord Eldon who alleged "municipal corporations were meant to have political influence and have the same right to use their funds as private individuals".

In the period 1882-1894 a pattern of local government was established which was, with minor changes, to last till the latter part of the twentieth century. In their day the reforms were a far reaching step forward. They abolished the myriads of single purpose authorities which had grown up towards the end of the nineteenth century:

70	improvement districts
1006	urban sanitary districts
2051	school boards
649	unions (aggregations of poor law parishes)
194	lighting and watching districts
14,946	poor law parishes
5064	highway parishes
13,000	ecclesiastical parishes

Municipal corporations were established in 1882 to govern the towns (239 in total). In 1888, 52 county councils were created to administer the affairs of counties replacing the justices who met quarterly in sessions for this purpose. County borough councils were also created for the largest towns. These were to have all the powers of both counties and boroughs. They were small islands of autonomy within the patterns of counties, all-purpose authorities of great power and importance. Originally only ten towns were intended to be created as county boroughs but in the upshot the Act of 1888 created no less than 61.

There was much rivalry between counties and the county boroughs. The problems which were felt in acute measure in the city regions, i.e. the large conurbations like Birmingham or Manchester, were felt to some degree by all county boroughs. Their areas were expanding yet their boundaries remained relatively unchanged. Proposals for changes were often fiercely resisted by the surrounding county council, and there were protracted battles in Parliament on the Private Bills promoted by county boroughs in their efforts to extend their boundaries to what, in their judgement, were more sensible limits.

In 1894 urban sanitary authorities became general districts of the county, and were classified as either urban or rural districts with councils of those names for each. Civil as opposed to ecclesiastical parishes were created to revive local life in rural areas.

Whilst the structure of local government in England and Wales changed little between 1894 and the second world war, the functions entrusted to local government grew enormously.

Victorian local government was largely concerned with the upkeep of roads, public health and sanitary matters, and the relief of poverty by the provision of poor law institutions. Housing powers sprang from the public health interests of local authorities in the early part of the twentieth century. Originally confined to dealing with overcrowded and insanitary conditions, the powers developed through wide slum clearance powers to a general power to provide housing for all those in need. So much so that in the post-war years approximately half of all housing in the United Kingdom was provided by local authorities and New Town corporations.

The town planning powers of local government also had their origins in considerations of public health. These powers were to be of little real importance until the passing of the Town and Country Planning Act of 1932. Since 1945, there has been abundant legislation about town planning, much of it concerned with efforts to gain for the public the financial benefit flowing to developers from the grant of planning consent for development (betterment).

Some functions which in other countries have stayed outside local government have been brought in the UK into the general powers of local authorities. School boards for example were abolished in 1902 and education has been since that date a local government function. Some of the last to be absorbed were the functions of poor law guardians, which were in 1929 transferred to counties and county borough councils.

If the period 1890-1945 was to see many new powers added to local government (libraries, food and drinks, weights and measures inspection, promotion of industry, promotion of arts and culture, open space and recreation, agricultural holdings and mental hospitals to name some of them) the next 20 years was to see a reduction in function. Whilst fire brigades were returned to local authorities after World War II, many other services disappeared from local control as nationalization proceeded. Hospitals were transferred to the National Health Service in 1946. Municipal Gas and Electricity stations were brought into the national network at the same time. The remaining health services of local authorities (largely home nursing and midwifery, school health and a variety of local health clinics) were vested in the National Health Service in 1974. Water and sewerage services likewise in 1974 were vested in the newly created regional water authorities.

(Police functions are partly under local control in that their budget is recommended by a committee consisting of county councillors (two-thirds) and justices of the peace (one-third) with however, safeguards for the Home Secretary to intervene if the county council refused to act reasonably.)

In 1939 a county borough council could be responsible for most of the community services—gas, water, electricity, buses, markets, schools, health clinics and so forth. In 1976 the list of activities is much reduced.

The desire for reform

The end of the War brought a new questioning spirit and reforming zeal into being. It was obvious that a local government structure which had lasted unchanged for half a century would need radical revision. The concept of the city region was not to emerge for another decade, but when it did, it added strength to the case for positive reform of the out-dated structure.

Reform was however too slow to come. The Local Government Boundary Commission set up after the War by the Labour Government was disbanded—reputedly because of quarrels over policy between its chairman and the responsible Minister.

In 1958 the Local Government Commission for England was set up to review the boundaries of counties, with powers to declare special review areas. This was largely a device to allow the problems of the city regions to be looked at in a more fundamental way than was possible under the Commission's normal powers. In fact one city region or conurbation area, the West Midlands, centred in Birmingham, was dealt with in this way by a Special Review Order. However, the Commission's powers were limited and its procedure necessarily protracted. On 31 May 1966 it was superseded by a Royal Commission under the Chairmanship of Lord Redcliffe-Maud to consider the structure of Local Government in England. London was excluded because it had been reorganized in 1965, and the first urban regional authority, the Greater London Council, had been created.

The Royal Commission reported in June 1969, after taking evidence from 2156 witnesses. It proposed the creation of 58 new unitary, or all-purpose, authorities and three metropolitan areas (Birmingham, Manchester and Liverpool) where functions would be divided between a metropolitan authority and a number of metropolitan districts. The metropolitan authorities were to be responsible for planning, transportation and major development. The districts were to be responsible for education the personal social services and housing. Although the Labour Government accepted the proposals in the Report, it did not stay in power long enough to induce the necessary legislation. The Conservatives who assumed power in 1970 introduced their own proposals. These to some extent built upon the report, but the essential point of difference was to establish a two-tier system everywhere. They also proposed a number of metropolitan authorities in which functions would be split in a different way to the rest of the country.

The desire for non-statutory improvement

We shall return in later pages to discuss the actual changes made in England by the Local Government Act 1972, particularly in relation to city regions.

We now need to consider the efforts which were made in England to deal with the problems of governing the city region during the period of stagnation just described. Between 1945 and 1970 there were many proposals and many attempts to induce reforms. Faced with so many abortive attempts to make real progress at Parliamentary level, several authorities or groups of authorities took action to improve the government of the city region by various devices involving cooperation of authorities and by measures not backed by statutory powers.

The actions taken were paralleled by those being taken elsewhere and in some cases were modelled on concepts in other countries which influenced official thinking in Britain: These are dealt with in the next part of this chapter.

The Rotterdam regional authority

One of the best known European experiments in the creation of a new authority for the area of a city region (some would call it a regional authority) was that for the Rotterdam area on the mouth of the Rhine (Rijnmond).

The timetable for the creation of this authority is interesting, because it shows the comparatively long period needed for an idea to be embodied in statutory form.

1958 — Committee of Inquiry set up
1960 — Report of Committee
1962 — Government introduce Bill into Parliament
1964 — Measure enacted and authority set up

The Rijnmond authority is responsible for an area of 150,000 acres (61,000 ha) and a population of 1 million. The authority has a chairman and 81 councillors drawn from the 23 Rijnmond authorities. It employs about 275 civil servants.

The Rijnmond public authority relies for its income on rating. Rates are levied on the 23 municipalities which are rated per inhabitant. However the Dutch government plays a part in the general financing—the salaries of the Chairman, the delegates and the Secretary are paid by the government and 25% of the salaries of the civil servants, and of the costs of housing the authority.

The authority has principally become famous for its attempts to monitor air pollution in the Rhine estuary. However, this was only one of the objects which motivated its creation. It was seen much more as a regional planning authority and its creation gave some impetus to ideas in the United Kingdom for more effective planning of regional, sub-regional and city regional areas.

The area of Rijnmond and the activities of the authority as described in the official publication are set out in Figures 9.1 and 9.2.

Metropolitan Toronto

In Canada, a much quoted example of local government of a city region is Metropolitan Toronto.

The present system originated in 1953, chiefly in response to pressures on municipal services brought about by the post-war population explosion in this, the largest population centre in Ontario.

The Provincial Government of Ontario consolidated the 13 municipalities in the area and reorganized them into two levels of local government—metropolitan and area municipal. There have been changes over the years, but the basic pattern remains unaltered—a metropolitan municipality, six area municipalities, and a mutiplicity of special purpose bodies and inter-governmental structures.

Local government in the metropolitan area is mainly financed by grants from the Province supplemented by local property taxes and other revenues such as licence fees.

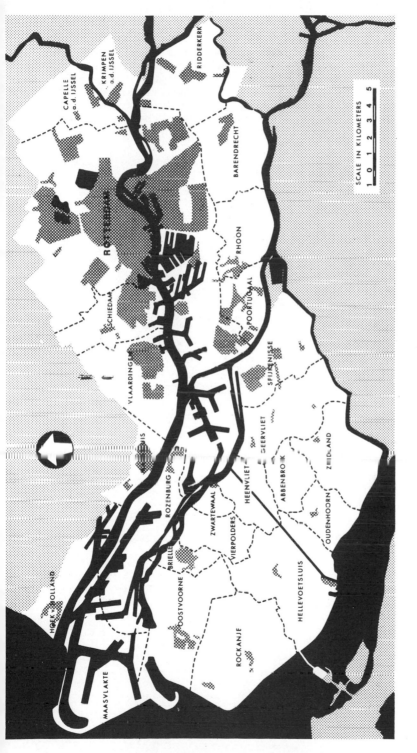

Figure 9.1. Rijnmond Regional Authority. Area: 150,000 acres (61,000 ha); Population: over 1 million; Council: 81 councillors; Civil servants: 275

1. Economics.

For the region an economic model has been developed, which makes use of regional input-output analyses. The model has already been used to determine a broad long term economic strategy (*Rijnmond in de Delta*), especially in view of the presently diverging trends of labour demand and labour supply. The model is continuously brought up to date and improved and may become a useful tool to evaluate in detail the consequences of certain policies with regard to the labour market, environment, housing, inland transport system, etc. etc.

---

2. Traffic and transport.

In order to evaluate future transportation needs a preliminary transportation study has been carried out for Rijnmond and the city of Rotterdam by Freeman, Fox, Wilbur Smith and Associates in London.
The transportation model now available is a very valuable tool in planning transportation facilities. A study will be started shortly to improve the model further by distinguishing peak and off-peak traffic and introducing relationship between speeds and the volume-capacity ratio of highways, roads and river crossings.
Such a study will give more information about the costs of congestion, it will improve cost-benefit analyses of different traffic solutions and in particular improve the evaluation of public transport versus private transport.

In 1970 Rijnmond published a report *Rijnmond on road and rail.*
The report contains a survey of needs for inland transport facilities (roads, railways and river crossings) for the Rijnmond area.
The plans include further extension of the underground railway line.
Studies and plans are carried out in close cooperation with the Rijnmond municipalities, the province and the government.

---

3. Physical planning.

As mentioned before, one of the tasks of the Rijnmond Public Authority is drafting the physical plan for the Rijnmond area. However, the Rijnmond area is not an independent entity, but part of north Europe and closely related to, in particular, the area between Antwerp and Rotterdam; *the Golden Delta.*
Therefore the future structure of the Rijnmond area must be adapted in relation to this much wider area.
The Rijnmond Public Authority has drafted a *structure plan* which is the first step towards a complete vision for the Rijnmond area and its surroundings.
Unlike previous plans the dynamic character of the development has been stressed and many mathematical models have been used.

Figure 9.2. Activities of Rijnmond.

At the metropolitan level there is a Metropolitan Corporation, governed by a metropolitan council consisting of a Chairman and 37 members. Council members are not directly elected. Their membership may stem from holding a position in the area municipal level of government, e.g. mayor, or they may be appointed by the area municipal council.

The Chairman of the Metropolitan Council is elected every two years, but need not be a metropolitan or a municipal councillor. His is a full time appointment and in 21 years there have only been four holders of the position. The Chairman is *ex-officio* a member of various metropolitan special purpose bodies and inter governmental bodies.

Much executive decision is undertaken by the Executive Committee of 14 members who have wide powers over municipal expenditure, contracts and officials. In addition to the Executive Committee there are standing committees to oversee the operation of line departments. These committees report to the Executive Committee and though influential have limited authority.

The governance of Metropolitan Toronto is distinguished (as is much of North America) by many special purpose bodies designed 'to keep local politics out' of their activities. Examples of these boards are as follows:-

(a) *Education*

This is one such activity. The Metropolitan Toronto School Board exercises authority, mainly fiscal, over the six area school boards. Its aim is to ensure high and uniform standards. The six area board chairmen are among the 20 members.

(b) *Public Transport*

The Toronto Transit Commission has exclusive responsibility for the development and operation of the public transport system, including the Grey Coach line but excluding railways and taxis. The board of the Commission is composed of five members appointed by the Metropolitan Council.

(c) *Police*

The Board of Commissioners of Police is the governing board of the public force. Of the five members, one is Chairman of the Metropolitan Council and one is appointed by that Council, the remaining three are appointed by the Provincial Government. The Board is primarily an agent of the province.

There are at least ten other metropolitan commissions or agencies

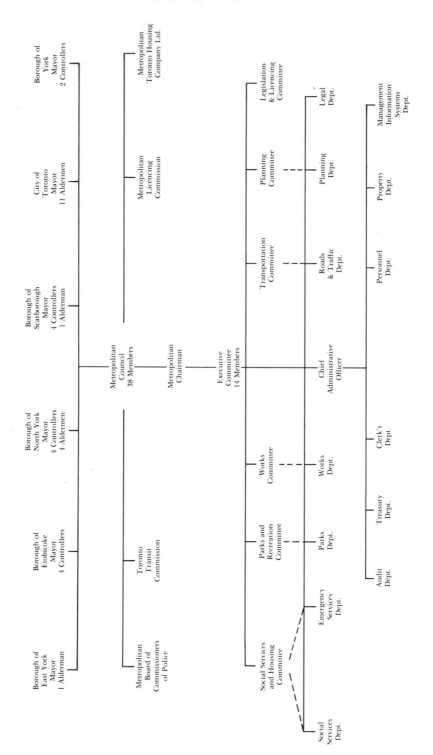

Figure 9.3. Council Committees and Departments of Metropolitan Toronto.

Exclusively Area Municipal Level Responsibilities

Retail distribution of electricity
Operation of public parking lots
Land use zoning
Public health services
Marriage licensing
Fire services
Building and building construction
  licensing

Responsibilities shared by both the Area and Metropolitan Municipal Levels

Exclusively Metropolitan Municipal Level Responsibilities

Public transportation (through the
  Toronto Transit Commission)
Chronically ill and convalescent
  hospitals
Homes for the aged
Ambulance services
Welfare administration including
  public assistance payments
Policing (through the Metropolitan
  Board of Commissioners of Police)
Licensing of businesses (through the
  Metropolitan Licensing
  Commission)
Emergency measures

Water Supply
Sewage
Garbage
Road Construction, Maintenance and Traffic Control
Planning
Elderly Persons Housing and Low Rental Family Housing
Elementary and Secondary Education
Parks and Recreation Centres
Libraries

Figure 9.4. Split functions in Metropolitan Toronto.

and numerous intergovernmental agencies for cooperation. Fig. 9.3 shows the committees and departments of Metropolitan Toronto, and the split of activities between metropolitan and municipal levels is set out in Fig. 9.4.

With the variety of governmental and inter-governmental structures, the overall picture is very complex. Land use planning, for example, is a responsibility shared between area municipal and metropolitan levels, and most decisions also require the specific approval of the province. Yet for all its complexity, the organization of local government in Metropolitan Toronto has proved to be effective and sensitive to the needs of the people it serves. But as the official background report concludes "However effective it may be, local government organization in Metropolitan Toronto is neither neat nor tidy".

(Further information is obtainable from the Royal Commission on Metropolitan Toronto, 145 Queen Street West, Suite 309, Toronto, Ontario M5H 2N9).

San Francisco Bay Area Government

A multiplicity of special agencies also characterizes the government of the San Francisco Bay Area—but with a difference, because the Association of Bay Area Governments (ABAG), the most comprehensive of these regional agencies, is a voluntary body. It is the council of local governments working at regional level with 85 of the 92 cities and seven of nine counties in membership.

ABAG was established in 1961 to tackle regional planning problems of mutual concern to its member cities and counties. ABAG is the comprehensive regional planning agency for the Bay Area, responsible for preparing and maintaining the regional plan. ABAG also reviews and comments on applications for a wide variety of federal assistance programmes. Through the policy framework of the regional plan, ABAG and its local governments have begun to implement policies for managing the Bay Area's growth and environment, notably pollution and open space. Fig. 9.5 shows the range of ABAG's activities.

The Association has a staff of 70 and serves an area of about 7000 square miles (18,000 km²) and almost five million citizens. Its work is financed by annual dues levied upon each member city and county, and a substantial proportion of these local funds is used to generate state and federal planning grants. Overall policy is set by a General Assembly, delegates to which are elected officials from member authorities. Each city and county has one vote and a majority of both city and county votes is required for action.

Whilst the General Assembly adopts the budget and reviews major policy decisions, most of the operational work is done by an Executive Committee of 35 members meeting monthly.

The Metropolitan Transportation Commission (MTC) established by State law, has been given the role of preparing a Regional Transportation Plan, as well as reviewing transportation projects. MTC has an adopted plan, which places stress on regional transit improvements.

Several agencies have been established to handle regionwide environmental problems. The Regional Water Quality Control Board is responsible for setting and enforcing water quality standards, while the Bay Area Air Pollution Control District is charged with a somewhat similar responsibility for air quality. The Bay Area Sewer Services Agency is empowered to plan and construct regional sewer systems.

The San Francisco Bay Conservation and Development Commission (BCDC), was established as a temporary commission in 1965, and made a permanent State agency in 1969. The San Francisco Bay Plan (1969) is a detailed policy plan for the protection and use of San

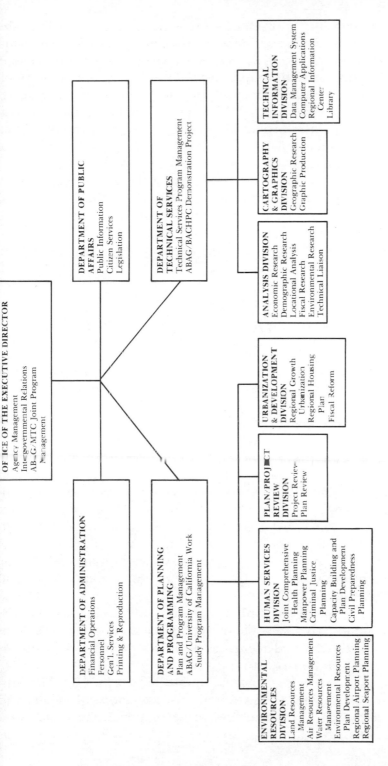

OFFICE OF THE EXECUTIVE DIRECTOR
Agency Management
Intergovernmental Relations
AB G/MTC Joint Program
Management

DEPARTMENT OF PUBLIC AFFAIRS
Public Information
Citizen Services
Legislation

DEPARTMENT OF TECHNICAL SERVICES
Technical Services Program Management
ABAG/BACHPC Demonstration Project

TECHNICAL INFORMATION DIVISION
Data Management System
Computer Applications
Regional Information Center
Library

CARTOGRAPHY & GRAPHICS DIVISION
Geographic Research
Graphic Production

ANALYSIS DIVISION
Economic Research
Demographic Research
Locational Analysis
Fiscal Research
Environmental Research
Technical Liaison

DEPARTMENT OF ADMINISTRATION
Financial Operations
Personnel
Gen'l. Services
Printing & Reproduction

DEPARTMENT OF PLANNING AND PROGRAMMING
Plan and Program Management
ABAG/University of California Work Study Program Management

URBANIZATION & DEVELOPMENT DIVISION
Regional Growth
Urbanization
Regional Housing Plan
Fiscal Reform

PLAN/PROJECT REVIEW DIVISION
Project Review
Plan Review

HUMAN SERVICES DIVISION
Joint Comprehensive Health Planning
Manpower Planning
Criminal Justice Planning
Capacity Building and Plan Development
Civil Preparedness Planning

ENVIRONMENTAL RESOURCES DIVISION
Land Resources Management
Air Resources Management
Water Resources Management
Environmental Resources Plan Development
Regional Airport Planning
Regional Seaport Planning

Figure 9.5. The ABAG Organizational and Programme Structure.

141

Francisco Bay. BCDC uses this plan, as well as State law (the McAteer-Petris Act) as a guide to the issuance of permits, which are required for any change to the Bay or to a 100-foot shore-line band. A somewhat similar California Coastal Zone Conservation Commission is now preparing a plan for the entire California coast, including the coastal zone of the Bay Area (but excluding the Bay proper). This plan, which includes a proposal for a permanent State Coastal Commission, will be presented for approval to the State Legislature this year.

The complexity and possible overlap of these regional agencies has brought forth numerous proposals for establishing some kind of multi-purpose regional government. To date, legislation to create such a regional agency has failed.

(Further information is obtainable from ABAG, Hotel Claremont, Berkeley, California 94705, USA.)

Strategic planning progress in the UK

In the light of moves throughout the World to improve planning of regions and conurbations, the British Government took certain initiatives in the early 1960's.

One of the best known of these was the publication in 1962 of the South East Study. This was a report summarizing the results of a study made by a group of officials from Government departments concerned with regional planning. It surveyed the London and surrounding area; appraised its principal characteristics and problems and suggested possible solutions to the more important problems. It was the first of several regional studies and did much to establish the concept of regional planning as an activity of Government. When Economic Planning Councils were set up in 1965, they were able to derive much help from the regional studies which had been initiated.

At city regional level, similar initiatives were being taken in the late 1950s and early 1960s. There were cooperative efforts by groups of authorities who had identified problems which could not be solved by one authority acting on its own.

A good example was the setting up in 1962 of a Steering Committee by authorities in the Liverpool area known as Merseyside, to consider transport problems and in particular the provision of a second crossing of the River Mersey. The Steering Committee was set up following a conference chaired by the Minister of Transport who made it clear that Government approval to any new river crossing must form part of a coordinated twenty year road programme. The extensive land use and transport study which was subsequently commissioned in 1965 is dealt with in some detail below.

Something similar had been happening at the other end of the Manchester Ship Canal in the great conurbation centred on Manchester. In 1958, the Government's Divisional Road Engineer suggested that all the road engineers and surveyors in the conurbation area should examine the problems involved in formulating a long term programme of road construction and improvement. A report was produced in 1962.

In October 1963 the Minister of Transport invited Manchester Corporation to convene a conference with other major local authorities in the SELNEC area to consider the establishment of a Transportation Study. The Minister said that "an essential basis for the right decisions about the future road pattern in towns and the best balance between public and private transport would be a sound and comprehensive Transportation Study in each of the main conurbations. This would enable an objective assessment to be made of the adequacy of existing road and public transport systems and planned improvements to them in relation to the growth of traffic, the likely changes in land use, the distribution of population and employment within the area of the conurbation and similar factors. Such a Study should clarify the nature of the decisions to be taken in both general and transport planning and enable the implications of them to be better understood".

A subsequent study in the Manchester conurbation is discussed below. Similar initiatives were taken in other conurbations. It is interesting that in many cases the initiative was taken by central government, and that it was largely transportation rather than land use problems which sparked off the initiative.

Merseyside Area Land use/Transportation Study

In 1962 the various authorities on each side of the estuary of the River Mersey set up a Steering Committee to consider traffic and transport problems on both sides of the river. This was in recognition that the problems of Liverpool, its associated port and the tunnel linking it to Birkenhead on the south side of the river needed to be looked at over the area of the city region.

In 1965, the Steering Committee on Merseyside Traffic and

Transport received a report indicating that an investment of £300 million in new highways might be needed by 1981 to keep pace with the growth in car ownership. At the same time, the report anticipated that the scale of investment could be significantly affected by the locations of new residential and employment developments and by the extent to which public transport services could be improved to offer an attractive alternative to the use of cars.

In recognition of this, the Steering Committee set up the Merseyside Area Land Use/Transportation Study to recommend a land use and transportation policy plan best suited to the anticipated growth of Merseyside over the next 25 years.

Consultants were appointed to prepare an overall programme of work for the Study; a study of long term needs was recommended and this was outlined in a project report submitted to members of the Steering Committee in February 1966. In summary it was proposed that the policy plan should be developed in two stages, the first being concerned with the adoption of a land use strategy plan and the second with the evolution in more detail of an associated transportation policy plan.

Work on the study started June 20 1966 and the first report was presented three years later in June 1969.

The Study was programmed to last three years and to cost £410,000. This cost was subsequently increased by £28,000 in view of the wish of the Steering Committee to test a wider range of land use plans than had been expected at the time the Project Report was prepared and to take account of the effects of devaluation of sterling.

One half of the professional staff engaged full time on the Study was seconded from local authorities. Equally important was the involvement of the planning engineering and public transport staff of the various constituent authorities.

The composition of the Steering Committee was such as to include all the local authorities within the study area as follows:

> The two county councils north and south of the river (Lancashire and Cheshire)
> The four county borough councils north and south of the river (Bootle and Liverpool; Birkenhead and Wallasey)
> The eight district councils all or part of whose area was included in the Study (Bebington and Crosby Borough Councils; Hoylake, Huyton-with-Roby, Kirkby; Litherland and Wirral Urban District Councils and Whiston Rural District Council)

The various transport interests (Mersey Tunnel, Mersey Docks, British Rail and two bus companies)

The Ministries of Housing and Local Government and Transport

It was a remarkable achievement that so cumbersome a body was able to mount a study costing over £½m and to agree upon the conclusions presented by the Study team three years later. The issues were of course complex. The first report of 137 pages and 50 plates relied heavily upon sophisticated computer techniques to analyze the results of interviews with 50,000 residents and 10,000 drivers of goods vehicles. It may well have been that besides the complexity of the report, the reasonable clarity with which issues were presented and the clear-cut recommendations for action led to ready acceptance by all concerned. A major achievement in cooperation was the extension of the study area for purposes of (a) transport analysis and (b) plan comparison. By any standard the MALTS study was a triumph of cooperation between authorities who had every reason, based on normal patterns of local authority behaviour, to refuse to agree. The study took place under the shadow of imminent reform of local government, when every authority was anxious to avoid prejudicing its future position, e.g. by accepting that it lay within the sphere of influence of the central part of the conurbation.

It is interesting that the boundaries of the Merseyside Metropolitan County Council set up by the Local Government Act 1972 were not markedly dissimilar from those of the study area.

The study of the Manchester conurbation

The work carried out in the Manchester conurbation was similar to that in Liverpool but was more restricted in scope and was later in point of time. The area was titled South East Lancashire and North East Cheshire (being more usually known as SELNEC).

The study was a transportation one and had a more limited land use input than the neighbouring plan in Merseyside. The Steering Committee was not set up until November 1963. This later start coupled with difficulties in getting technical help, delayed production of the study report until 1971. Whereas the MALTS exercise was carried out by consultants, the SELNEC exercise was in the hands of technical officers employed by the constituent authorities and seconded full or part time or specially appointed for the study. However, some of the early work was carried out by consulting engineers.

The composition of the Steering Committee was very similar to that established at Merseyside. It consisted of two representatives each from the county councils of Lancashire and Cheshire, the county boroughs of Manchester, Salford, Stockport, Bolton, Oldham, Rochdale and Bury, British Railways, the Ministry of Transport, and the Ministry of Housing and Local Government, and one representative each from the borough of Ashton-under-Lyne, the Ribble Motor Services Limited, the North Western Road Car Company Limited, the Lancashire United Transport Company Limited and the Stalybridge Hyde, Mossley and Dukinfield Transport Board.

The area chosen for the study was 413 square miles (1067 km²) and was largely determined by the limits of the conurbation which housed some 2½ million people. Within this area lived the large majority of people who travelled daily to work in central Manchester. However, because the settlement pattern had emerged from the growth of a number of separate industrial towns, rather than simply from the expansion of Manchester there were many important centres of employment dispersed throughout the conurbation.

Traditionally Manchester was the commercial centre of an encircling ring of other manufacturing towns, each possessing its specialist trades. The result was that Manchester had become a commercial and administrative centre of international importance, but the outlying towns remained greatly dependent upon manufacturing industry.

From the information gained in the field surveys it was possible to develop a mathematical model of the trip-making patterns of the area. Following the example of other transportation studies this process was broken down into the four main stages (or sub-models)

    (i) generation
    (ii) distribution
   (iii) modal split
   (iv) assignment

The structure of the SELNEC model was very similar to that used in other studies.

The mathematical model of travel behaviour used in the SELNEC study and its associated suite of computer programs were developed by the Mathematical Advisory Unit of the Department of the Environment. As with Merseyside, the study area proved to be a good forecast of the eventual area to be entrusted to the metropolitan county of Greater Manchester.

The work done may have had less of a pioneering flavour than that achieved in Merseyside. It nevertheless showed what could be done by cooperative effort. It brought together a number of local authorities who otherwise would not have worked together with an acceptance that there was a common problem transcending local government boundaries.

City regions and reformed local government

As we have seen above the Labour Government accepted in principle the proposals made in the Royal Commission's report. That Report was largely based on accepting the principle of the city region. The following is an extract from the short version of the Report (9.2) and it clearly shows the importance which was given to the whole concept of the city region by the Royal Commission. In the end the Report suggested a new structure which was a compromise between three considerations (a) the pattern of life and work (b) the needs of democracy and efficiency and (c) the existing boundaries.

"In considering this question, we first concentrated on the 'city region', since this was the idea strongly advocated for the whole country by the Ministry of Housing and Local Government, the department with chief responsibility for English local government. We examined various possible local government maps of England in turn, and the following points emerged:

The city region idea has value because it takes account of the fact that people are now much more mobile than they were, and that activities in town and country are much more closely interlocked.

Witnesses put forward a variety of possible areas as city regions, ranging in number from 25 to 45 for the country as a whole. This suggested that the city region was not an idea which could be applied uniformly all over England, and in some parts of the country it did not seem to us to fit reality. In a number of areas it does provide the clue: around the great urban concentrations of Birmingham, Liverpool and Manchester, and also in areas where a big town is the natural centre for a wide area of surrounding countryside and smaller towns. But in others, such

147

as the south west, insistence on the idea of the city region seemed to mean creating artificially constructed areas whose people have no sense of looking to a city centre or of sharing interests peculiar to themselves; and in the south east the idea leads to no clear local government pattern because the influence of London overshadows that of other centres.

Many suggested city regions would be so large as to need a second and lower level of authorities if local government is not to be too remote for effective contact between the elected representatives and the people. But many of these second level authorities would be too small to find the resources needed for the main local government services; and in any case the present splitting of personal services which ought to be concentrated in one authority would be reproduced over a large part of the country".

The Conservatives when they came into power, produced their proposals in a White Paper in February 1971. This was based upon producing two forms of operational authorities. In the Conservative party's view some areas needed wider areas of administration whilst others were best dealt with by authorities more closely in touch with local conditions. A *county* was the word chosen for the wider areas needed for some services. The more local areas were titled *districts*, with an indication that the historic title of borough would also be retained.

The White Paper in 1971 (9.3) paid some regard to the general concept which lies behind the thinking about city regions as the following paragraph shows.

"The areas of many existing authorities are out-dated and no longer reflect the pattern of life and work in modern society. The division between counties and county boroughs has prolonged an artificial separation of big towns from their surrounding hinterlands for functions whose planning and administration need to embrace both town and country. There are too many authorities and many of them are too small in area and resources to support the operation of services to the standards which people nowadays have the right to expect. The present division of responsibilities between authorities is, in some fields, confusing and illogical.

If local authorities are to provide services effectively and economically, their areas should be large enough in size, population and resources to meet administrative needs, including the maintenance and development of a trained and expert local government service:

boundaries should be drawn so that areas take account of patterns of development and travel: and services which are closely linked should be in the hands of the same authority."

It will be realized at once that the White Paper proposals did not go nearly as far as the Royal Commission in accepting the principle of a city region as the base for each new local authority. However, in practice, new authorities were usually created with more sensible boundaries than the ones which they replaced. The reduction in the number of authorities from 1397 in England and Wales (excluding London) to 456, in itself improved the general structure enormously.

The conurbations

One matter about which both political parties agreed was the need to deal in some special way with the really large city regions. The Royal Commission, it will be recalled, had proposed three areas for such special treatment: Birmingham, Liverpool and Manchester. The Labour Government, in accepting the report of the Royal Commission had suggested that further areas would have to be dealt with by the setting up of the special type of metropolitan authority proposed by the Royal Commission. The Conservative Government's proposals in 1971 had this to say about the problem:

"The Metropolitan Counties. In the Government's view a metropolitan type of structure would be appropriate in Merseyside, South-East Lancashire and North-East Cheshire (Selnec) and the West Midlands and, in addition, West Yorkshire, South Yorkshire and the Tyne and Wear area. These six areas need to be treated as entities for purposes of planning transportation and certain other services; at the same time the districts into which they divide would all be big enough in population and resources, and sufficiently compact in size to be responsible for education and the personal services, as well as the more local functions.'

"The Government are therefore of the view that the metropolitan type of structure should be adopted in the six areas referred to in paragraph 30, and not elsewhere. The boundaries of these areas should include all the main area, or areas, of continuous development and any adjacent area into which continuous development will extend. It may be right to include closely related built-up areas, too. But none of these proposed metropolitan counties can practicably contain the solution of all the planning problems of the conurbations and, where it is impossible to meet all housing and

1 Tyne and Wear
2 West Yorkshire
3 South Yorkshire
4 Greater Manchester
5 Merseyside
6 West Midlands

Figure 9.6. Metropolitan Counties. 1. Tyne and Wear; 2. West Yorkshire; 3. South Yorkshire; 4. Greater Manchester; 5. Merseyside; 6. West Midlands.

redevelopment needs within the county boundaries, the answer will lie in development well outside the metropolitan area, in accordance with a carefully worked out regional plan." (9.4)

The six areas are shown in Fig. 9.6.

Functions of the Metropolitan Counties

There was a considerable area of disagreement about the functions which would be appropriate for the metropolitan authority. The Royal Commission intended that the metropolitan authorities would only be responsible for planning, transportation and major development together with functions relating to the police, fire services, refuse disposal and promotion of the arts. The Labour Government, in accepting the Royal Commission's report, proposed that the metropolitan councils should also be responsible for education. The Conservatives produced legislative proposals which were based more nearly on those in the report of the Royal Commission. They allocated education, social services and housing to the

County Councils (Outside Metropolitan Areas)
and Metropolitan District Councils:
Education
Personal social services
Libraries

Metropolitan County
Councils only:
Passenger transport authorities

OTHERWISE:

County Councils

Planning
Structure plans
Development control
(strategic and reserved decisions)
Acquisition and disposal of land for
planning purposes, development
or redevelopment (1)

Highway authorities

Traffic

Transport coordination

Housing
Certain reserve powers, e.g. for
overspill

Consumer protection
e.g. weights and measures, food and
drugs

Refuse disposal

Museums and art galleries (1)

Parks and open spaces (1)

Playing fields and swimming baths (1)

Police (3)

Fire (3)

District Councils

Planning
Local plans
Most development control

Acquisition and disposal of land for
planning purposes, development
or redevelopment (1)

Maintenance of unclassified roads in
urban areas

Public transport undertakings

Housing, including
House building
House management
Slum clearance
House and area improvement

Building Regulations

Environmental health (2)
e.g. clean air, food safety and hygiene,
nuisances, slaughterhouses, port
health, Offices, Shops and Railway
Premises Act

Refuse collection

Museums and art galleries (1)

Parks and open spaces (1)

Playing fields and swimming baths (1)

Cemeteries and crematoria

Notes:
(1) Concurrent powers exercisable by county councils and district councils.
(2) Future administration of water supply, sewerage and sewage disposal
provisionally put at the district level (including provision for joint boards)
pending long-term decisions regarding water organization.
(3) Some counties will need to be amalgamated for police purposes and possibly for
fire.

Figure 9.7 Allocation of main functions in England.

metropolitan districts leaving the metropolitan county councils with planning and highways functions together with fire, police, refuse disposal and consumer protection. The detailed split of functions in reorganized local government in England is set out in Fig. 9.7. The reorganization of local government in England has accordingly recognized the problems of the conurbations and to that extent the new structure has been designed to meet some of the problems, experienced over past decades, in running the large city regions in the country. The six largest city regions have each been given a distinct identity. The sort of cooperative arrangements which existed in the 1960s should no longer be needed in these areas. In assessing the success or failure of the present proposals it is ironic to note that the heaviest criticism has been levelled at the six metropolitan authorities. Yet this is the one area upon which all parties were agreed. Whilst there was disagreement about the functions to be entrusted to the county and to the district neither the Conservatives nor the Labour party, nor for that matter the Royal Commission, dissented from the view that special arrangements needed to be made for the densely built up and urbanized areas of England.

The Greater Manchester County Council

In order to understand more clearly how the new system of governance of the city region works it will be helpful to examine one of the largest, the Greater Manchester County Council in some detail.

The Greater Manchester Council is responsible for a population of 2,729,900. It has ten metropolitan districts the largest being Manchester with a population of 530,000.

The council hold office for four years, as do the councillors in non-metropolitan counties, and retire together.

The Council comprises 106 members whose present political composition is as follows:

Labour	69
Conservative	24
Liberal	13

The Budget of the Council is detailed in Fig. 9.8. It will be seen that the revenue budget was nearly £110 million in 1975/76. This budget is not much larger than that of the metropolitan districts in the county, who have major commitments to education and housing.

| | 1973-4 | 1974-5 | | 1975-6 ESTIMATES | | | |
| | Actual | Estimate | Revised Estimate | Submitted to Committees | Approved by Committees | Approved by Finance Committee | Total reductions (-) (Col 6-Col 4) |
	(1)	(2)	(3)	(4)	(5)	(6)	(7)
	£000	£000	£000	£000	£000	£000	£000
1. Consumer Protection	13	815	732	1,156	1,156	1,106	50
Finance -							
2. County Treasury	73	384	271	494	494	303	191
3. Computer Systems Development Unit	7	20	90	151	151	151	—
4. Other Financing Expenses including Debt Charges on New Schemes	Cr. 28	408	459	1,843	1,843	1,837	6
5. Probation and After-Care Committee	—	289	316	387	387	377	10
6. Other Precepts	—	1,000	1,094	1,133	1,133	1,126	7
7. MAJC—Deficiency Contribution	—	—	—	165	165	165	—
8. Fire Services	55	7,190	7,696	9,416	9,416	9,256	160
9. Highways	72	20,801	23,945	27,573	26,189	26,189	1,384
10. Planning	167	1,018	973	1,995	1,398	1,353	642
11. Police	161	14,408	15,593	17,511	17,511	17,381	130
12. Policy	380	1,987	1,913	2,776	2,673	2,460	316
13. Recreation and Arts	—	415	406	970	845	845	125
14. Transportation	—	12,560	14,661	21,500	21,500	29,500*	+8,000
15. COMMITTEE REQUIREMENTS	900	61,295	68,089	87,370	85,161	92,349	−3,021 +8,000
16. Revenue Contributions to Capital Expenditure	—	5,000	3,500			6,776 -	
17. Contingencies	—	3,752	425			9,910	
18. Balance brought forward	—	303	181			95	
19. TOTAL REQUIREMENTS	900	70,350	72,195			109,130	
Less Income							
20. Transport Supplementary Grant		—	—			12,595	
21. Yield from Precept	719	70,350	72,100			96,535	
22. TOTAL INCOME	719	70,350	72,100			109,130	
23. Balance carried forward	181	Nil	95			—	
24. Precept (pence)	0.25	17.5	17.5			21.5	
25. Yield from Precept of 1p	2,876	4,020	4,120			4,490	

* includes supplemental estimates approved by Finance Committee on 14 January 1975.

⸗ includes allocation of TSG agreed by Council 29th January 1975—08M PTE support:
01.176M grant for ongoing Capital Schemes. The Transportation Committee figure
in Col. 6 includes a sum for rail support which in earlier columns was paid direct to
Passenger Transport Executive from Department of Environment. The figures,
therefore, are not directly comparable.

Figure 9.8. GMC Revenue Budget 1975-76-Summary.

The staff employed by the Greater Manchester Council is as follows:

(1975/76 established posts)

Administrative etc staff 3167
Police (uniformed) 6628
Fire (establishments) 2324
Manual workers 2029

In fact, in common with most local authorities in the UK in 1975, the number of posts actually filled was less than establishment. Only 75% of administrative posts, 83% of police posts and 84% of fire were filled at February 1975.

The number of administrative posts filled can be broken down as follows between departments:

Department	No of Posts Assigned	Posts Filled as at 3.2.75	
		No	%
Chief Executive's	82	70	82.4
Prosecuting Solicitor's	111	106	95.5
County Treasury	167	158	94.6
County Secretary's	110	82	81.2
County Planning	210	169	80.5
County Engineer's	619	304	49.4
County Fire Service	152	143	94.1
County Val. and Est.63		42	66.7
Consumer Services	238	168	70.6
Greater Manchester Police	1369	1097	80.1
Rent Officer Service	50	45	90.0
TOTALS	3167	2384	75.3

The number of manual workers were allocated as follows:

Department	No. of Posts Filled	
	Full-time	Part-time
Chief Executive's	7	14
County Secretary's	14	53
County Engineer's	213	821
County Fire Service	135	81
Consumer Services	11	4
Greater Manchester Police	390	286
Totals	770	1259

The GMC meets in full council 12 times per year. It has established 10 standing committees with 19 sub-committees.

Areas of activity of GMC

Clearly a completely new authority requires time to develop its role. In particular on the highways side, the council has granted extensive agency arrangements to metro-district councils to carry out road maintenance and agreed improvements. The Transport Policies and Programme (the TPP) submitted to the Government and on which grant is based, severely restricted finance available with the result that many schemes were deferred.

Planning

The GMC have agreed schemes with the districts for development control and local plans. Structure plan work is proceeding on a number of fronts, e.g. shopping offices and industrial locations, car parking policies. The Planning Committee are continuing the reclamation programmes started by former authorities and subject to capital finance hope to reclaim about 500 acres (200 ha) per annum. The council share the Joint Reclamation Team with Lancashire. The rehabilitation of river valleys is also a fundamental plank in the programme.

Recreation and Arts

The GMC support financially the major institutions, e.g. Halle Orchestra, Northern Dance Theatre, 69 Theatre. The GMC and the districts have agreed to the GMC paying the whole of the North West Arts subscription. This is a Regional body which exists for the promotion of the arts in the North West—visual, musical and cultural. The GMC are offering revenue support to the Manchester Museum, North West Museum of Science and Industry and the Whitworth Art Gallery and are devising a scheme for the financial support of other museums and galleries in the County which make a significant contribution to the cultural life of the County as a whole. They are grant aiding DALTA (Drama and Lyric Theatre Association) and Glyndeborne. They are also making arrangements for the BBC Camerata Chamber Orchestra to tour the County and are in touch with the BBC to develop a working relationship on the promotion of music. Next year the council's aim is to promote cultural and recreational activities and events in the county.

Transportation

A number of papers dealing with the transportation issues and strategies for the County have been prepared. The council are giving financial support to bus and rail operations and are examining very closely the relationship and costs of different forms of transport. They are actively promoting the Piccadilly-Victoria underground rail link line which was one of the recommendations of the SEL-NEC transportation study previously referred to.

Consumer Protection

Apart from the statutory services such as Weights and Measures the GMC have been promoting the concept of consumer advice. The aim is to open Consumer Advisory Centres in each of the ten districts to deal with not only consumer complaints but also to give pre-shopping advice. The council are working closely with Citizens Advice Bureau and the Manchester Consumer forum which represents consumer interests in the voluntary field.

Industrial Development

There is an industrial development unit in the Chief Executive's office working out, with the districts, policies for the encouragement of industry to the county.

General liaison with the Districts

The Greater Manchester Association of Metropolitan Authorities (GMAMA) has been established with equal representation from each of the ten districts and the county. The Chief Executives meet as a Coordinating Working Group at two monthly intervals (in between meetings of the GMAMA). To deal with concurrent functions in the Recreation and Arts field, meetings are held regularly with the districts to discuss the interrelationship between the County and District for the support and promotion of arts and recreation. *Ad hoc* meetings are also held when necessary to deal with specific topics, e.g. housing problems and needs in Greater Manchester.

Summary and assessment

We have seen that local government in the United Kingdom altered little in structure between 1892 and 1974. During this period the functions entrusted to it expanded steadily. The nineteenth century authorities were concerned with roads, public health and the relief of poverty. At the end of World War II, some county borough councils were providing nearly all the community services. These ranged from public utility functions like gas and electricity through health, planning housing and environmental functions to roads, parks and markets. The period in question was one of steady urban growth. The boundaries of the larger towns increasingly failed to reflect modern patterns of life and work.

Some considerable efforts were made in the 1960s to deal with the planning and transportation problems of the conurbations by

establishing on a voluntary basis, cooperative working arrangements. Steering committees representative of the different local
authorities were set up often at the suggestion of the then Ministry of
Transport. In smaller towns there were often Advisory Committees
to plan over a wider area than that of the old central urban core.

However it was not till the passing of the Local Government Act
1972 that a new system was introduced which created new statutory
authorities for areas more nearly approximating to the needs of the
time. Six large urban areas or conurbations were selected for special
treatment with the title of metropolitan counties. Elsewhere strategic planning and transportation were placed in the hands of 39 new
county councils. Their areas did not correspond in all cases to the 24
to 45 regional units or city regions which were identified in England
by expert witnesses to the Royal Commission on Local Government. However in most cases the areas were improvements on the
old, if only because there were no autonomous islands of urban
development such as resulted from the creation of separate authorities for the 62 largest towns in England in 1888.

The new system is a compromise. The reduction in number of
local authorities was not so great as to make the district councils
totally remote from their electorate. Some district councils are quite
small and some quite large but well over half are in the population
range 75,000-150,000. The counties have been changed, but not too
drastically. They are mostly recognizable even if some have disappeared in the process of reorganization.

Most criticism of the new boundaries has been levelled at the new
metropolitan counties. This is ironic as the creation of metropolitan
authorities was the one issue upon which all were agreed in principle.

On the plus side of the new metropolitan counties, their supporters might say:

> the area in each case is large enough to do most things effic-
> iently;
> planning at strategic level is in the hands of one authority
> instead of several working together as best they could. So also is
> transportation and roads;
> there is a single new authority to promote the interests of the
> conurbation as a whole;
> by restricting the area to the identifiable built up parts, any
> tendency to encroach into adjoining countryside will be mini-
> mized.

The critics of the new metropolitan county concept might say:

at councillor level there are not enough 'human interest' type services to retain the interest of the best councillors;
the metropolitan district councils are relatively large and powerful with wide ranging functions. This may help to promote a feeling that the new county council is not really needed and that its functions could somehow be done by the districts working in collaboration. It is productive of friction;
the area within the metropolitan envelope is not large enough. In particular the new counties, say critics, should have a rural area within which to plan recreation and leisure for its inhabitants.

The truth is that it is too early to make judgements about the new system. It may take a long time to make changes in local government. It also takes a long time for the changes to be accepted by those affected.

References

9.1   From the First Report of the Municipal Corporation Commissions, 1835, cited in WEBB, S. and B., *English Local Government from the Revolution to the Municipal Corporation Act*, Part II, 1924.
9.2   *Local Government Reform*, Cmnd. 4039, HMSO, 1967, p.6.
9.3   *Local Government in England*, Government Proposals for Reorganization Cmnd. 4584, HMSO, 1971.
9.4   *ibid.*

Further reading

CRAVEN, E., (Ed.), *Regional Devolution and Social Policy* published for the Centre for Studies in Social Policy, Macmillan 1975.
SENIOR, D., *The Regional City*, Longman, 1966.

PART THREE

CHAPTER TEN

The Location of
Industry in the City Region

W. F. Luttrell

Introduction

My emphasis will be on dynamics: the changes, the causes of change, and the policy implications for future change, in the spatial pattern of industry in large cities and city regions. By industry I mean not simply manufacturing, but all forms of economic activity and thus all kinds of employment.

There are two basically different approaches to the analysis of these changes; that of the 'dynamic geographer' and that of the economist or socio-economic analyst. (Some may dispute the titles, but most would agree that the approaches are quite different.)

Two approaches

The first method is that of direct analysis of the observed changes. The sequence may go like this. First, observe and record the changes in the spatial pattern over a period of time; the measurements may include places of work and of residence, their densities and changes over time; journeys to work; spatial pattern of different types of job; incomes. Secondly, find variables that can be associated with these changes: they might include rent and land value gradients; stock and availability of premises; labour availability; managers' or others' preferences for residence; transport improvements; government policies and planning controls. Thirdly, try out and check for 'fit' formulations that will 'explain' the changes that have been observed to have taken place.

The second method is to try to discover the underlying causes of change. These will be both internal and external to the organization which is undertaking the economic activity in question. For example, in manufacturing the techniques of production change over time, and these changes affect economies of scale, size of plant, mix of skills and other factors such as reliance on outside services. Office operations are also changing internally and so are retailing methods. But all these activities are also influenced by changes which are external to them but may be internal to another industry, such as in transporting techniques. For a number of reasons, also, the sizes of organizations have been changing: the general trend has been for local enterprises to be overtaken by or absorbed into national enterprises. There has also been a secondary effect of devolution within large organizations, both public and private, to reduce over-centralization; but it does not reproduce the previous pattern. In parallel with all these changes in the units of economic activity, there are various changes in the social patterns of individuals, partly caused by higher incomes and better education, partly by changes in attitude and opinion, but also partly in response to the techno-economic changes already referred to.

This second method, of examining the underlying causes of change, does not produce a neat overall analysis and 'explanation' of spatial change. This is largely because it is difficult to provide reliable measures of the advantages of concentration: for example, the cost advantage to a certain enterprise in having a specific service available to it within a given distance. It is known to be advantageous to its efficiency, but the effect is difficult to quantify. (In contrast it is relatively easy to measure some of the disadvantageous effects of urban growth.) For the same basic reason, it is difficult to combine the first and second methods I have referred to: inputs from method two cannot be easily produced and neatly fitted into the kinds of category used in method one.

Strategy selection

My own inclination is towards the second method, partly perhaps because more is at present written under the heading of method one. Each is at present imperfect; method one may be accused of being superficial, method two of being indeterminate. Eventually they may be brought together. Meanwhile, it seems to me that the best course is the following. First analyze the underlying causes of change, both economic and social, and consider whether they will continue and what form they will take. Secondly, consider how well they agree with or are accommodated with the present urban and spatial framework. Thirdly, consider what social and other disadvantages there arc in the existing or developing urban patterns, and how they might be avoided. Fourthly, consider alternative urban and spatial patterns which would meet the economic requirements so as to provide a rising standard of life, but would at the same time remove or minimize the environmental disadvantages and provide improving social conditions. Fifthly, select a course which will make for continuous improvement: a dynamic plan rather than one for a fixed future date.

This approach differs from that of most urban planners on two grounds. First, it is based primarily on an attempt to discover the underlying causes of change, which are to a great extent economic, and to reconcile plans with them. Secondly, it is inherently dynamic: it considers changes of need on the one hand, but it also considers all plans as changing patterns rather than eventual patterns. While I can perhaps claim that this approach is especially suitable for considering the dynamics of industrial location, I must admit that in this Chapter I shall be straying into wider implications for urban planning as a whole. But this I must excuse on the ground that the basic reason for the existence of cities is economic, and job-location should be an integral and important part of urban planning.

In general, people in cities have better employment opportunities than in the remainder of their countries: it is chiefly for this reason that cities have grown, and the proportion of urban population is still growing throughout the world.

Nevertheless, there are certain contradictions, and certain ways in which job opportunities are worsening in some large cities. One reason appears to be that the economic pattern is changing; and the town planners, or perhaps I should say those responsible for policy, have not always adjusted their thinking to the new problems. I try to illustrate this by over-simplified models of the old and the new.

The old pattern

In the last century most cities, though they had single-activity streets or districts, included many functions in their central areas: commerce, shopping, entertainment, manufacture and wholesaling. Mixed up with these functions were sub-areas of housing for both rich and poor.

A great deal of the manufacture was in relatively small workshops of skilled craftsmen, whose jobs were related to specialized retailing in the same city, from clothing to jewellery to small industrial and household goods; and this pattern is common today in the cities of developing countries. But there were also large factories with houses clustered closely round them within the urban fabric, and some of these still survive in Britain's older industrial towns.

In the same way, wholesale distribution, warehousing and the bulk handling of goods, were internal city functions. Based on railway station yards, and (for towns with water access) on docks inside the city, the warehouses and wholesale markets, with their attendant jobs, were all well within the urban orbit.

The other special functions of a large city were regional or national administration, commerce and finance; the higher levels of cultural and entertainment activities, with hotels and catering and specialized shopping; higher education; and the higher levels of all professional activities, such as medical and legal.

The changing situation

In recent decades, much of this pattern of activities, and of jobs, has changed, for reasons which come primarily from changes in the operational techniques of production, handling and transportation.

Distribution

First, wholesale distribution and the bulk handling of goods has moved (or is fast moving) right out of the cities. As more goods are handled by road instead of rail, it is more convenient to have the wholesale distribution points on the main road network outside the cities. For water-borne goods, with new methods of shipping, the old urban docks are being adandoned and specialized facilities are developed outside the city, where there is sufficient space for extensive mechanized handling of cargoes. Also, wholesale produce markets are tending to move out of cities for similar reasons. Ideally a large market of this kind is fed by both rail and road, while the onward distribution is nearly all by road; the best location is therefore outside the city, in some cases with one on either side of a large conurbation. For all these changes there are sound reasons which hardly anyone disputes.

Manufacturing

Secondly, manufacturing has been moving out. There have been two causes. First, a much higher proportion of manufacturing is in full-scale factories rather than small workshops. Second, modern production plants require spacious single-storey buildings, with further space for handling goods and suitable access for road transport. The old congested and often multi-storey factories inside towns were therefore unsuitable. But in moving out from inner-city and middle-city sites, many factories (in Britain at least) have moved right outside the travel-to-work range of their city of origin. Some of the largest factories have gone to quite distant places where there has been heavy unemployment, the so-called development areas, and these moves have accorded with government policy. But many others have gone to smaller towns around the conurbation, at distances of between 20 and 100 kilometres from it.

The question may then be raised whether it is advantageous to remove a great deal of manufacturing employment from the great cities, as against relocating on the periphery where the wide range of skills of the urban population can be drawn upon. From the viewpoint of the skilled employee, also, there may be advantages if his job is in a large city, if it means there is a choice of employers where he can apply his special skill. The outflow can be large: it is estimated that London lost 400,000 manufacturing jobs, 25% of its total, in the decade 1961 to 1971, and as many as 70,000 in 1972.

Attempts have been made to analyze which types of manufacture are most appropriate to a large city, though without very definitive results. In considering an optimum distribution pattern of manufacturing, a large part of the comparison will rest on the alternatives to be considered in the smaller towns, such as the degree of specialization in a single group of products or skills, as against diversification. However, I think the major distinction will probably be between the routine production of standard products, which can have a wide choice of locations, and those factories which undertake prototype work and the development of new products, often in the more advanced technologies. There are of course many examples of such work being successfully located in medium-sized towns, especially where there is a local specialization. But they are also very suitable for the periphery of large cities, with the further advantage that the other members of a worker's family, who may have quite different skills, should also have appropriate job opportunities.

Office-type functions

The third type of activity which has been moving out of large cities is, perhaps surprisingly, that of office employment. This is not to say the numbers of office workers in cities have declined absolutely; indeed they have often increased somewhat. But there have been two reasons why office functions appropriate to a large city have tended to grow. First, there has been a general trend to more office-type jobs as against manual jobs in all sectors of the economy. Second, more enterprises have been combining together, or one absorbing others, so that a larger proportion of economic activity is handled by organizations with a regional or national coverage as against simply a local one, and these enterprises need to have a controlling office in the provincial or national capital. The consequent increased demand for offices in city centres has sometimes led to developments which have destroyed some of the historic fabric of the original city. For this and other reasons, opposition to further office jobs has built up. In London, for example, employment of this kind has remained approximately static in the Central Area, while the increase in demand has been catered for by a policy of dispersion, and severe restraint on more offices in the centre: increases in floorspace have been largely balanced by the trend to more floorspace per worker. As a result, some headquarter-type offices have been scattered in the rest of London, while many others have been persuaded to go to towns right outside London. In the public sector, some central government offices have been moved to towns hundreds of kilometres away. Nevertheless, the continuing pressure of unsatisfied demand has kept rents at the centre still very high, as much as five times above those of offices near the centres of quite prosperous cities 100 to 200 kilometres away.

It could I think be argued that office-type jobs are often attached to a headquarters office (whether in the public or private sector) which have no need to be there, and that unnecessary congestion and external diseconomies may result. From this viewpoint, some pressure to remove unnecessary activities is healthy, and higher

166

rents could be one of the means. But it should be remembered that the clustering of central offices has an important rationale: the need for frequent face-to-face meeting between decision-takers in related activities. Where this is the case, there will be a loss of effectiveness if the offices in question are scattered over a large area, even within one conurbation, and more so if they are forced to go to distant locations.

There are two ways in which office jobs can be removed from city centres with no loss of efficiency, and even with some gain. There are some activities which are genuinely footloose in that they have rather few contacts with other central offices, and their only real need is to be in a suitable catchment area for their employees: an example would be an office which did nearly all its business by post or teleprinter, or within its own branches rather than needing contact with other headquarters. But these have mostly moved out already.

The second approach is by internal reorganization: by delegating responsibility to regional control offices and retaining fewer decisions for headquarters. This can apply both in the public and private sectors: indeed, if it is applied in the public sector, by devolution of more power to provincial or regional authorities, it becomes easier for large private sector enterprises to do the same. Of course, this requires a political decision which will not be taken on town planning grounds. Its first effect would be to transfer growth from national to provincial capitals rather than to smaller towns. (In Britain, on the contrary, we are moving national offices of central government to a variety of provincial towns without changing their functions.) Another reorganization, especially in the private sector and in multi-activity enterprises, is to transfer more authority from central headquarters to divisional headquarters, which will often be in the part of the country where the division in question has most of its activities.

Nevertheless, the central office functions of a large city, whether a national or provincial capital, are likely to be increasing, and I discuss later whether they should be accommodated or resisted.

The city's population

At the same time as the job pattern and the kinds of activity have been changing, so has the resident population of some large cities. In some cases there has been an apparent decline simply because the city is spreading, and it is measured by a municipal boundary which is no longer realistic. But in others, such as London, there has been a genuine decline. The inner boroughs, which coincide roughly with nineteenth century London and are fairly close-packed, are being redeveloped to lower densities: between the Censuses of 1966 and 1971 they consequently lost over a tenth of their population; while the outer boroughs (the newer suburbs, with some small towns that have been absorbed) hold unchanged numbers. The trend is continuing, and Greater London is expected to decline by about two million from its peak of around 8 million.

Also, the constitution of the city's population is changing. For a long time higher-income people have been moving right outside London, and commuting daily to jobs in the centre. More recently, parts of the inner boroughs are being 're-colonized' by middle- and upper-income people, which has increased the trend to lower densities on redevelopment. Meanwhile, lower-income people who wish to retain jobs in London are finding it increasingly difficult to get accommodation they can afford.

It might be argued that if in a large and mature city both people and jobs move out, a new balance could be struck with a smaller population, and there would be no disadvantage in a continuing decline. It can be agreed that there is no single optimum size for a capital city, and that redevelopment of outworn housing will lead to lower densities. But it does not follow that a continuing reduction will be advantageous.

First, one should look again at the functions of the city. In London over one-third of all the jobs, about 1½ million of them, have been estimated to fall into the categories of national, central and head-office-type functions. While some of these jobs could no doubt be moved out to advantage, by the methods I have described, it is likely that there are at least an equal number of activities that would gain by being in or near the centre of this city and have been frustrated. These jobs are nearly all non-manual and do not cater for all the population. The local service jobs, whose numbers are related to the population and which account for around 40% of the whole, do of course include manual and unskilled jobs. But manufacturing, now accounting for rather under a quarter of all jobs and declining, could supply a high proportion of skilled manual and technical openings.

Secondly, I would express a personal opinion that there are advantages in a large city which cannot be matched elsewhere. It may be argued that among the middle-aged it is chiefly the upper-income and professional people who reap the gain, both in job opportunities and amenities. But among the young I think it is apparent that the advantages, of both kinds, are appreciated much more widely through all classes. I may say that this view is by no means shared by all, many of whom think in terms of towns that 'small is beautiful'. However, I would suggest that many who prefer living in a small town appreciate the amenities of the large city. They would also prefer to have a more thriving national economy, and I suggest that a properly functioning city makes an important contribution to it.

At the same time, large cities run into great problems of congestion, communications, and imbalance of living places and jobs. The problems are severe but in my view not insoluble. In suggesting some of the implications for action, I take the perhaps simplistic view that it is useful to look at the functions of the city, and consider how they can be made to work. If we can arrive at some principles, even over-simple ones, it may be better than being overwhelmed by the size and complexity of the tasks. There are of course other problems of the great city, chiefly social ones, discussed elsewhere in this book; but I do not think their solution will be incompatible with these suggestions.

Possible solutions

In discussing possible solutions, I am not in any way suggesting there should be a single physical pattern for all large cities, but simply that the adjustments to a city's pattern should take account of its functions and the ways they are changing, as well as of changing living requirements, so that the two aspects can be coordinated.

The needs

A compact central area

The most important functions of a large city are in its central area. It chiefly exists because it can bring close together groups of people who need constantly to communicate with each other. These are headquarters staffs of large organizations, whether in the private or public sector, and the supporting technical, commercial, or financial and other services. If any of these offices (or detachable parts of them) do not need to have this contact with others, they should move right out. If they do need it, they should be close together, so that the area should be as compact as possible.

There are advantages in having also in the central area, very close to the Central Business District just referred to, other central functions: restaurants, entertainment, highly specialized comparison shopping, cultural centres like art galleries. These also can be grouped fairly tightly.

Secondary nodal points

In a large city, it is advisable to have a few important secondary centres, also well placed on the public transport system, which will provide services for the city's resident population. They would therefore have shops and personal and professional services equivalent to those of a fairly large independent town. Since they would have quick access to the city centre, they could also take some of the headquarter-type offices which needed to be near, but not necessarily right in, the city centre.

Manufacturing

In my view it is unnecessary and wrong to force all industry right away from large cities. Much modern manufacturing, while it needs spacious sites, is clean and non-polluting. Especially for the plants using a variety of high-level skills and services, there are advantages in their being sited on the periphery of a big city, with good access to the external transport system, but also able to draw on the city's varied labour force and services. Some groups of industrial estates towards the edge of the city, convenient for both public and private transport, should achieve this.

The urban pattern

In the simplest form for exposition, I am suggesting that the city's jobs, and its urban form, can be regarded under three headings.

Central and national functions

These would nearly all be in the central area, which should not expand spatially but could often have higher job-density under the conditions I mention below

Local and regional service functions.

Many of the local service jobs will of course be scattered throughout the city; but their higher-level functions could be concentrated in a few secondary centres with a fairly full range of urban services.

Manufacturing

Manufacturing would be concentrated at groups of large sites on the edge of the city, with good access to its resident population.

Transport implications

The first essential need is a full public transport system into the city centre, with complete priority over other road users on specified routes through the city, as well as a wholly segregated system such as an underground. It should be remembered that many going to the central area will be coming right through from collection points outside the city, others from the outer suburbs and inner residential areas. Despite the high concentration of journeys, it is in fact easier with a public transport system to organize journeys to and through a concentrated centre than to a great variety of destinations. The central area should also have major public transport links with the secondary nodal points I have referred to. Lastly, in the central area itself there should be an efficient public transport circulatory system: this will preferably involve either the complete removal of private transport in this small area, or certain fully segregated routes for public transport which cannot be impeded by other vehicles.

Central area implications

If the functions of a central area are fully recognized, it could often accommodate more jobs, not fewer. The problem in planning its development is that it is often associated with historic buildings and streets which should be preserved. The result often is that an unresolved battle continues, with developers (and even public bodies) gradually nibbling at the parts that should be preserved, while there is general reluctance to allow the needed development in the whole area. In my view this is a field for firm decisions: some districts of a central area should be preserved as a whole, and the aim should be restoration rather than development. Other districts of the centre, especially those well placed for public transport stations, could go to very high densities. The preserved parts will mostly revert to cultural and entertainment uses, with specialist shops and small offices. In any case, if the central area is kept very compact as it should be, these activities will all be close to each other.

But if this kind of policy is followed there is an important implication for housing. The central area development is often vitiated by trying to provide conditions for family living and children at the same time. In my view (though many disagree with me) one should recognize the specialized functions of a central area. It can well accommodate, at high density, the people who like central urban life, young people without families, bachelor types, and those whose families have grown up. It is impossible in such an area to provide proper conditions for young children, with play-grounds, schools, low-rise housing and so on. It is therefore better to recognize this and move towards a policy of central-type residential living in the centre, and proper conditions for family life and children in the main residential parts of the city.

Residential area implications

The main residential areas of the city will as far as possible provide a suitable environment for families with children, and not be interspersed with large offices or factories. They will be planned around secondary urban centres which will themselves provide a fair range of jobs as well as services: local and regional shopping and personal and professional services, as well as some independent offices. They will also be on rapid-transit routes, both to the city centre and outwards to points near industrial jobs.

An important aspect, if the central area housing policy just mentioned is to be implemented, and if there is to be physical mobility for people as their jobs and family need change, is that there should be a freely-moving housing market, allowing people to interchange easily between the central area, the inner residential family areas and the outer suburbs.

Industrial job implications

In a large city, factory-type jobs are likely to become a smaller par of the whole but can still be important. They will in some cases be associated with research work in related fields, and some peripheral areas of the city may develop such specializations. But an increasing proportion of the less-skilled and less well-paid manual jobs are likely to be in the services (catering etc.) which will be scattered through the city. To assist this pattern it will be helpful to have residential income-mixes in various parts of the town, rather than class segregation. The other need will be housing mobility within the city for its residents at all income levels, as I have mentioned.

Conclusion

A live city must be ready to change in accordance with social and economic requirements. I suggest here that it can adapt to these requirements rather than simply opposing them, and can provide both better living conditions and better job-ranges if the pattern of change is recognized and suitable policy steps are taken.

To revert to the earlier part of this chapter, where I outlined a possible approach to urban planning, I have attempted above to carry out two of the required stages. First, I have outlined broadly what I regard as the underlying forces for change and the characteristics of the job requirements that follow. Secondly, I have suggested some of the implications for the spatial pattern of activities in a great city such as London, and its immediate surroundings. What I have not done is to sketch out the adaptive and dynamic plan by which such objectives could be achieved within a defined time-scale.

CHAPTER ELEVEN

Function and Form of the City Region

Marcial Echenique

Introduction

The intention of this Chapter is to demonstrate the relationship between changes in the functional base of the city region and the resultant changes in form. For this purpose a simplified conceptual model of the city region is used as a point of departure to analyze the changes through time. By varying the inputs to the model, in order to reflect the changes in the economic base of the city region, the resultant change in the spatial organization can be ascertained. This process gives us some guidelines for the most appropriate pattern of urbanization.

The model used

Models are representations of reality and, as any representation, they are somewhat 'unfaithful' (11.1) to the portion of reality under observation. The purpose of models is to present a simplified and intelligible picture of the World in order to understand it better, thus by their very nature models cannot be very accurate. There are many types of models which can be classified according to what they are made for (intentions), what they are made of (substance) and how

174

the time factor is treated (11.2). The model used here is derived from the work of Lowry (11.3, 11.4), and its main intention is to derive conditional predictions given certain inputs. It is a conceptual model in which the elements of the city are represented by variables and their relationships expressed as mathematical equations. It is also a static model, which means that, given an input, the model finds the equilibrium value for the outputs; but it can be used with a time dimension if the basic inputs to the model are changed through time.

The most important idea behind the model is its systemic framework, that is to say, that all the elements represented throughout the model interact with all the others. In this form the final state cannot be deduced by the addition of each part.

In order to conceptualize this model, it is useful to classify the elements of the urban system into four major components. The first two components relate to the activities of the population: within-place or localized activities and between-place or flow activities (11.5). The second two components relate to the stocks of infrastructure necessary to support these activities: adapted spaces or land for the containment of within-place activities and channel spaces or networks for the containment of between-place activities (11.6). A change in any of these elements will produce changes in all the others. For example, a change in network provision not only affects the transportation flows and the utilization of the network but also affects the distribution of activities through space, thus changing the use of the land.

The model distinguishes three types of within-place activities: basic employment, service employment and residential activities. The basic employment can be defined as city-forming employment, because it brings money into the region by selling the goods and services that it produces outside the region. This money supports the necessary services for the population and buys goods which the region cannot produce by itself. The remaining employment (educational, commercial, recreational, etc.) can be defined as city-serving employment because the primary role in the city's economy is to serve the basic sector and the residential population (11.7). Residential activities are the activities that the employees and their dependents perform at home.

The Lowry model is structured such that, given an input of basic employment spatially located, it is possible to locate the resultant residential population generated by this employment. Knowing the location of population, it is possible to locate the demand for services. These services generate more employment, which in turn generates more residential population and so on. The service employment can be classified into three hierarchical levels: level one, or regional services; level two, or district services; and level three, or local services. The population demands different quantities of each level. This process is repeated until the system approaches an equilibrium state, that is to say, that no more increments of population or services are generated (see Fig. 11.1).

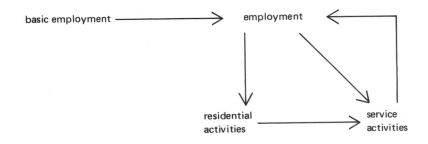

Figure 11.1. The structure of the Lowry model.

The allocation of residential population and service employment gives rise to two types of between-place activities: journeys from work to home and journeys from home to services. These flows can be further classified by the mode of transport used (pedestrian, public transport, private car, etc.) and allocated to the network.

The stocks of infrastructure can be classified corresponding to the classification of activities. The adapted spaces or land developed for the activities can be subdivided into basic employment land, residential land and service land. The channel spaces can be classified according to mode of travel, each one having a different speed of travel.

Inputs

The model is applied to a homogeneous region (idealized plane). This region is subdivided into zones of equal size. The zoning system used is hexagonal, which is the nearest subdivision to a circle, but covers the entire space without overlaps (see Fig. 11.2). The activities (i.e. number of employees or number of people) are allocated to individual zones. The channel spaces connect the centroids of these zones by a link representing a particular mode of

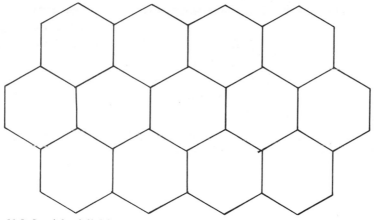

Figure 11.2. Spatial subdivision used.

transport, thus a time can be computed for travelling between any pair of zones. The model also gives the flows between zones and the land use of each zone.

The time dimension is given within the model by changing the basic inputs, that is, the location and type of basic employment and the utilization of transport technology. Fig. 11.3 shows the changes through time of basic employment as a percentage of total employment. As can be seen, the basic employment over 200 years changes from 70% to 40%, with the resultant increase in service employment. This change reflects the increase in productivity of the employment with the consequent increase in service provision.

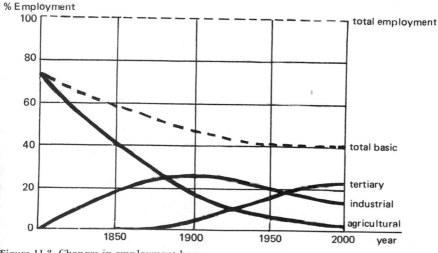

Figure 11.3. Changes in employment base.

Also it can be seen that the composition of the basic employment changes from predominantly extractive industries (agricultural, fishing and mining) to manufacturing industries, to tertiary industries (government, research, etc.).

The changes in transport technology are shown in Fig. 11.4. The percentage utilization of individual modes of transport changes from 100% pedestrian or horse back travel, with an average speed of 5 km per hour, to 10%. Public transport (i.e. trains, suburban railways, buses) increases to a peak of 70% utilization, declining to 25% with the emergence of the motor car. The average speed is 15 km per hour. The private car increases and stabilizes at around 65% of the total utilization with an average speed of 30 km per hour.

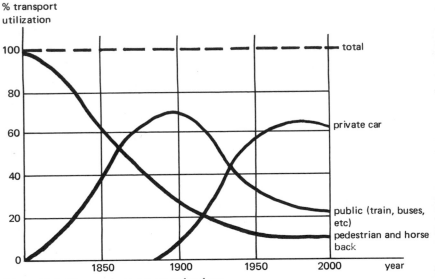

Figure 11.4. Changes in transport technology.

Four basic runs through the model are done: the agriculture based region (around the year 1800), the industry based city region (around the year 1900), the tertiary based city region (around the year 1950), the post-industry based city region (around the year 2000). Each run contains specific locations of basic employment and specific locations of channel spaces with their corresponding utilization.

The agriculture based region

In the first run, the basic employment of the region is agricultural,

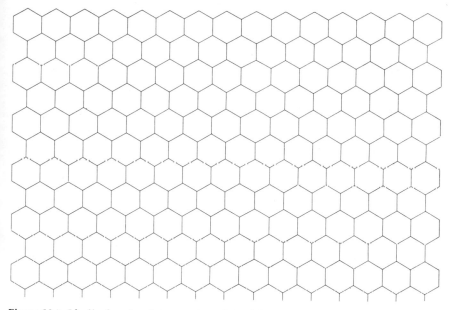

Figure 11.5. Idealized region (hexagonal spatial subdivision).

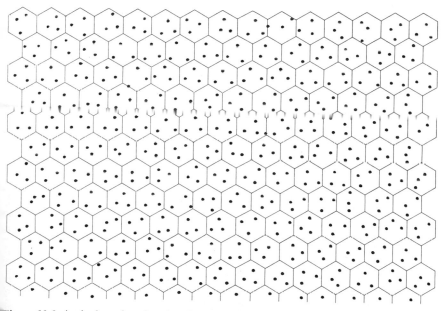

Figure 11.6. Agriculture based region: location of agricultural employment.

homogeneously distributed amongst all the zones. In real life this pattern is distorted because of topographical barriers (mountains, rivers, lakes, etc.). Fig. 11.6 shows the location of the agricultural employment and Fig. 11.7 shows the location of the transport

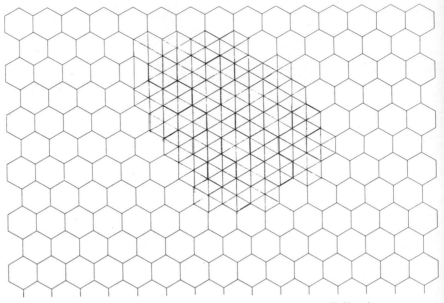

Figure 11.7. Transportation network: pedestrian or horse back in all directions.

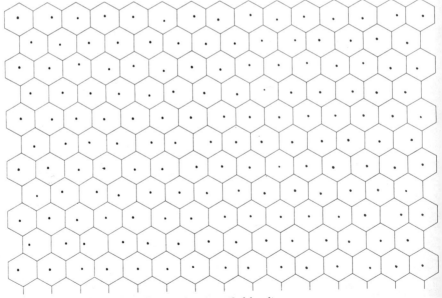

Figure 11.8. Location of service employment (3rd level).

network for pedestrian or horseback travel in all directions of the plane.

The population generated by the basic employment demand services at the three different levels shown in Figs. 11.8, 11.9 and 11.10. These services constitute the hierarchies of villages, towns and

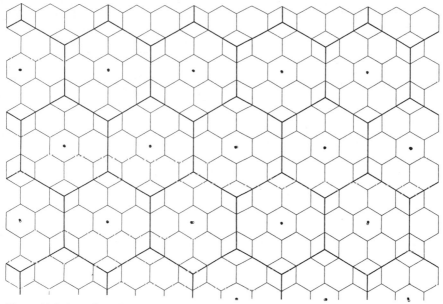

Figure 11.9. Location of service employment (2nd level).

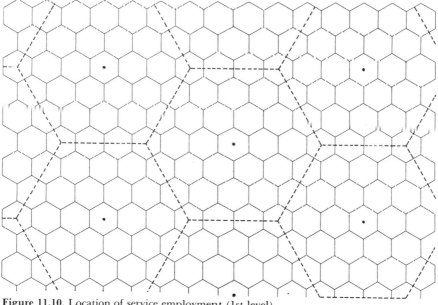

Figure 11.10. Location of service employment (1st level).

cities in the region, forming a pattern similar to Christaller's central place (11.8) with nested hexagonal market areas. The total service employment is shown in Fig. 11.11. The resulting residential population depending on both types of employment is illustrated in Fig. 11.12.

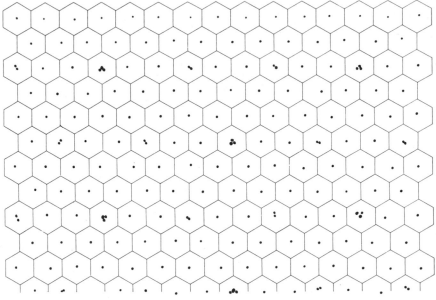

Figure 11.11. Total service employment location.

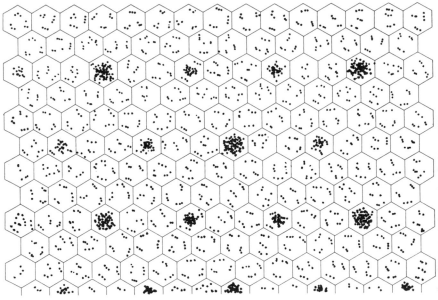

Figure 11.12. Location of residential population.

The industry based city region

The second run of the model simulates the emergence of indus-

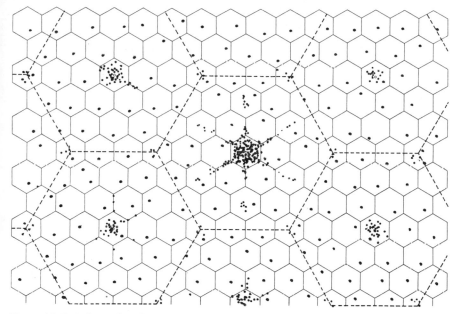

Figure 11.13. Industry based region: location of agricultural and industrial employment.

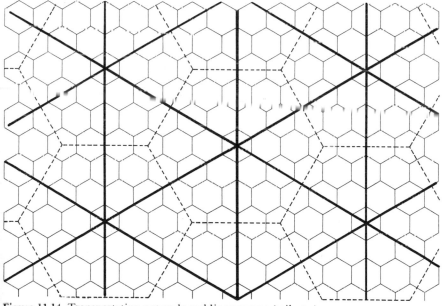

Figure 11.14. Transportation network: public transport (rail, etc.).

trial activity as the main form of basic employment. As shown in Fig. 11.13, this employment is centred in certain zones due to their accessibility to markets and labour (mainly in towns and cities). However, there is some industrial employment randomly located in certain zones due to availability of raw materials or energy resources. The agricultural employment is reduced, generating migration from rural to urban areas. The main forms of communication are now railways and channels with certain directionality. In Fig. 11.14 this is shown as a network connecting the main cities of the region. As a consequence of the introduction of this new form of transport, the accessibility of the zones changes, generating a much more concentrated distribution of services and population (see Figs. 11.15 and 11.16).

The tertiary based city region

The third run of the model simulates the decline of industrial employment and the emergence of the tertiary sector (government, office employment, etc.), concentrating at the point of higher accessibility to labour, markets and other forms of employment (see Fig. 11.17). The transport system is now strongly orientated towards the private car, which is channelled in a denser network connecting small villages. This is shown in Fig. 11.18, where the primary network runs parallel to the main public network, but a secondary network interconnects more zones directly. The resulting service distribution follows the pattern of accessibility generated by the

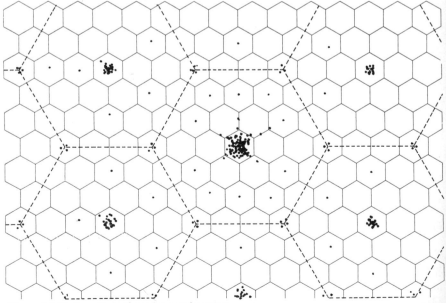

Figure 11.15. Location of service employment.

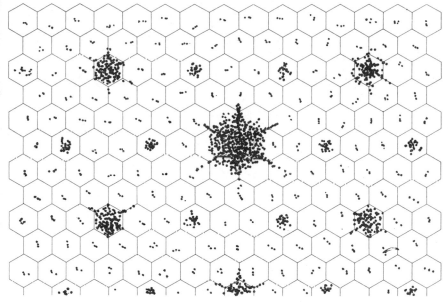

Figure 11.16. Location of residential population.

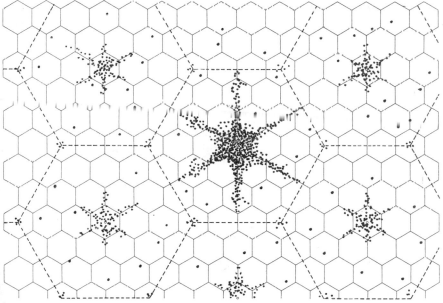

Figure 11.17. Tertiary based region: location of agricultural, industrial and tertiary employment.

transport and the population is dispersed in the suburban areas. Figs. 11.19 and 11.20 illustrate the emergence of a star shaped metropolitan area, and the conurbation effect as the urbanization starts to incorporate the villages and towns adjacent to the main city.

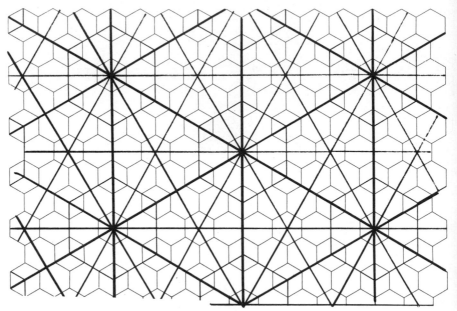

Figure 11.18. Transportation network: car and public transport.

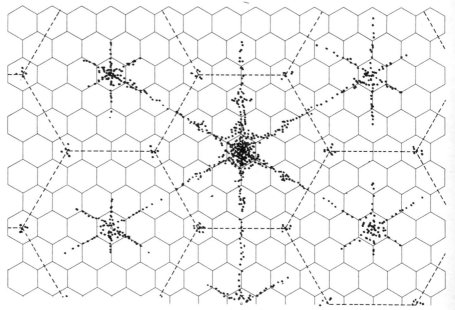

Figure 11.19. Location of service employment.

The post-industry based city region

The final run shows the effect of congestion in the central areas.

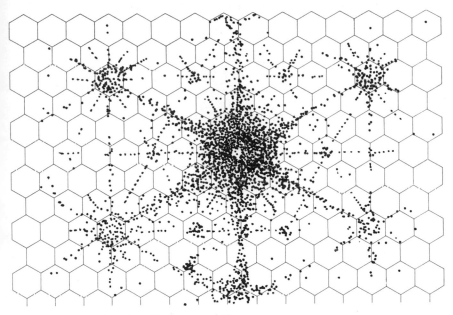

Figure 11.20. Location of residential population.

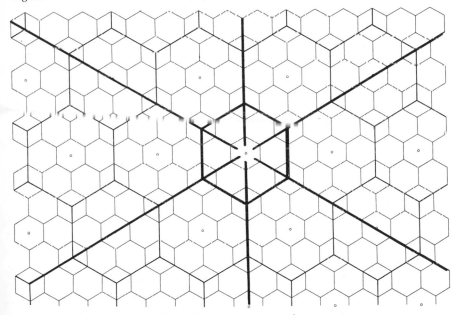

Figure 11.21. Effect of congestion in the transport network.

As can be seen in Fig. 11.21, the congestion caused by high car ownership reduces the accessibility of the central areas. The resulting ring road to move passenger and goods vehicles from one place to another, increases the accessibility of the suburbs, generating a

187

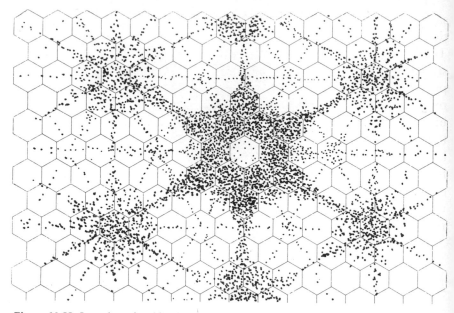

Figure 11.22. Location of residential population.

further decentralization of jobs and people. Fig. 11.22 shows the decline of the central area and the continuous 'ex-urbanization' of the surrounding countryside.

Conclusion

In all these runs, the previous basic employment and forms of transport remain but much reduced in importance. These produce the complex overlapping of activities and transport networks. At each stage of the development of the city region, the physical form of the overall pattern can be illustrated. Also the land use and transport utilization can be deduced.

It can be seen from the resulting pattern in the city region that a wide variety of life styles will be possible. Because of the increased mobility of the population and dispersal of jobs and services, people will have more choices in the environment they prefer to live: from high density old towns to low density exurban surroundings. Naturally this exercise, being of an abstract nature, does not take into account other 'pulls' which may exist in real life, such as proximity to coastal resources, national parks, etc.

The effect of increasing travel costs, due to high cost energy, is the

same as the one illustrated by the final run on the effect of congestion. This will produce a higher rate of dispersal of the city region.
The reason is that with high travel costs journeys will tend to
shorten, producing a patronage of service centres near the suburban
population. The service employment accounts for 60% of employment and if this moves closer to the population, it should produce a
bigger dispersal than hitherto has occurred. Finally, it is important
to reiterate that the functional base of the city region, that is to say its
basic employment, will be a combination of types of employment,
but predominantly based in the tertiary sector. This sector, by
definition is an exporter of services outside the region and may have
markets at the national level (government, universities, etc.) or at the
international level (insurance, banking, finance, research, etc.).

References

11.1 BLACK M., *Models and Metaphors: Studies in Language and Philosophy*,
Cornell University Press, 1962.
11.2 ECHENIQUE, M., Models: a Discussion, Working Paper No.6, LUBFS,
University of Cambridge, 1968.
11.3 LOWRY, I.S., A Model of Metropolis, RM-4035-RC, Rand Corporation, 1964.
11.4 For applications of models to planning practice see: BAXTER, R., ECHENIQUE,
M. and OWERS, J., (Eds). *Urban Development Models*, LUBFS Conference Proceedings No. 3, The Construction Press, 1975; PERRATON, J. and BAXTER, R., (Eds),
Models, Evaluations and Information Systems for Planners, LUBFS Conference
Proceedings No. 1, MTP Construction, 1974.
11.5 CHAPIN, S., *Urban Land Use Planning*, University of Illinois, 1965
11.6 LYNCH, K. and RODWIN, L., 'A Theory of Urban Form', *Journal of the
American Institute of Planners*, November, 1968.
11.7 GARNER, B., 'Models of Urban Geography and Settlement Location' in
Chorley, R.J. and Haggett, P., (Eds.), *Models in Geography*, Methuen, 1967.
11.8 CHRISTALLER, w., *Die Zentralen Orte un Suddeutschland*, Jena, 1933, English
translation by Baskin, C.W., *Central Places in Southern Germany*, Prentice Hall,
1966.

PART FOUR

CHAPTER TWELVE

New Towns in the Future City Region

David Lock

The New Towns programme

There are 33 New Towns in the UK (Fig. 12.1), including four in Northern Ireland that are now administered by a central authority under the Planning Order (Northern Ireland) of 1973. The towns have been created using legislation first enacted in 1946 and taking its most recent form in the New Towns Act of 1965. Most of the New Towns were begun in the period of enthusiasm that had lead to the legislation in 1946 (and to the Town and Country Planning Act 1947 and National Parks Act of 1948) and although there have been a number of designations in the years that have since passed, the clear trend (see Fig. 12.2) has been to the expansion of existing settlements rather than in the continued development of new ones. The reasons for this trend are set out clearly in Frank Schaffer's *The New Town Story* (12.1) and may be summarized as being based on arguments of economy, a desire for social balance, and a loss of faith in the ideas that had fired the programme from the first. The economic argument is that it is patently cheaper to extend an existing system of urban services than to build a completely new system, though time has yet to tell whether this was a short-term economy that will cause problems of maintainance and obsolescence in the 'core' system. The desire for social balance arises from the criticism of the population structure of the first New Towns which was mainly young and

Figure 12.1. Map showing New Towns in Great Britain and Northern Ireland. (*Reproduced by kind permission of the Town and Country Planning Association.*)

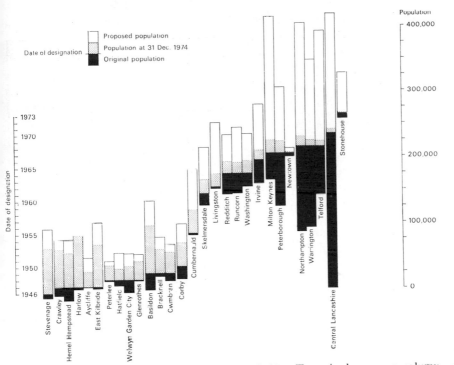

Figure 12.2. Population of the New Towns. Each New Town is shown as a column proportional to its population past, present, and proposed, and arranged in chronological order. (*Reproduced by kind permission of the Town and Country Planning Association.*)

economically active; and again only time will tell whether the critics should await the natural growth of the towns from this first generation stock into a diverse and balanced community. As far as the loss of faith is concerned, this is evidenced by the words of Baroness Sharp in her book on her experiences in the Ministry of Housing and Local Government, who as early in the programme as the 1950s had to "fight for the life of an apparently poor and much too demanding child" (12.2), and by the ever-increasing difference between the intentions of the legislation and the uses to which it is put: the scale of Milton Keynes 'New City' is far removed from the small human-scale settlements envisaged by the pioneers of the New Town idea; and Central Lancashire New Town is a 'New Town' in name only, for it embraces an entire sub-region and several extensive industrial settlements.

The original promoters of the New Town idea had completed much of the essential thinking by the early 1900s. There had been a general revulsion against the squalid urban conditions of Victorian industrial development, and this revulsion was manifest in the work of the intellectual giants of the time such as Patrick Geddes as well as in the thinking of lesser men. One such was Ebenezer Howard, a short-hand writer, who wrote an analysis of urban evils and a peaceful method of correcting them in 1899, in his *Tomorrow—a Peaceful Path to Real Reform* (12.3). This brief text is disarmingly clearly argued and its simplicity captured a popular imagination that other, more sophisticated thinkers, never attained. Howard and his supporters followed the promotion of the ideas in this text with a demonstration New Town at Letchworth, begun in 1903. A later demonstration occurred at Welwyn Garden City in 1919, though it was not until the destruction of the cities during the 1939-45 war that politicians were prepared to accept radical solutions to the housing problems and imaginative attempts to improve the quality of urban life: hence the New Towns Act of 1946.

A full and impassioned account of the evolution of the New Towns programme from the pioneer days of 1903 to the Government's post-war enthusiasm may be found in Osborn and Whittick's *New Towns—the Answer to Megalopolis* (12.4). The point to be stressed in this Chapter, however, is that the New Towns were intended to be settlement nodes within a clustered city region: small settlements in the hinterland of the metropolis that could individually offer a human-scale and economically viable style of life, and which collectively could support the sophisticated benefits of a metropolis. This view of the existing city as the hub of a potential city region (a 'social city', to use Howard's term) was conceived with the intention of rescuing from the sprawling, congested conurbation a system of settlements that would of themselves be better places in which to live, but which would, by the planned dispersal of population, allow a reconstruction of the old city in more spacious and human-scale proportions. These two parts of the idea are important, for they were rapidly forgotten and some, notably F. J. Osborn, have felt that the idea was never grasped by the politicians at all; if it had been, the city region would in the 1940s have become the basic unit of local government, permitting the organized dispersal of population to New Towns and the reconstruction of the old city to have gone hand-in-hand. The profitable activity of building New Towns in which increased land values are taken by the state would have been used to subsidize the expensive reconstruction work. The policy of encouraging growth in New Towns would have been matched by powerful policies preventing growth elsewhere. The New Towns would have been more numerous and closer together, and the regions' transport network would have been tailored to the settlement strategy rather than the reverse.

Instead of the implementation of these original ideas, we see but eight New Towns in the so called 'London ring', and those include Welwyn Garden City itself. We see New Towns financed, constructed, managed and popularly regarded as isolated planning projects, divorced from the mainstream development programme of the nation and as luxury investment that can only be afforded in times of economic growth. There is no true reflection of the city region in local government organization, and there is no more detailed settlement strategy for the areas that surround the conurbations than the vague accommodation of projected trends of development based on assumptions of mobility and population growth that are questionable. With so few New Towns and the absence of any city-region understanding, it will be no surprise to discover that they have contributed only 4% of the national house-building programme, and that in the South-East the New Towns have only accommodated 30% of those moving from the Greater London conurbation: "Too few and too late may well be the verdict of history on the first twenty years of work under the New Towns Act" writes Schaffer. People still live in appalling housing conditions in the old cities, and we have moved but a few steps towards the goal of providing a satisfactory local environment with home, workplace and amenity in reasonable proximity. The New Towns are places which show by example the advantages of planned settlements and the results of a development programme which puts the interests of the people above other considerations.

With this somewhat depressing summary, it may well be asked if New Towns have any relevance at all for the future city region. The intention of this Chapter is to show that they have immense potential significance: as tools for city region structuring and development; and as examples of the legislation that may be needed in managing the planning strategies of the future city region.

Some functions of New Towns in the City Region

Relief of the old city, to permit reconstruction to new scale

It has been mentioned earlier that New Towns were originally intended, by their promoters if not by the Government and its legislation, to permit the reconstruction of the old cities by attract-

197

ing population away from the congested centres to new, attractive and relatively stimulating places. There was also the awareness that the population was increasing in number, so New Towns were also given an *overspill* function, whether or not old city densities were relieved. Perhaps the best planning representation of both the policies of relieving the old cities and coping with their natural population increase was Abercrombie's Greater London Plan 1944 (12.5). This plan accepted entirely the arguments of the New Towns thinkers and pioneers of Letchworth and Welwyn and presented the New Town solution after an accurate analysis of London's problems. Growth was to be concentrated in a ring of New Towns, and constrained elsewhere by Green Belt policies that held agricultural land inviolate; and the existing structure of village and town settlements worthy of some infill and marginal expansion were to form 'nodes' in the city region. His plan was never fully executed and was soon made obsolete by the impact of the motor car and the effects of increased mobility on the spatial scale of the London city region. It was also frustrated by an absence of regional administrative machinery that caused the settlement strategy to be vulnerable to compromises hatched between the London government and that of the outside areas affected by the policies. And by the New Towns Act itself which is, as is discussed below, managed by Central Government and by neither the 'exporting' old city, nor 'importing' local authority in the region's hinterland. Nevertheless, the Abercrombie plan warrants study today for the clarity of its contents and for its representation of the ideas of the original New Town promoters. An interesting fact of recent years in the UK (fully tabulated in the PEP. work *The Containment of Urban England*) (12.6), is that although the New Towns have catered for only a small proportion of the post-war population increase (as overspill) and have enticed only a small proportion of the old city population away from their homes (to relieve the old city and permit reconstruction), the old cities have lost a considerable proportion of their population to their hinterlands. Rising national affluence and the mobility brought by the motor car have led to the voluntary evacuation of the old cities by thousands of people. The slum clearance programmes needed to cope with obsolescent housing after the war has also caused the evacuation, this time less voluntarily, of thousands to new municipal developments of either new estates of housing on the fringes of the built-up area, devoid of employment, shopping or recreational opportunities, or to high density schemes built on the cleared land in the old city. The New Towns, in the context of these two vast movements of private house-buyers and municipal tenants, have had foisted upon them the unjustified blame of the faults of both these movements. Thus the problems caused by the evacuation of the employable from the old city areas are blamed on the New Towns: it being argued that the policy of dispersal to New Towns leaves a rump of the aged, infirm and unemployable, regardless of the fact that so few of those leaving are going to the New Towns. As for the movement of municipal tenants, the critics see the investment that the New Towns attract from Government and compare it with the help given to old-city authorities struggling with slum clearance and re-housing, and blame the bad results of the latter on the success of the former. This scape-goat role for New Towns is an important one to note, for it shows how 'too few' New Towns, 'too late' in the development of the conurbation, and financed and developed in isolation from it, can to a certain extent discredit the idea of New Towns as an essential element in the structure of the evolving city region. The first wave of New Towns, though ostensibly designated to cope with the overspill of an expanding population, were also founded on the principles of Abercrombie's plan, being intended to relieve the land-use pressures on the London conurbation and permit its reconstruction at the human scale that had been so singularly lacking before the war. The London New Towns which fulfilled this role were Stevenage (1946); Crawley, Harlow, Hemel Hempstead (1947); Hatfield and Welwyn Garden City. An inspection of the early reports justifying their designation provides the raw material of evidence

Population retention

New Towns have also had the role of retaining populations in areas subject to great outward migration. Historically, the migration has been from rural regions to conurbations (in the manner so much in evidence in the developing world), but these movements have continued even in post-war UK. The designation of a New Town in such a region allows the concentration of limited Government investment in an attempt to provide work and homes as a counter attraction to the traditional conurbation goal. Two factors have emerged which bring this use of New Towns into the discussion of the future city region: first, that mobility has widened the sphere of influence of the city region to embrace, in the UK at least, most of the rural hinterlands; second, as the system of allocating regional investment becomes more sophisticated, the debate between the competing claims of urban and rural regions is highlighted. By way of illustration of these points, the influence of the West Midlands conurbation on the economy of Mid- and North-Wales has increased rapidly: tourism, second-home ownership and day recreational excursion has caused deep shifts in the economic structure of many Welsh districts, and made them vulnerable to the economic fortunes of West Midlands' industry. Second, the investment claims of rural regions has historically been for agricultural development. Now the claims of these regions include transport subsidy, housing investment to permit local people to compete in the market with potential second-home owners, and support for the payments of social benefits to cope with the seasonal fluctuations of an economy based on tourism. With diminishing national investment available, the Government makes claims upon the European monies intended for regional development, and this has a direct effect on the city region which finds itself at a disadvantage when in competition with subsidized rural regions. The people of the West Midlands now ask for State assistance in attracting new industry because the motor-vehicle industry is in recession, arguing that the advantages they can offer a new industry are beaten by the advantages offered by rural and developing regions (12.7). This debate is, however, a very recent one, and the UK New Towns located in rural regions have been developed with little concern about the possibility that they may have come within the orbit of an urban region. An example of a New Town with this role is Newtown in Mid-Wales, designated in 1967 with a target population of 13,000. This may be compared with the 'overspill' New Towns listed above, with target populations of 70-80,000.

Re-population, and military strategy

New Towns have been used not only to hold populations in an area subject to outward migration, but also to populate regions vacant either by accident of history or by evacuation in earlier times. There is no example of a New Town performing this function in the UK, though it was much discussed during the 1950s when the fear of nuclear attack led politicians in both the UK and USA to consider the merits of repopulating rural regions to achieve a dispersal that would prevent total loss in case of attack. This reasoning seems out-of-date in the UK now, but dispersal for reasons of military strategy is being pursued in the Middle East. Another reason that may justify the repopulation of rural regions by New Towns is that of economics: it is argued that land at present unproductive must be made productive, and New Town programmes to this end are discussed frequently in the planning literature relating to the USSR and to China (12.8), and to parts of Malaysia.

Stimulating regional development

A further distinct role for New Towns that may be found in the UK is that of stimulating regional investment from the private sector and improving the economic structure of depressed regions in a general sense. Though sometimes the towns may be planned to take overspill populations in addition to a pursuit of this policy, an inspection of the reports of designation show the priority. Washington (1964) and Peterlee (1948) are both examples, where the new town is intended to attract varied industry to a region dependant on coal mining. Although the most recent example is Stonehouse in Scotland (which Government now intends to de-designate), the largest and most obvious is Central Lancashire New Town.

At the date of designation (1970), the population within the area of this New Town was 235,638 living in 14 settlements. The plan is to provide for a target population of nearly 500,000 grouped around the five existing towns within the area (Grimsargh, Preston, Walton, Leyland and Chorley): this is a scheme that really bears no relation to the New Towns of previous years, but is one designed "to generate prosperity on a sub-regional scale using the New Towns Act", to quote the Outline Plan (12.9). The view of the Town and Country Planning Association is that "the role of New Towns as carefully designed and located growth points especially in the assisted areas (i.e. those areas so economically depressed that they attract Government subsidy) has proved to be one of their most successful. The combined impact of population growth, economic development, and investment in infrastructure associated with a New Town can be of sufficient scale and duration to influence the balance of activity between the regions" (12.10).

Fulfilling social objectives

One further rule of the New Towns programme is in attaining objectives of social policy, of which the greatest has been the desire to provide a better living and working environment for as many people as possible. It has rarely been argued that New Towns are *intrinsically* better places than big cities, but by having the New Towns within the city region, the qualities of the central city can be enhanced and be better enjoyed by more people. A second social objective has been to demonstrate how a planned urban environment, with what the professional planners may call 'a better ordering of urban spatial relationships', can lead to the enhancement of human, community and civic values. It is difficult, for example, to experiment with innovations in education, welfare and medicine in existing cities, and New Towns have proved ideal for demonstrations and experiments in these fields.

Aspects of New Towns legislation

A full description of the legislation may be found in Schaffer's work and in numerous publications. There are particular aspects of the legislation which commend themselves when considering the future city region.

The development corporation

The Development Corporation is the body that actually builds the New Town and manages the land acquisition and development. Unlike the sophisticated and well-established local government system which has administrative responsibility throughout the UK, the Development Corporation is not an elected body. It is appointed by the prevailing Government and it is charged with the sole duty of building the New Town. To do this it hires its own staff and has a single-mindedness of purpose which frankly astonishes and irritates the elected members of local government in whose area the Corporation can suddenly be placed. The Development Corporation is only in a locality for a relatively short period, perhaps 20 years (though it may be longer), and it therefore attracts to its staff the architects, planners, and other professionals who are interested in the creation of a new community and who usually have drive and initiative. Managerially, the Development Corporations are staffed by people with particular entrepreneurial skill and commitment, and these qualities are needed in order to achieve the building of the town. The activities of the relatively aggressive Development Corporation contrasts with the work of the local authority which has been administering the area historically, and enough friction has been generated in this way for political pressure to have developed pressing for a change in the way that Development Corporations are structured. It is argued that they should contain elected representatives only and not Government appointees, and secondly there is political pressure to reduce the amount of control that Development Corporations have over land acquisition and town management.

These questions are important. Because the Development Corporations have been successful as institutions for getting new development under way there has been talk of using them in other circumstances.

For example, the concept of an *Inner City* Development Corporation that could be used to solve the problems of London's 5000 acres (2000 ha) of derelict docklands, which by accident happen to be within the boundaries of five local authorities, has been mooted. If that whole area were put under the control of one Development Corporation, then a New-Town-in-town could be built in the manner originally envisaged by the promoters of the New Town idea.

Another idea is that of the *roving* Development Corporation in regions such as the South West of England, which has low industrial investment, a small population and inward migration of old people requiring a lot of investment in social services and yet yeilding nothing in terms of production. A roving Development Corporation could use its powers of land acquisition and development initiation to stimulate development and growth in appropriate parts of the region, uninhibited by the traditional boundaries and attitudes of local government.

Powers of land acquisition—disposal

The powers of land acquisition and disposal are a major aspect of New Towns legislation. The financial success of the New Towns is based on the powers of the Development Corporation to acquire land at its existing market value rather than at its development value. The increase in the land values thus accrues to the Development Corporation, allowing the repayment of the capital investment to the Treasury and financing new investment in the town itself. Perhaps the most dismal aspect of this process is that the Development Corporations' profit is returned to the Treasury instead of being ploughed into the modernization and improvement of services in the exporting city regions. Such financial links would allow the Inner London Boroughs, for example, to cope with the high land values that at present inhibit satisfactory redevelopment. This sensible cycling of investment, where new communities are helping to finance the restructuring of the old, is an essential arrangement in the future social city region.

The Community Land Act, 1975 (12.11) introduces the power of land acquisition at existing use value throughout the UK: in other words to give this Development Corporation advantage to every local authority. In planning terms this is an extremely attractive proposition, allowing a proportion of the development profit to be taken by the local authority and used for investment in services, and development, whilst the remainder goes to the Treasury. The ability of all local authorities to handle the acquisition and disposal of land without causing delay and even corruption has been questioned. Other doubts about entrepreneurial ability and skills may be justified, as many of the people with the appropriate talents for land acquisition and management are either working in New Town Development Corporations or in the private development industry.

A further flaw in the New Towns legislation is that, upon completion of each New Town, the Government is able to retain its interest. Upon attainment of its target population, the management of the New Town is, theoretically, given over to the local authority in whose area it has been built. The Development Corporation is then wound up, but the Government has, in the past, retained its ownership of the housing stock and industrial land that the Development Corporation developed, entrusting this capital to the Government-controlled Commission for the New Towns. This body has become the principal landlord in the completed New Towns, causing much irritation to the locally elected council.

For example, two years ago the Government changed the way that rent calculations were worked out to prevent New Town local authorities from subsidizing the rents of municipal housing: there was considerable political opposition, but with the Government owning the majority of property in the New Towns the law was enforced, creating havoc with attempts to keep rent levels at levels designed to attract the people they wanted. There is now pressure (12.12) to have the Commission for the New Towns wound up and to transfer the property to the local authority: an eminently sensible and realistic thing to do.

The potential of New Towns in the future City Region

There is much discussion about the planning implications of the current decline in growth in the UK, and the New Towns programmes are sometimes suggested as appropriate sacrifices in such circumstances. There is no doubt that the financial success of New Towns has rested on their effect on land development values within the designated area, but there can equally be no doubt that this effect and resultant profitability will remain whatever the prevailing economic climate, though the time span between initial investment and profitable return must obviously extend if economic growth falters. The essential mechanism, that land for development is more valuable than prohibited land, must surely remain constant. Thus in taking land at its existing undeveloped value and either selling or leasing it for building, the Development Corporation must make a profit that should offset its own expenditure on services. For industrial land, the Development Corporation is forbidden from selling at all, and disposes on lease which reverts at a later date at consequential higher value. Of all forms of investment in new development (including redevelopment in old city areas), that in New Towns has been the most productive. Thus in times when the available investment is reduced the financial advantage of New Towns investment should be evident. Development Corporations have shown themselves to be most efficient in realizing the development at great speed and the New Towns have the real bonus of greater social benefit returns, both intrinsically and within their city region, than other forms of urban investment.

Furthermore, if economic growth declines to the extent that there is no state finance available at all, then the New Towns programme will presumably proceed on the same basis as the day-to-day burden of redevelopment in the existing cities. In the absence of either central or local government assistance, the inhabitants would have to carry out such improvements and developments as they could individually and cooperatively undertake. Those most in need would be those least able to act.

If this injustice caused the State to intervene then, (for the reasons given earlier) New Towns would be the most viable form of planning intervention. It is worth mentioning that both Letchworth and Welwyn Garden City were substantially completed without State assistance, and were based particularly on the merits of cooperative organization. Letchworth managed to retain, by special Act of Parliament in 1962, the same control over land values that the government has for its own New Towns. (The company had been threatened with asset-depletion when control was lost to interests anxious to capitalize on the land holdings.) This town now returns a healthy surplus each year (£60,000 in 1973) for the use of the people of the town. All this supports the view that the New Town idea need not only be considered viable when the initiative of the State, and that in other circumstances designations could proceed with the interests of private capital and cooperative endeavour in mind.

Then there is the question of *industry* itself. Some argue that the industrialized system of the Western World is at an advanced stage of inevitable collapse, and there are those who hope this to be so for the health of the natural ecology. The original concept of small clustered New Towns would have much to commend it in such circumstances. Small settlements with an agricultural economy would provide the most robust structure for organized society in the face of economic collapse and could perhaps, as Kropotkin argued, elevate the spirit of man by re-establishing his essential relationship with the land (12.13). China is following this concept in her decentralized development.

The existing New Towns in the UK have been places of industrial as well as social innovation. The building of small workshops and 'nursery' factory units to enable new enterprise to take off has been undertaken for some time: this symbolizes an appropriate approach to some of our economic problems.

Next there is the question of increasing mobility. Here an assumption must be made: either that when current forms of energy are exhausted new forms of power will safeguard existing mobility, or that mobility will fall with the exhaustion of liquid hydrocarbons. Either way, as Meyer Hillman has shown so clearly, we are less mobile as a society than we think: a large majority of the population does not have the use of a car, and there is less public transport available every year as unprofitable routes are closed and apparent economies made (12.14). These matters are crucial for the future city region; they affect its spatial scale and efficiency of operation. But in planned settlement strategy that encourages a high degree of local employment, the economics of public transport become more favourable. In the New Towns themselves there would be scope for either a return to the scale suggested by Howard of 30,000 population (based on desirable densities in an area described by a maximum 15 minute *walk* to town centre and, in the other direction, to the countryside) or a development of the present form which is of small neighbourhoods within walking range and public transport links to the town centre of the Stevenage 'superbus' (12.15) kind.

Last, there are the problems caused by population change. In the UK the population is approaching stability: a balance between live births and deaths. Too much is being made of this at the moment, however, as the larger age groups are those in the early years of fertility and there is yet to be growth before there is stability, assuming the statistical balance between births and deaths continues. In circumstances such as these New Towns have immense potential in the future city region: so long as there is any overall population increase they remain the most satisfactory way of accommodating it; so long as existing cities remain congested, they remain the most satisfactory way of accommodating overspill; and so long as an existing population through mobility increases its land-use demands they are the best way of ordering such consumption.

Having threaded our way through assumptions about growth, *administration* remains to be cleared. It has been explained (Chapter 10) that the UK has not, despite reforms, yet ordered its local administration to reflect the city region in spatial, financial or social terms. The point was nearly reached following the Redcliffe-Maud Royal Commission on local government in England and Wales which reported in 1969, and most particularly following Derek Senior's *Memorandum of Dissent* on regional boundaries and organization (12.16). When local government was reorganized in April 1974, the many faults were evident, of which the most significant are: the continuation of historic boundaries regardless of social, economic, administrative or geographical realities; the drawing of tight boundaries around the conurbations; and the two tiers of planning activity at county and district level which cause wasteful duplication of staff and effort and much delay in negotiation and political competition.

The need for city-regional local government is being expressed again in evidence now being given to Layfield's Commission on Local Government Finance (12.17). In considering the future city region it has to be hoped that the necessary reforms will come about.

Assuming then, a future administration based on the city region, what applications are there for a New Town programme? We have assembled a formidable array of strategic planning options using the New Towns concept: accommodation of overspilling population from existing cities; relief of land-use pressures on existing cities to permit reconstruction; the holding of population in parts of a region that may be vulnerable to outward migration; the dispersal of population to unpeopled areas for reasons of economic promotion or even defence strategy; the stimulation of regional regeneration by focussing investment; the fulfillment of social objectives relating to the quality of urban life; the innovation in social and economic activities by experiment. We have also touched upon the financial return that New Towns might bring to the existing cities to assist them in their reconstruction; and upon the uses that the legislation might be put to help regional strategies; the *Inner City* Development Corporation; the *roving* Development Corporation; the powers of land acquisition and disposal. There is much to commend from this wealth of experience obtained in the relatively few years since the enthusiastic months of 1946 and 1947 in the U.K.

References

12.1 SCHAFFER, F., *The New Town Story*, Paladin, 1972.
12.2 SHARP, E., *The Ministry of Housing and Local Government*, Allen and Unwin, 1969.
12.3 HOWARD, E., now published as *Garden Cities of Tomorrow*, Faber and Faber, 1975.
12.4 OSBORN, F.O. and WHITTICK, A., *The New Towns: the Answer to Megalopolis*, Leonard Hill, 1969.
12.5 ABERCROMBIE, P., *Greater London Plan*, HMSO, 1945.
12.6 HALL, P., and others, *The Containment of Urban England;* Vol. 1 *Urban and Metropolitan Growth Processes or Megalopolis Denied;* and Vol. 2 *The Planning System: Objectives, Operations, Impacts*, Allen and Unwin, 1973.
12.7 'A Time for Action' and 'Current Developments in the West Midlands Economy', West Midlands Metropolitan County Council, 1974.
12.8 See chapters of Wilsher, P., and Righter, R., *Exploding Cities*, Andre Deutsch, 1975.
12.9 See LOCK, D., 'Central Lancashire 1973', *Town and Country Planning*, January, 1974, p. 75.
12.10 'The British New Towns Programme' TCPA evidence to the House of Commons Sub-committee of the Expenditure Committee, *Town and Country Planning*, January, 1974, p. 77.
12.11 The Community Land Act, HMSO, 1975.
12.12 Transfer of Rented Housing in New Towns, Department of the Environment, 1975.
12.13 WARD, C. (ed.) and KROPOTKIN, P., *Fields, Factories and Workshops Tomorrow*, Allen and Unwin, 1974.
12.14 HILLMAN, M. and HENDERSON, and WHALLEY, 'Personal Mobility and Transport Policy', *Political and Economic Planning*, 1973.
12.15 See further examples in 'Travel in Towns', *Town and Country Planning*, July/August, 1975, p. 359.
12.16 *Royal Commission on Local Government in England 1966-1969;* Vol. 1 *Report;* and Vol. 2 *Memorandum of Dissent by Mr D. Senior*, HMSO, 1969.
12.17 The Royal Commission on Local Government Finance is continuing its work at the time of writing.

CHAPTER THIRTEEN

Scenarios of the Future Part One: Future Fun

Maurice Ash

Why should the future itself hold such fascination for us? Futurology, after all, has been something of an intellectual cult of recent years; and, particularly in Britain (whose future seems so uncertain), it has aroused much morbid interest. Thus, whilst I have felt flattered to make my own pronouncements on 'Scenarios of the Future' for urban planning, yet at the same time I find I hold my own motives in some suspicion.

Now, our contemporary presumption about the predictability of things is at a notable extreme from the pre-industrial, pre-scientific mentality of Europe. As Lewis Mumford has suggested, it was with the bells which counted the hours, from the belfries of the thirteenth century onwards, that the modern mind emerged. Till then, the World was only an ante-room to eternity and tomorrow was no different from today. Since then, however, time and space have been dissected and, therewith, the mastery of the present World has become our ruling passion. Yet we have now reached a moment when the Western mind has become notoriously uncertain of itself; or, at least, in Yeats' words,

"The best lack all conviction, whilst the worst
Are full of passionate intensity."

Hence, one cannot but wonder whether the hold this presumption about the future now has upon our minds does not also relate to this malaise: whether it is not a symptom or our somehow flawed grasp of the World? Were this so, it seems to me, it might also serve to illuminate the very uncertain ground on which urban planning stands—and on which, with a palpable loss of confidence, it now knows it stands.

It follows, then, that what little I have to say will be less concerned with some vision of the urban future, mechanistically arrived at, than with how our idea of knowledge itself affects how and where we live. For it is this idea of knowledge, it seems to me, that imbues our urge to realize it 'tomorrow', in ways and with consequences that were unthinkable before the bells began to tell the time.

It would perhaps be as well to admit, straight away, that the predominant influence over British planning is an utopian one. Let me hasten to add—what is scarcely necessary—that ours is an utopia gone sour: than which, alas! I can think of nothing more sad. In Britain we now have, that is to say, a gigantic planning machine, but one which works only negatively and destructively of creative development. (Its energies seem consumed in concocting innumerable reasons why things should not be done.) Of course, such is the pervading belief in a mechanistic universe that there may be some who still believe this planning machine is justifiable in its own terms. The majority, rather, probably accept it apathetically as an inescapable norm of life today.

Be that as it may—and regardless of the reasons that have destroyed our particular utopia—the utopian influence upon planning has only been a special case of that strain of ideological thought which has increasingly dominated the European mind for a hundred years now. This ideological strain, then, was itself brought about by the 'counter-Copernican' revolution, wrought by Hume and Kant, whereby Man himself was put back at the centre of the universe of ideas. For, once finding himself there again, the obligation was felt to establish absolute social standards against which to measure his actions—such that ideologies (revealed by the supposedly dispassionate process of history) were developed for this purpose.

It is the very totality of ideology that has commended town planning to it. For a city or a town holds the promise of representing a total society. Therefore, not only has the ideal city held sway over our minds; end-state planning also has sanctioned exclusive prescriptions for its realization. The very isolation of the city (by a Green Belt) has been the pre-requisite of its definition, and its centre—the one and only—has been where its identity was to be established and its urban essence concentrated—if necessary, to the discomfiture of its inhabitants.

Now, that being hinted at, I would be the first to admit there remains a strong strain in British thought resistant to this ideological rigour. Just as it was Hume, in the second half of the eighteenth century (when it was becoming clear, through the Industrial Revolution, what Man's knowledge of the external world was doing to Man himself) who undermined the Cartesian framework of the World by a kind of atomistic personalism: so, also, the British have not taken readily to the later intellectual tyranny of ideological thought. (Indeed, the original strain in British planning was a concern for public health and civic engineering, with all their particularisms.) But nor, it seems, have we put very much in place of ideology, or had much intellectual capacity to clear the undergrowth of all the nonsense wherewith it has obstructed commonsense. Certainly, as the Garden Cities movement shows, there is still a considerable humanistic reservoir in Britain; but we can also display our own inhumane, monolithic developments, to set against the Karl Marx Hofs and the Evrys of the rest of the World. Perhaps, like latter-day Greeks, our confused personalism causes our responsibilities to weigh too heavily upon us. At all events, a kind of decadent, and above all lazy, idealism is perhaps what chiefly informs British planning today. It lacks, not so much an ideological, as an intellectual rigour.

Please do not infer from this I think other countries are necessarily better off. Rather, I think the lesson is to eschew universalistic analysis. I think, for instance, the American mind is now as different from the British as the latter is from the French or German—let alone the Islamic, or the Asian. To consider America for a moment, since she is sometimes thought (erroneously, I think) to presage our own future: she, like Rip van Winkle, slept for a hundred years and thus mercifully missed the European age of ideologies, but also (and de Tocqueville is here our guide) remained stuck with the Cartesian focus upon externalities and hence on technology. Coming, as America now is, up against external limits at last, she yet has the opportunity to start afresh, against all the new problems of the age, with a relatively clean intellectual slate.

America, I think, is clear-eyed enough to recognize—at least, her young people are—that capitalism and communism, for instance, are only variations of materialism and hence are equally conducive of alienation, that real sickness of the West. Perhaps significantly, it is in America that the main ferment of ideas about community has of late been generated. Perhaps only coincidentally, this has been paralleled by a bewildering yet abortive set of United States Govern-

211

ment urban programmes. The urban process, after all, seems for the moment out of control there and formless. True, the city (in America, as elsewhere) becomes romanticized the more it decays— just as, ironically, 50 years ago rural life was being romanticized in Britain. But this is a weak force to set against the social fragmentation and the sheer physical size of cities generated by America's mode of knowledge, as this, in every possible way, exploits the external World.

Will the city in America yet be recovered—or any other form of urban life there—as her idea of knowledge comes to turn in on itself, as surely it somehow must? Such a prediction would be foolish, if only because we cannot say what new forms of urban life a new mentality might establish. One can only feel confident, at least in America's case, of the vitality for change. In another 50 years we might begin to 'prophesy'.

By extension, I think there are many scenarios of the urban future. Perhaps that is the unifying point, the only possible generalization. The genius loci should come into its own again. And this but follows the trend of philosophical thought (as I understand it)—for the discussion has turned, from knowledge itself, rather to meaning. The mighty reversal of thought by Wittgenstein is what has signalled this: words cannot reflect some reality, even could we at last uncover this; rather, the meaning of a word must be its use in the language. Our 'knowledge' has indeed generally driven meaning from our lives—and, perhaps above all, in our post-industrial cities, those hothouses of alienation and deprivation of personal identity.

So, perhaps one cannot usefully depict the manifold future, yet one can suggest the forces that will bear upon it. I think, then, the present era of the quantitative will turn into the qualitative (a return to Aristotle?): or rather, where till now only some one measurement of anything has ultimately been deemed valid, increasingly we shall accept the simultaneous use of several different languages, each equally valid—and not least, the social, the personal and the physical languages: as also we shall turn away from the nonsense of reducing all measurement to money. This implies, above all, the development of environmental thought, of concern for all that lies in the interstices between specialist knowledge: between what also defines one thing from another. And this means casework: knowledge, that is, not by abstract (and academic) thought, but rather learning by doing, by involvement in actual problems. This in turn points to the question of scale, and particularly to the reduction of urban size to the humanly comprehensible. Again, the future points less to growth, with all its daemonic numeracy, and more to balance—not as somehow quantitatively defined, but as honestly recognized as subject to dialogue, to the language game.

Indeed, this moves me to hazard that, if Western civilization is to survive its profound contradictions at all—and by this I do not mean a return to before the bells began to tell the time—it must do so by putting this very idea of the game at its centre, as a civilizing force. Our dominant idealistic (but so humourless) mode of thought, after all, has produced this century's notorious tyrannies, and ultimately made of Man himself only an object. That life must either be interplay, or else a living death, almost suggests itself by now. (In this context, I would comprehend a symbiotic relationship of Man to Nature—so contrary to Descartes' hatred of Nature.) In this event, then, I would see the urban game as one of the foremost we need to play: the making of where we live, that is, by the play of minds to cultivate every kind of urban form—a cultivation that could not idealistically be imposed, because it would also need to be generally understood and hence accepted in being acted upon.

And the name of the game would be planning: not utopian planning, but planning by rules which cheerfully respected the needs and uses of everyday life, and celebrated these. I should be surprised if in such a game villages of various kinds (and perhaps Garden Cities, as well as Ujima villages) did not play a significant part, as also if these were not adorned by vegetation and new landscapes thus made, not only out of countryside but out of the wastelands of old cities. (We shall soon be pulling down the tower blocks we have just put up, of that I am sure.) But what matters is that these games about our future communities should indeed be played; that the very process of making our towns, cities, villages should be one enjoyed for its own sake. No doubt the prince, the aristocratic patron, once enjoyed his patronage in bringing places into being. That same enjoyment should now be more widely shared. The rules of this game, I think, must centre on the forms of urban life to be created. This will demand a new calculus of values, and the language of these forms has been largely lost and must be rediscovered. But I am certain these matters generally ought to hold an increasingly important place in our lives.

Scenarios of the Future Part Two: A Guide to Futurologists

John Davoll

Scenarios of the future should not be confused with predictions. A scenario is an aid to the imagination, something that gives us a sense that there are different possible futures from which we can make deliberate choices. To serve this purpose, it is often necessary to fill in details with greater precision than prediction could legitimately aspire to; indeed, looking retrospectively at history one has a powerful sense of how rapidly radically different futures could have diverged from microscopic variations in a single event, such as the conception of Adolf Hitler.

A determinist might argue that no event *could* have occurred differently, and writers such as Olaf Stapledon have speculated that perhaps all physically possible alternative events do, in some sense, occur, producing an infinite series of four-dimensional cosmoses exfoliating from each point in their own proper times into multi-dimensional space. Although it is of metaphysical interest as to how this would differ, as far as we were concerned, from a deterministic universe, the fact remains that none of us is a determinist in practice; we strive to inspect possible futures and allow their imagined content to influence our *choices* in the present.

In the more distant past, when the pace of change in human affairs was slower than now, men doubtless accepted that the future would be much like the present, and indeed the past. Now we live in chaos and doubt, and more and more people seem to be giving up the struggle to influence what is happening—"things are in the saddle, and they ride mankind". If our experience of passing events is not to shrink to a narrow band between a discredited past and an unknown, but vaguely menacing, future, we need to develop a sense that a hundred years from now only one of our possible futures will have happened, and what will then be locked into the crystalline rigidity of the past will depend on our choices now.

This felt need to reach into the future manifests itself in two principal ways.

One the one hand, governments and industries would like to know as much as possible about the future, particularly over the near term of 5-10 years; so that their planners know what to provide when it takes well over 5 years to plan and build a nuclear power station or a major road development, day to day judgements are not sufficient.

On the other hand, as the total human impact on the environment increases exponentially, the need for some assessment of the consequences of our actions over a longer time becomes clear. In fact, there is still far too little appreciation of how far ahead one needs to plan in dealing with matters such as the growth of populations or industrial demand.

In practice, the two areas of study seem to attract different types of futurologist. Forecasts made for industry and government departments are usually 'surprise-free'; they are characterized by a relatively uncritical acceptance of present trends as a guide to the future and carefully ignore awkward, unquantifiable factors that might make nonsense of the whole exercise. Thus, forecasts are made of traffic levels without much thought being given to the possible actions of the oil-producing countries as they see their only source of wealth being depleted at rapidly escalating rates. Economic forecasts are made that the rich countries will go on getting richer, without any consideration of the reaction of the poor majority of the World's population as they see the gap widen between their poverty and the affluence of others. The technological optimism that pervades the background thinking of this type of futurologist is essential if he is to be able to ignore problems that threaten to make his work meaningless.

Desmond King-Hele expressed it well: "The survival of the fittest applies to futurists as well as insects, and establishment futurists (i.e. those paid by society) survive by conforming to society's optimistic requirements. They predict the predictable—what society allows to be predicted. Shy of taboos, establishment futurists steer clear of chemical and biological weapons, and shirk scenarios in which the humans destroy themselves, and other creatures take over as Earth's lords and masters, though evolution has seen many such upsets, e.g. the dinosaurs. So the real future is unlikely to resemble the scenarios of establishment futurists" (13.1)

The second main type of approach has been that exemplified in *The Limits to Growth* (13.2) and it is important to emphasize that these studies do not claim to be predictions, but projections: that is, they say '*if* we continue to do these things, *then* these other things are likely to happen'. This gives society a chance to look at alternative courses of action and choose those that lead to a desired future state. Rather than being warnings of inevitable doom, they claim to give advice on how doom may be avoided.

In principle, of course, this is common sense. A motorist approaching a sharp bend at high speed may be said to make a projection of a future in which he does not slow down and wrecks the car. This projection feeds back into his planning with the result that he applies the brakes in good time and the projected accident does not occur. Unfortunately, human affairs are more complex, and opponents of the *Limits to Growth* approach claim that we can rely on technological developments to avoid disaster; that before the motorist actually reaches the bend he will have time to modify the car's suspension and so improve its cornering abilities. Although the *Limits to Growth* advocates might reply that this is a hazardous approach to planning, and certain to eventually lead to catastrophe, the argument is dismissed by the sufficiently optimistic, and no real reconciliation of views has so far occurred.

This seems to me to be unfortunate, as the surprise-free projections by establishment futurists are usually based on facile optimism, and need to be sobered up by a more serious consideration of the possibilities set out by *Limits to Growth* writers. I suggest that their forecasts would be more realistic and valuable if they conformed to the following conditions:

1. Major factors likely to affect the future should not be ignored just to simplify the procedure of forecasting. Thus, if a projection of trends for this country shows a substantial increase in the consumption of resources and energy, we should assume that other rich countries will be behaving similarly and that the poor countries will be trying to catch up with them. Can the combined demands be met? Before the oil crisis of 1973, the United States, Europe and Japan each planned to import, by 1985, an amount of oil equal to the total 1973 output from the Middle East. I suspect that similar thinking, if

that is not too kind a word, is now being applied to the supply or uranium for nuclear power stations.

2. If the projections assume major new technological developments, realistic assessments for the cost and feasible rates of installation of these should be given. The mainstay of much technological optimism is abundant nuclear power to replace oil, although a careful examination of technical constraints—quite apart from present and future environmental hazards—shows that this is not feasible within the probable lifetime of the oil resources.

3. The consequences of failure of the hoped-for technological developments to materialize should be stated. For example, in the UK relatively little importance has been attached to protecting agricultural land from development, partly because it has been assumed that we can continue to import almost half the food we consume, and partly because it has been thought that we can continue to raise the productivity of agricultural land almost indefinitely. Thus, Edwards and Wibberley (13.3) wrote: "Even accepting the authors' *more cautious* (my emphasis) judgment that output of food is likely to increase by 110 to 120% between 1965 and 2000, no serious conflict arises unless the demand for food grows by more than 70% and land lost to agriculture exceeds the forecast loss of 10% of food production potential". However, the first assumption could easily be proved unjustified by World population growth, and it is then instructive to think very seriously about what will then happen if—as now seems likely—the promised increase of productivity cannot be attained.

4. The degree to which one course of action effectively forecloses other options should be made clear. The purpose of this condition is to counter the self-fulfilling tendency of much planning; for example, planners study trends in traffic growth and conclude that more roads will be needed; as the roads are built they encourage more traffic growth and the planners congratulate themselves on their foresight. In this process alternative options that could have been planned for are foreclosed; for example ones involving provision of more facilities locally with a consequent reduction in the need for mobility.

5. The widest possible variety of scenarios should be set out, including ones submitted from outside the planning apparatus; the aim would be to provide alternative goals towards which society might choose to move. The effect would also be to prevent unstated

assumptions that 'progress' is synonymous with 'technological advance' from limiting possible choices; if the pursuit of undifferentiated material growth has to be abandoned as a guideline for society, vigorous debate about possible alternative goals is essential if a pervasive sense of defeat—already clearly perceptible in society— is not to become widespread.

References

13.1   KING-HELE, D., 'From Prophecy to Prediction', *Futures*, December, 1974, pp. 512-518.
13.2   MEADOWS, D.H., *et al., Limits to Growth,* Earth Island, 1972.
13.3   EDWARDS, A.M. and WIBBERLEY, G.P., *An Agricultural Land Budget for Britain 1965-2000,* School of Rural Economics and Related Studies, 1971.

CONCLUSION

CHAPTER FOURTEEN

The Education of Planners

David Eversley

Introduction

This Chapter is concerned with education in an academic sense, not with vocational instruction. The subject matter, then, is not the skills the planner must learn in order to perform a specified number of tasks (like development control, design of shopping centres, road junctions, or master plans for new towns) which traditionally form the greater part of the planner's activities. Traditionally, also, these skills can be acquired by people who do not possess an education beyond, at most, a secondary set of courses leading to a school-leaving examination at 17; certainly only relatively few planners until recently had any university education, let alone post-graduate qualifications (14.1). The tasks they were set did not necessarily call for a high order of judgement, ability to communicate in speech or writing, and certainly what they did was unconnected with the making of policy—an activity always reserved, in Britain, to those with higher education, preferably in an irrelevant subject from one of the older universities. The planner was in the same relationship to members of the administrative class of the civil service as the surveyor, the road engineer, the book-keeper or indeed any other specialist employee of national or local government of whom matters of judgement could not be required.

There were two kinds of exception to this general rule. First of all,

221

modern professional planning always had a small cadre of very highly educated men at the centre (usually ex-architects) who were able and willing to communicate, who conceived and explained ideas, and whose plans were written in terms of a general social and economic policy, whether for cities or the countryside, regions or the whole country.

Secondly, the most important new ideas in planning have, for a century or more, come from men who were amateurs. That is to say, not necessarily totally untrained in any even remotely related subject, like George Cadbury, but often coming from subjects which touched on planning only at one or two removes, like Geddes or Mumford (14.2).

The professional element, indeed, grew up in a different atmosphere altogether. Architecture and civil engineering were recognized as professions, though neither, until very recently, required higher education for the practitioner (14.3). The rise of the professions, and their recognition, when for so long only the priest, the doctor and the lawyer had been able to claim the social status of the professional man, is a different story (14.4). But it should be noted that although planners were anxious to secure such status for themselves (and this is shown in the history of their Institute, culminating in its acquisition of the Royal prefix to its name) (14.5), they were in fact exceedingly slow in thinking out what was involved in achieving the social status they sought. Looking at their handbooks of professional practice, and their training syllabus, such was their preoccupation with technical competence (coupled with the usual admonitions regarding incorruptibility) that they altogether failed to see that the one decisive dividing line between professionals of superior and inferior status, i.e. a code of *ethical* responsibility, was entirely lacking (and probably still is). Excellence, in the professional planner's eye, consisted of smoother functioning, an outwardly pleasing appearance of their work, and perhaps financial accountability. Originality was reserved for the very few, innovation in social form mostly, as we have said, the work of amateurs, and the social and economic consequences of their activities a matter for politicians. Thus they had to seek status by other means—by exclusivity in the matter of admission to their Institute, by the practice of excluding, from the right to call themselves 'planners' all those who did not have the necessary paper certificates, by pressing for the establishment of separate planning departments in local authorities, with someone of chief officer status at the head, and similar organizational devices. That these have done little or nothing to make the planner respected in society, in the way a doctor or an architect, let alone a senior officer or church dignitary command respect, may of course be a reflection on the society in which we live rather than the planning profession (14.6).

It still leaves us with the question of why it is that planning education has apparently been unconcerned with the question of the place of the planner in modern society, and why it seems to have so consistently, with each revision of its syllabus, ensured that its products did not receive the recognition they felt they should have. To be sure, if one possesses a good degree, preferably in a traditional subject from one of our older universities, and follows this with a two-year course leading to a master's degree in planning, one is then automatically placed in the elite, and considered suitable for employment in almost any capacity within local and national government, private practice, academic research institutions, and, again, employment unrelated to planning. In contrast to the position of the educated person, who happens to be a planner (though not of course admitted to RTPI membership on the strength of these degrees), the early school-leaver who can work his way through part-time courses to the necessary external examinations and eventually present a thesis to the Institute, probably based on his own current work, can be fully recognized as a Planner, without any education in the real sense.

It is these anomalies which have led to so many examinations, in the last few years, of the role and status of the planner, the constant attempts to revise the syllabus of examinations, but, or so it seems, without any real understanding why such tinkering with the basic weakness of the planner's professional status is self-defeating (14.7). The outsider who tries to analyze the annual attempts of the RTPI to promote a new image and a new syllabus always looks forward to the arrival of a new President, renowned for his liberal and progressive views, and is then disappointed when such a potential ally once again fails to shift the deadweight of opinion. There is in fact, very little difference in the outcome of the years of office, close to each other in time, say, of one of the most enlightened social science orientated corporate planners of our time, and that of an old-style geographer wedded to traditional land use planning techniques in the recreational field. One therefore feels justified in regarding the attitudes described here as monolithic and almost irremovable.

To assert this is not to claim that, for good or ill, the professional planner has not left his mark on our built and natural environment. Progressively, for the last 70 years, the law has given tools to national and local government, which, in the hands of planners, have profoundly affected the way we live. The fact, again, that so much of this activity has been negative, or has apparently restricted the freedom of individuals, has not helped to raise the esteem in which planners are held. Even more so, the association of planning with destruction and the creation of monstrous new buildings is deeply ingrained in the public mind. 'Planning', then, means at best, development control, refusal to build on a particular spot or for particular purposes, comprehensive redevelopment, the destruction of historic buildings, the driving of motorways through urban centres, the erection of unwanted office blocks, and a total disregard for human scale, individual liberty, and the dignity of mankind. That this is a gross libel on the profession is easy to see if one happens to work on the inside; or if one is a planner, one may feel totally unaffected by such charges as one can blame the others—the politicians, the road engineers, the housing architects. But such disclaimers serve no purpose. It is basically because the planner has no positive *raison d'être* in our society, that he is considered a superfluous fifth wheel recently introduced largely in the interests of privileged classes and large business interests, and this is common ground between historians, aesthetes, and left-wing agitators.

Predictably, many of the younger generation of planners have themselves revolted against the system which they have been trained to operate, and have become overt or under-cover rebels, agitators, and advocates of the cause of planning's victims (14.8). But even this over-reaction has no logical basis—it is instinctive, emotional, and thoroughly unprofessional. Both the indifference of the vast majority and the bitter opposition of the young radical minority can be traced to a common cause, that planning education is unsuitable for the planner's real tasks. The purpose of this Chapter is to examine what these tasks are, and to see how far past or proposed changes in planning techniques and syllabuses are likely to improve matters in the future. For this purpose we draw heavily on a mass of existing literature, without however examining it in detail, since we are here concerned only with principles (14.9).

The main task of planning

Nobody has undertaken an analysis of the time spent by practising planners on different activities, as a whole (as opposed to local O

& M type studies). It is therefore quite possible that quantitatively it is still true that the majority of planners spend the greater part of their time examining applications for planning permissions or designing streets, neighbourhoods or whole new settlements (14.10).

Qualitatively, however, the planner's task must be ranked quite differently. Moreover, as Britain moved from the years of rapid growth, of population and economic expansion, especially in the 1960's, to the present decade of stagnation, these qualitative assessments (necessarily based on value judgements) threaten to become also the quantitative measure of planning performance. To say 'threaten' is in itself to make yet another value judgment, since the state of non-growth has long been advocated by many sections of the intellectual elite as well as the self-appointed intelligentsia which now acts as a kind of watchdog over our national heritage. The acceptance of non-growth or even decline is no part of the planner's business as such, though circumstances may force him into inactivity, wholly negative activities, or, most wasteful of all, the nugatory attempt to produce designs which are bound to be rejected (14.11). (Hence the strong contrast between the INLOGOV (14.12) view of the number of planners which may be required, and a widespread if vulgar view that no harm would come of it if the planning profession were totally abolished).

What is the nature of these new, important tasks? First of all, in times of scarcity of resources, the planning function is essentially an allocative one—i.e. making a decision about priorities as between conflicting claims for land, labour and capital. This has always been so, but tends to come to prominence more in times of recession (when capital is scarce) rather than of affluence (when land and labour are likely to be the most limiting factors). In other words, at all times the planner performs an *economic* function, and since he is generally not trained to do this, he tends to leave the judgements underlying this type of activity to his political masters. This may in some sense be a proper 'democratic' process, but since most planners are not even in the legitimate civil service position of being able to point out to their political masters the socio-economic consequences of deciding on this or that piece of action (or inaction), we can reject the disclaimer from the start. Everything that is now added to the stock, or every improvement that is applied to existing stocks, is bought at the expense of something else not done, and the planner's role is pre-eminently to clarify the consequences of alternative plans of allocation. Clearly, when a sizeable proportion of the population still lives in unfit housing and a generally squalid environment in old cities, then the allocation of large resources, let us say, to a mixture of new private speculative development, green field New Towns, and the further expansion of existing settlements already in good environmental shape, whether with public or private resources, can only be justified if it can be shown to benefit those whose present style of life is undesirable (14.13). Yet the planning of New Towns, town expansion schemes, fresh private developments in villages or market towns, is carried out as if it were totally unconnected with the fate of people in Lambeth or Liverpool 8. Whilst unemployment grows in areas where manufacturing industry has died, or from which it has been removed by regional policies, planning often encourages the growth of fresh economic activities (offices, factories in more remote areas, out-of-town shopping centres) to which the urban employed have no access (14.14). Whilst urban roads decline in carrying capacity, and public transport is neglected, inter-urban motorways may proliferate. Although such statements may sound just like the judgments of the vulgar critics of planning, quite often these actions can be defended on one ground or another. The point is that most planners are simply not educated even to see the connection, and proceed with their own small piece of design, allocation, or permission outside the totality of the resource-allocating process.

The second new activity concerns the relationship of the planner to the planned, to use the hackneyed but quite accurate phrase. In less than ten years, we have gone from the acceptance of the Skeffington report (14.15) (which merely recommended, by and large, that the public should be informed of what was intended to be done and have adequate time for raising objections) to a situation where it is virtually conceded that any group of people, whether directly affected by a planning proposal or not, has the right to hold up the implementation of such a proposal indefinitely, by any means short of overt violence. (Mere obstruction, in or out of courts, hearings or inquiries, however, is permitted.) It is impossible to say whether such a state of affairs would be allowed to continue were it not for the fact that in the mid-seventies, it suited national and local government eminently well to delay the execution of public works projects almost indefinitely, in order to combat inflation and the rise of taxation associated with high interest rates and an increasing volume of activity in the preceding period. Even disregarding the most extreme manifestations of the 'no to everything and hands off' movement, we can see that the planner's first task, in relation to any project of construction, demolition, or alteration, is to come to terms with the 'community'. The fact that nobody has yet explained what 'the community' consists of, in relation to a particular process, is merely a reflection of the planner's lack of attention to such matters. In this respect, he needs to be a sociologist of a type that probably does not yet exist: one who understands the structure of society sufficiently well to allow him to choose, for the purposes of consultation and participation, which individuals and groups represent legitimate interests in respect of any one particular plan (14.16). Thus, spontaneous neighbourhood groups, exogenous agitators, societies for the prevention of this or the promotion of that, academics, professional organizations, chambers of commerce, or simply individuals with a sense of mission, are all equally permitted to join in the business of protesting. Structure plan hearings are more orderly in this respect: there it is decided, according to fairly well understood rules, who may or may not make representations, or rather which representations should be given the dignity of being 'heard' (14.17). This is in contrast to, for instance, inquiries into a motorway route which have become in recent years, focal points for the voicing of discontents of quite diverse groups of interest, just as the arrays which opposed the third London airport, first at Cublington, and then at Maplin, consisted of bodies of quite disparate standing (14.18).

In this situation, the role of the planner is to decide which are the legitimate and affected interests, to ensure that the community is alerted, informed, represented and heard, and that there is finally a positive conclusion, as opposed to a mere abandonment of the project out of despair in the face of undifferentiated clamour, which is a fairly normal characteristic now. But to learn to enter into a genuine dialogue with the planned is not a matter of academic social psychology, but of educating eyes, ears and brains to a sensitivity to the feelings of people whose lives are affected by changes ordained by government, and the ability to involve such people in the process of plan-making and plan-execution. To pursue the professional analogy with which we started, the planner has to be educated to enter into a new, and egalitarian relationship with his partners, just as doctors, academics and even school-teachers have to learn to do, and as the best practising architects are now advocating. This, however, is not a matter of stereotyped techniques, but of a process of education.

The third new role of the planner is more general. It is concerned with equity—the distribution of well-being in society. For planning to be effectively part of a process of creating a more just society, he must see himself as a member (and probably a leading member) of a team of what is fashionably called corporate management by objectives, and which, more soberly, takes the form of concentrating activities, resources, and political attention on priority areas (whether one uses this term in a purely spatial sense or in relation to any particular group in society). This is not the same thing as our first new task, that of rational overall allocation, although clearly the two activities bear some relation to each other. Basically, the third task is connected with the positive identification of disadvantaged groups in the community and the positive steering of advantages in their direction, with a view to improving their life chances (14.19). Who these groups are, (14.20) we all think we know, but so far the attempt to promote a system of corporate planning which yields results has proved largely abortive. Coloured commonwealth immigrants, single parent families, large families, the handicapped and chronic sick, the unemployed and the permanent low wage earners, all figure largely in the literature and one assumes that planners are educated to understand the social and political processes by which some amelioration might be achieved. Generalizations are easily made: all we need is for planners, architects, housing departments, educators, agencies concerned with the promotion of employment and economic activity, health authorities, water authorities, voluntary associations, treasurers and social service departments to pull together—and the job is done. Clearly there are as yet no examples of this happening, and perhaps it never will. Education here means political education,—knowing how our society works through its institutions, its vested interests, and how it is hampered by geographical boundaries, departmental demarcation disputes, hierarchical bureaucratic systems, and the weight of tradition, inertia and social conservatism which always makes it easier to pursue existing spending and activity patterns, than to change them, however much such continuity may aggravate inequality.

To sum up this general overview, one would say that planning is now one of the social sciences, and has lost most of the affinity which it once had with what where once quaintly called 'the mechanical arts'. Yet there is scarcely any recognition of this change: only one planning department in a British institution of higher education was, in 1975, part of a Faculty of Social Sciences (14.21). Most courses paid lip service to the new ideas by fitting subsidiary economics and sociology courses into odd corners of their curriculum, and almost everywhere the radical younger generation of planning teachers infused an element of political understanding into the student mind. Unfortunately, theirs tended to be an over-reaction, so that the social science component was as often as one-sided a presentation of the 'realities of planning' as the older core syllabus of physical design. If anything, the student, torn between the extreme traditionalism of those who taught planning starting with Italian cathedral cities, French fortresses and German *Residenzen*, and, on the other hand, those who presented planning purely as a special manifestation of the excesses of dying capitalism, has tended to be more confused than ever.

The new planning techniques

When we come to examine, in detail, the changes in the syllabus of planning schools in the last few years, we do indeed find innovation—but of a kind, it will be argued here, which will tend to help to perpetuate formalistic approaches to the art or science of civic design, regional planning, or urban social planning, in just the same way as the old teaching of the original large planning schools.

It is difficult to give a general name to these new techniques, because they are in fact rather varied in origin, discipline affiliation, relevance to the real world, and in their relationship to the social science component which this Chapter has put at the top of the list of desiderata (14.22).

Their common feature lies in the attempt to make planning more of a science, rather than a social science. The distinction is import-ant. If it is assumed that planning is after all, an activity in the tradition, of, say civil engineering, then it is entirely proper that the modernization of the subject should follow the same paths as those now being pursued in engineering and other forms of production. If planning is a managerial activity, it is right that its reform should run parallel with innovations in management. Our difficulty is that all these changes may take place, and lead the planner still further away from what I have identified as his main task.

The central idea of the 'new' planning is that the whole of society, and the relationships of the people who live in an area, with its built and natural environment, can be reduced to some form of schematic representation. Whether we call this activity model-making, or (as in geography) spatial analysis, whether we explain planning in terms of systems theory, or cybernetics, the key activity is always the same: we reduce the complexity of the observed relationships to a series of abstractions, which we can express either in a purely formal and even mathematical way, as stylized diagrams of linkages and flows, or we can operationalize them by collecting data and make the model 'work' by changing the inputs. This is a very rough and ready picture of very diverse activities, many of them first invented in the United States, and then brought to Britain, and familiar to every student of planning through the work of authors like J.B. McLoughlin, G.F. Chadwick, and Jessop and Friend (14.23). (The selection is arbitrary, and implies no value judgements or even the association of particular authors with any part of these ideas.)

The common denominator, however, to all these attempts to make planning more rational, more scientific, is that it must lead to education of the planner away from the tasks which have been previously outlined, unless the assumptions which lie behind the new scientific handling of problems are carefully explained for what they are: deliberate abstractions, over-simplifications, attempts to assume that people (clients, communities) will behave, or want to behave, in a more or less rational manner; that, in some cases, there is something like an optimal technical solution to a technical problem which is worth implementing because it is by definition the best use of scarce resources, and so on.

The pre-supposition, behind these thought processes, is that we do indeed have, or can acquire, a knowledge of how human society works, that we can predict how people will behave at some future date when incomes, tastes, technology and economic organization may all have fundamentally altered: in short, that we can link scientific observations about the past, and surveys of the present, with better informed guesses about future behaviour which we then call planning.

In principle, this attempt to instil some tidiness into the process is not a bad thing. It is when the precise conceptual tools, the welter of mathematics and pseudo-logical abstractions, threatens to divorce itself entirely from the real world, that we run into trouble. To educate someone to be a mathematician, a logician, a philosopher, is clearly as worthy an activity as to bring him up to be a linguistic analyst or a theologian. It is when the abstract activity is being taken as a substitute for the real world, and when the future practitioner infers, perhaps not by the intention of his masters, that his diagrammatic representation can help him to understand the processes of the real world, that the disasters begin.

We have to be clear about what we mean by 'understanding'. Let us take an example. A household lives nearer to a minor shopping centre B than to a first order centre A. B can only be reached by private transport, it offers less choices and its prices are higher, but the atmosphere in its small shops is more friendly. A can be reached by public or private transport, though parking is difficult. Prices are lower, there is more competition and other activities can be combined with shopping. Behind these banal facts we observe, lurking as it were and competing for our attention, two entirely different approaches to planning: one, rational scientific optimizing, presenting us with networks, gravity models and the theory of intervening opportunity; the other, leading us to observe the fundamental irrationality of human behaviour, the impossibility of predicting what people will do next, even in the face of the most obvious pushes in the 'right' direction by the planners, when they exercise their choices, or their tastes change with their incomes. Now so long as we know that we have to 'understand' shoppers' behaviour in both senses, no harm is done. Unfortunately, since planning is taught mostly by minor practitioners relying on other people's textbooks, the formal approach tends to prevail, and the unnecessary complications involved with the other, more humanistic form of 'understanding' goes by the board.

Let us take another field. We know that government is a chaotic mess of pressures and counter-pressures, special interest groups, sometimes complicated by changes in boundaries, allocation of functions, not to speak of corruption or sheer, everyday incompetence at all levels. The 'new' planning's answer to this is to set up extremely tidy prototypes of management systems, usually borrowed from industrial organization. It is here that cybernetics has played such a large role. The result has been the introduction (and speedy withdrawal) of devices which bore fashionable names, like government (or management) by objectives, Planning, Programming and Budgeting systems; corporate management. Following a number of official investigations into the practice of government (from Mallaby through Maud to Bains) (14.24), local authorities have slavishly tried to adopt this or other re-structured system of administration, paid lip service to the desiderata of the academic textbooks—but, it appears, have in practice carried on as before.

Although some of the most recent texts of the 'new management' school have become more elaborate, one also detects a fresh note of modesty in some of the better ones (14.25), based on the early experience of those authorities which have attempted, perhaps halfheartedly, to put some of the new techniques into practice, and found them to have validity only in the hands of practitioners already endowed with a degree of experience, perspicacity, critical faculty and commonsense, that the text book teaching was almost superfluous, whereas in the hands of the uninitiated (and especially the student), good advice becomes a prescriptive instruction, and leads to doomed attempts to apply on the ground the neat diagrams of the treatises.

Now we have observed that very often those who were charged with putting the new management into practice were re-educated on post-experience courses, sent to staff colleges, (or later to the new School of Advanced Urban Studies set up following the Sharp Report, etc. at Bristol) (14.26) or any one of dozens of short conversion, instruction or indoctrination exercises which every university or polytechnic seems to offer. So why was this education not enough? Because it was too short? Hardly, since some of these courses lasted for a year or more. Because its recipients were not intelligent enough, or the teaching too superficial? It seems unlikely.

It is far more probable that it was the sheer irrelevance of the formal systems that are presented at these institutions that made the graduates forget very quickly what they had learned, when they returned to the real life situation. Sometimes, they would admit that they benefited because, thanks to their formal analysis training, they were able to think more clearly about the nature of the actual muddle they face in their daily lives. This is laudable. It is an attitude of mind, however, which can probably be equally well instilled by playing chess, learning computer programming, or doing crossword puzzles. However, once this aid to systematic thinking is made to appear as if it were an attainable end-state, or if the impression were created that the model was in some ways related to the real world as that of the Double Helix is to the structure of protein, incalculable harm is done.

Of course, this substitution of an artefact derived from first principles by a deductive process is not confined to the new managerial and scientific planning procedures. We find it equally in the generalizations of modern urban sociology, especially of the Marxist variety, where the most complex events and relationships are reduced to extremely over-simplified and sometimes downright crude assertions of states which are simply labelled 'state capitalism' or 'neo-colonialism' or 'racism'. In some senses the sociologists are even worse when they resort to this kind of abstraction, because whereas in the managerial 'sciences' there is emerging something like a corpus of agreed knowledge, which has even been empirically tested in the laboratory-like atmosphere of experiments in firms, the sociologists insist each on inventing his own system, his own language, and producing yet another 'model' of urban society, each as untestable as its predecessor, and as irrelevant as an analytical tool. To say that regional policy is a form of neo-colonialism has a slight flavour of bizarre originality about it, but it does not actually help the planner to think systematically about the objective of regional economic policy, or to evaluate results, since the object of a 'sociology of regionalism' of this sort is simply to prove that a late capitalist society is incapable of planning anything except in the form of yet another desperate attempt to save itself from extinction by revolution.

However interesting one may find the suggestions contained in these words, their overweening claims to explain how 'the system' works invalidates them. Naturally, the student welcomes books which explain everything there is to be known between two hard covers, or better, of which a bad teacher can claim that they are the 'key' books—a claim the authors would often repudiate. There is in fact an interesting contrast between the relative modesty, the reservations, the admitted constraints and limited applicability, the warnings about taking every suggestion as normative, which abound in the best of these new planning books, and the exaggerated deference which is paid to usually vulgarized abbreviations of their main conclusions, in the way they are used.

The way to a balanced education

Almost every one of the numerous publications dealing with planning education, which have appeared in the last few years, has used the word 'unbalanced' in relation to the existing syllabus. But such a negative agreement does not imply that the various authors could agree what constitutes 'balance' (14.27). In the end, as has been said, agreement could only be reached on the formalistic content of the course: the 'new' planning methods. Perhaps, let it be said, this is the fault of the immature social sciences: since no consensus could be created, especially amongst sociologists, as to a proper syllabus for intending planners, one could only fall back on the 'scientific' system of analysis. Thus, from the start, a new imbalance was built into the way planners were educated.

Let us take the systems approach as a starting point. Those familiar with Brian McLoughlin's *Urban and Regional Planning: a Systems Approach* are almost universally full of praise for its logic, its relevance, and its educational value. It is, arguably, the most widely used planning textbook in British institutions. Yet the interpretation of what McLoughlin has to say seems to fall short of his own ideals. Briefly, if the teacher (or pupil) has the wide humanistic background, the broad interests, and the catholic reading of the author, then such a book is invaluable. Behind all the scientific lay-out there is the over-riding assertion: *nihil humanum mihi est alienum*. But if the reader knows nothing of the human condition, the systems approach, which is to be seen as an aid to analysis, becomes planning in itself, and that was never intended. By now, the use of the word 'system' has been so vulgarized, away from the original test, and reduced to an entirely illegitimate analogy with 'systems' as seen in engineering production, that the educational advantage has been quite lost. To some extent this may be said to be McLoughlin's fault, because of his own (sometimes apparently uncritical) acceptance of cybernetics as his starting point, because of his admitted admiration for systems engineering, because of his facility for diagrams which to the casual observer, who cannot be bothered to read the qualifying text, *appear* to reduce the whole complexity of the urban structure to something that is comprehensible in a single page. (In the work of G.F. Chadwick, this danger is even greater, as it is in all those who attempt to give mathematical rather than diagrammatic expression to this structure.)

The common limitation to these approaches is that insofar as they represent anything, it is only the process, not the objective (or the end product), let alone conflicting objectives or obstacles to implementation. Much as McLoughlin stresses this point, it is overlooked because that part of the planning progression is mostly *not* reducible to diagrams or equations, or only in terms of simple financial or resources trade-offs. The essential message of inter-relatedness, which is indisputable, undoubtedly penetrates, but shorn of its most important concomitant: that the strength of the direction of pressures, and therefore the end result, is of itself a different phenomenon from the existence of the linkages.

The same is even more true of the management approaches. The odious line-diagrams which adorn every cheap primer on urban organization have left their mark on the badly-trained planner. He believes, implicitly, in the correctness of a certain structure: it seems rational, complete, effective in terms of the identifiable tasks. There is no fault to be found with the sequence of events which lead from the first identification of a planning 'problem' to the final implementation of a scheme, as almost all the systematic authors portray this sequence. The fact that they differ from each other quite fundamentally is not in itself a reproach; often the number of times a feedback loop is required, or for the sake of simplicity a two-way flow of information and decision-making is reduced to a *sens unique* (because the draughtsman did not want to clutter the diagram too much), are matters of accident. And, textually, verbally, and in their own practice, these authors invariably point out that in the real world every situation is different, both direction and strength of communication within the decision-making process are determined by the strength of individuals, historical accidents of seniority, inertia, or even political chicanery and corruption. It follows that such 'systematic' learning *must* be counter-balanced, not only by a prior knowledge of the real world, but also by the guidance of other disciplines which take it for granted that such abstractions are meaningless by themselves. One remembers the great shock, as a student, of finding, not only that competition, in the economic world, was by no means perfect, but that there was an 'Economics of imperfect competition' (14.28), and later still, that monopoly, oligopoly, and downright fraud on the consumer, who was far from sovereign, were the norm.

This brings us to another general point. We still stick far too much to the peculiar British system where a man or a woman goes to school once (quite often now for 21 consecutive years) and then never again. Having been divorced from the real world from his kindergarten days to the award of his MPhil, he then finds the world he enters so utterly different from that portrayed by his textbooks and their incompetent interpreters, that he discards almost everything, and starts from scratch, but with such ineradicable cynicism and disbelief now built into him by this simple transition that he never uses the excellent ideas of some of his texts again. It was the recognition of this likelihood that led to Lady Sharp's report, and the establishment of the School for Advanced Urban Studies, in Bristol, to other post-experience courses, staff colleges and so on. But the basic lesson was never learnt: that planning can only be taught to someone who has already been educated in the very broadest sense, who then goes out into the real world for a few years, and then returns to approach his vocational training with scepticism rather than cynicism. Every planning teacher knows the difference. The most un-rewarding students are those who swallow the formalistic abstractions wholesale, whether they emanate from Britton Harris, Karl Marx or Max Weber.

None of this is new. In their succinct publication, *Education for planning,* the authors and editors, who included McLoughlin and other leading exponents of formal methodology, were clear about what was required:

"The kinds of choice with which planning is concerned are broadly: choice as to goals and objectives: where we want to go and when we want to be there;
choice as to policies and programmes that will get us there (and selection of information and methods of analysis to be used in generating policies);
choice as to means: raising and allocating resources to implement the policies and programmes;
and finally, choice about organisation itself, the nature of its management structure and planning processes.
Beyond that, however, we have to determine with what characteristics this planning principle will endow the governing process, and our reading of current opinion and our own views led us to the following formulation. We believe that the community is likely to seek a planning process whereby urban governance will become: 1. anticipatory, 2. analytical, 3. objective-oriented, 4. evaluative, 5. innovatory, 6. apparent, 7. responsive, 8. connective, 9. effective and 10. adaptive" (14.29).

Did the authors of these admirably compressed maxims not realize that the normal planning education process will simply ignore that which is not reducible to simplistic formulae, and concentrate on what can be compressed into diagrams and equations? In other words, is it because the discussion about the future of planning was entrusted to people who could never sink to the depths of social illiteracy displayed by many practising planners, and even planning teachers, that they are so little concerned about the way their own advice would be interpreted?

Every competent planner will of course, when faced with a real-life situation, concentrate on consciousness (or awareness) and push the formalistic approach firmly into the background. Planners will tolerate a high degree of abstraction for the purposes of model-building, and put up with the most absurd assumptions in order to make the model computable, but they will never accept the print-out as anything more than a guide to what would happen if the real world did not exist. (A good analogy is the position of a demographer who will cheerfully write a programme for a population projection on any assumptions one chooses to give him, or he chooses to write into his preface, about the continuation, or otherwise, of existing trends. He will then obtain his projection, and if pressed, will give his personal opinion as to which of the underlying assumptions, if any, stand a chance of deserving the epithet 'probable', or 'most likely'. Beyond that he will not go. (14.30)) This of course is exactly what the best authorities tell him to do, and the standard textbooks and United Nations Manuals on the subject tend to devote as much time to stating their special assumptions, caveats, and reasons why projections are unlikely to be usable as forecasts, let alone prediction, as to the projection techniques themselves. On the face of it, retreat into academic isolation becomes respectable, and indeed mandatory, and the model planner sees no reason why he should not follow the same road.

But in our world, planners were brought up on the great urban land use and transportation models of the fifties in the USA and the sixties in Britain, which cost more than all other forms of planning research and education put together, and which turned out to be practically worthless, because they assumed that the world would go on as it was. In rather simplified words, planners, of all people, who are concerned with creating an environment to last at least for two or three generations, have been brought up to believe in the most static of all dynamic processes: where indeed the world changes but according to constant trends, and where political decisions can safely be taken on abstractions culled purely from past experience, or worse still, from a single point-in-time survey. Anything more unscientific it is hard to imagine. The acceptance of these models proves more than anything to the total inadequacy of planning education: they should have been rejected as mere *jeux d'esprit* before they were ever put on a computer. But we do not learn from past experience. At the time of writing, there are still many people who believe, not in Jay Forrester's *Urban Dynamics* (14.31), but, worse still, in the so-called models computed by his disciples, like the Meadows (14.32), with their total disbelief in any learning process, deep pessimism about the human ability to change, adapt, react, let alone invent and innovate.

If planning is about anything, it is about change, and the inadequacy of the vulgar interpretation for the formal approaches lies in the predisposition of the reader to assume that change is either impossible or uni-directional modified only by invariant feed-back processes.

The in-bred profession

If one reads what the authors of the apparently rigid systems produce (whether they call themselves planners, spatial geographers, or urban sociologists is immaterial), one realizes that they can only survive because they totally shut themselves off, not just from the evolving world, but from scientific principles of the most elementary kind, let alone from the precepts of a teacher like Karl Popper for whom (if he has ever had time to read them) those closed approaches must be as horrifying as his own worst examples of inventors of structures for closed societies. In other words, it is only by assuming away the idea that planning is for, by and about people, that one can believe in the diagrams and equations. Now such a sentiment is in itself brash, obvious, vulgar, and only serves usefully as a choice for titles of books which play variations on this theme (14.33). But there is a deeply serious side to it. Once the student is encouraged to take a critical stance outside the planning process, either as it actually takes place, or as it is portrayed in the texts, he can begin his synthesis of learning. But since this would lead him to question the easily learned paradigms, he is not encouraged to go outside. Every planning teacher remembers a graduate student who begins his essay: 'Faced with the last desperate attempts of dying monopoly capitalism, Gladstone introduced some regulation of the railway companies, even threatening them with nationalization if they did not conform'. One then asks, as gently as one can, what is meant by 'dying'.It turns out to be a term without time scale, without any intention even to produce an analogy, let alone a prediction, and to be simply an epithet much of the kind which delighted Homer, for whom no dawn could be anything but rosy-fingered. But then he did not live in contemporary England, any more than the believers in the formalistic and normative approaches to planning.

Yet it is precisely some of the inventors of the 'new planning' and again notably McLoughlin, who have shown the way out of this dilemma, who have done most to modify the ridiculous assumptions which their casual readers used to digest their books. (Just as Willmott and Young, who in their book on Bethnal Green (14.34), were supposed to have 'killed' the idea of urban renewal, have done more than anyone to remind us there is not a single pattern, or urban structure, for which a single planning prescription will hold good. (14.35))

It is precisely when we are exhorted to be 'problem-orientated', when every single handbook on structure plans, on management, on model-building even, tells us to begin with objectives, that the game is given away before we have begun to play. In hungry times, children had to eat pudding (i.e. suet, flour and water) before they could touch the exiguous amount of meat that their parents could afford. The systems approach, cybernetics, network analysis, these are meaty dishes. But let the prentice planner first eat his pudding— the problem, the objective, and when he has digested this lump, let him loose on the rest. But the problem is shrugged away as being there anyway, and not worth discussing, just as the objective is dismissed as being a matter for political decision-makers.

But this will not do. The successive stages of research, data accumulation (or retrieval), the identification of alternative modes of procedures, the formulation of choices to be made; the strategies to be outlined and the methods of implementation to be taught, all depend, in themselves, on problems, and the objectives in relation to these problems: they have no life of their own. And this is where planning education falls down because it constantly pretends, in practice, that this separation (which as we have said the protagonists of the new approaches would never allow themselves) can exist in fact. The theory (if any) behind this assumption is that it is quite immaterial whether the problem is one of congestion or empty space; whether it is one of excessive growth or no growth at all, whether the objective is one of maximum GNP or its more equitable distribution; all this is a matter of no moment: the systems approach is, after all, applicable under all circumstances. So it is, once one realizes that it is not a single approach, and that no single diagram can serve the different situations. Thus, in the good old days, when the public did not exist in the planner's consciousness, procedures appropriate to an autocratically run and highly automated munitions factory, or the conduct of a war, were perfectly acceptable. When planning has to start from the community or the grass roots (questionable as this demand may be), the sequence just outlined does not apply, nor can it be stood upon its head by starting with implementation. We have to go back to Robert Owen for that to be possible (14.36).

Secondly, because of the intense desire to avoid the inevitable, 'problems', or 'objectives', when mentioned at all, are invariably reduced to second or third order types. Traffic bottlenecks, lack of open space, polluted water courses or an absence of indoor lavatories do not present problems, nor is their removal an objective, or only of a very primitive kind. Tactically of course it may be important that ambulances should be able to get from an accident at Marylebone Station to University College Hospital in three minutes, or that 15 species of fish should be theoretically swimming under the Albert Bridge. Aesthetically, the preservation of New Scotland Yard may be of first order importance to some art historians. But such short-term localized, matters are for tactical consideration. The underlying problems are those connected with the choices to be made, at the start, of a distributional nature (and this again is stressed over and over again, both by the politically neutral advocates of a particular systems theory, and by the extreme advocates of *laissez faire*, or state control, or community control).

The trend one observes is towards more extreme polarization of views, so that what looked at one time like moving towards a consensus—perhaps at the time of Daniel Bell's *End of Ideology* (14.37), is now again resolved into extreme positions. Milton Friedman may write for large popular audiences, and F. von Hayek can be dismissed as a superannuated Austrian survival of a World that died in 1914, but this would be dangerous. In Britian, people like Alan Walters have resurrected the virtues of the market economy, partly with the help of the Institute of Economic Affairs, so that the do-nothing, subsidize-nothing, prohibit-nothing, encourage-nothing stance is once more becoming respectable, in the face of apparently irrefutable technical proof that the market can sort out the preference of individuals better than planners (14.38). Conversely, the more extreme left wing demands for the total takeover, not indeed by the State, but by 'the people' or the 'community' are becoming more insistent, and signs are multiplying that if this cannot be done peacefully, it may be done by violence masquerading as industrial action.

So there are still choices to be made, and only when this has been done, and always remembering that they may change over time, we can begin to think about the process. That all this is aggravated by lack of economic growth, is by now commonplace in most countries which have recently begun to suffer recession or even just stagnation, but it applied equally in periods of growth (14.39). And with this realization there goes overboard any pretence to neutrality, value-free modelling, or lack of concern with end-states, however intermediate they may be.

Then to take refuge behind words like 'flexibility', 'the need for robustness', 'constant monitoring', 'annual reappriasals', is merely to shirk the issues: either we really keep the situation open, and therefore destroy the value of the fixed diagram or equation, or we close it off and shut our eyes, as we do in war-time. Either we assume that an optimal allocation of resources can be made centrally, or we say that devolution is now so serious a matter that any orderly process of central decision-making must go by the board, so long as people can make their own mistakes. Sometimes, at this stage, the planning texts pray in aid the supposed guides to human behaviour—games theory for instance. Sometimes, bereft of any other mathematical approach to a situation which already had more equations in it than the computer can handle, we talk about stochastic processes. We talk about cities as if, like radio-active substances, they have a half-life, giving the planner the option of concerning himself only with the first small slice of their total existence, leaving the remainder to timeless speculation. Irritating as it may seem, science just misleads us in these circumstances. But we should not be irritated by the fact that planning is not scientific, just because it deals with the response of human beings to an intolerable, or at least, unsatisfactory, environment. That response can be resigned, cowed, passive, conditioned by years of authoritarian rule, or it can be revolutionary, or at least non-accepting, obstructive, to the point of standstill. We have seen both varieties in the UK in the space of ten short years. Only very poor planning education, or poor education before planning training, could produce such a surprise.

The planner's office requires him to be constantly aware of the changes in the world around him. But these changes require him to rethink his assumptions, strategies, tactics. One famous model-maker, whose London economic model is said to have had 1700 variables built into it, was reputed to have said that he could produce a new (land use and resources allocation) plan for London in a day, if you told him which inputs to change. In his isolated world, this was true. But in the world we live in, the completion of the Kingston By-Pass according to the 1930 plan will take 40 years, or 60 years to translate the Birmingham Inner Ring Road from the drawing board into an actuality, all too visible (14.40). This is the nub of the matter. When we are dealing with large, indivisible, objects, we either stick to the implementation of a plan almost regardless of its relevance by the time it is put into effect, or we resort to total inactivity, as being both cheaper and politically less dangerous. (In case planners have not noticed it, they are far more often, and more viciously attacked, for doing something, or even planning to do something, than for doing nothing, because the opponents of action are educated, articulate, single-minded, and successful, and those who would gain from action are cowed, under-privileged, unorganized and poor.)

The advocates of systematic planning will say that all such trivial generalizations are perfectly subsumable under the headings they have created, and every model-maker will say that all he needs to do is to build a delay fuse into his feed-back loop labelled 'consultation'. But these are not answers to the central dilemma. What the architects, the civil engineers, the self-taught geniuses and the amateurs once could do (create splendid cities, landscapes, amenities, plan, water, dry out and change beyond recognition), the modern professional planner apparently cannot do. Some would say that this is progress. Some would claim that it is societal changes that have made this profession redundant. One must not believe this, because there are 'plans that pleased', (14.41), and in some places houses, schools, shops, and recreational facilities are still being built, landscaped, inhabited, used and enjoyed, especially in other countries, some of which have no planning profession at all. One should therefore resist the temptation to absolve the planner from all blame. But especially one should cut off his refuge, the fantasy world he has created in the shape of the 'new syllabus'.

When we discuss the relevance of these new techniques, we are of course assuming that we are dealing with enlightened people who really wish to play a role in society. That in itself is a dangerous assumption. The great mass of traditional planners (who by definition make up the majority of the membership of the professional institute,) must ensure three things: one, that they are not labelled backwoodsmen because they do not understand the new planning; two, that they are not ousted from their posts by those who would make planning a social science; and three, that they fulfill their promise to those whom they have attracted as recent recruits to the profession, culled from the uneducated, that they shall have as good a chance in life as the initiated. The first two objectives may be selfish, the third laudably altruistic. It is useless to speculate, but one must quote what the Institute itself says:

"The social, economic and physical aspects of the broad planning process are intricately interlinked and interacting. Here it is assumed that the RTPI's professional concern is with that part of this process which focusses on the physical environment, both urban and rural, and the functioning of society within it, and hence with the education of professional planners in such ways as may fit them to deal with the matters involved.

242

'However, this concern cannot be narrowly confined to the physical environment alone, which constantly changes and requires modification in relation to society's needs; it must also extend to include the identification of social and economic needs and the means for their satisfaction insofar as these are related to the physical environment and, conversely, with the regulation, and if need be with the limitation, of the impact that the satisfaction of society's expressed needs will have on the physical environment," (14.42).

To reject the social management role is to be arrogant, not humble. Arrogant, because it assumes that technology is superior to the hesitant process of thinking about one's social aims. To ask that physical planning should have 'regard' to social desiderata is like saying that the practising doctor should have 'regard' for human life—the rest is technology. This is clearly nonsense, for the doctor begins from the assumption that the normal human body is healthy, functioning, and enjoying this functioning, and all else is pathological.

"Some test of relevance in relation to general objectives may be helpful in determining, within the context of a particular course, the range and depth of treatment required for any one of the elements set out above. While the Institute does not feel it appropriate to lay down detailed rules concerning minimum contact-hours or the precise manner in which individual subjects and courses should be developed, they will need to be satisfied that the internal structure of any course, as a whole, clearly reflects the following principles concerning the relevance and scope of the subjects to be covered:

(a) That the major focus of interest throughout the course is planning for the physical environment in relation to the needs of society and that other subjects are considered in relation to this central theme.
(b) That in each field of knowledge a satisfactory balance is maintained between the academic (theory and principle) and the professional (practice and procedures) aspects of the subject so as to ensure that candidates receive a broadly-based treatment which is at the same time directly related to the professional practice of environmental planning.
(c) That the range of planning skills should be developed specifically in relation to the environmental planning process" (14.43).

Towards a constructive alternative

Criticizing other people's planning ideas or syllabuses is of course easy. It is the mainstay of our literature. Therefore one is bound at least to make the effort to put something else in the place of what has been rejected or held up to ridicule.

Are there, indeed, elements in the education of the planner which can be identified as having such permanent value that one can confidently put them forward for serious consideration by planning schools? Or is it just back 25 years to the Schuster Committee (14.44), calling for the planner as a whole man, rejecting the amalgamation of skills so satirically dismissed by Alonso (14.45), and saying, in effect, planning is a game that anyone can play, provided they have a good general education, are observant, receptive, and know enough of the rudiments of other skills to be able to give adequate instructions to lower species of specialists, like draughtsmen and computer programmers, and to judge the adequacy of the output of these principal helpers? This would be merely a studied insult to pay back a score incurred a few years ago when a few social scientists were invited to a TPI meeting because of the importance of their 'ancillary skills'.

To begin with, nothing can be excluded *a priori*, on the grounds that it does not concern the planner, if we have started planning with the notion that it is an all-embracing activity. However, simply because we do not have time to do everything, we have to make the same sort of choices which, professionally, we have postulated the planner himself must make in the exercise of his profession. I believe the same rules apply. In other words, it is not possible to say that relevant planning education syllabuses can be made permanent. If, on the other hand, we keep on changing the syllabus to adapt ourselves to new circumstances, it is also self-evident that every planner brought up in a different world must go back to school as it were, and learn what the new situation requires. The fact that at present he neither thinks he needs it, nor is enabled by near-bankrupt local authorities or central government departments to take advantage of such courses as are offered, is relevant in the long run. Planning can only succeed if at any one time, every member of the team, from county directors down to administrative assistants, is aware of the changing circumstances, of new approaches, ideas, and especially changes in direction in other fields of urban management with which the planner must associate closely.

One would begin, I believe, with a knowledge of the history, and evolution of the ideology of planning as a professional activity (14.46). Only as late as 1975 did we see the beginnings of a study group to look at the history of planning in an international, comparative, and analytical way. Courses on planning ideology tended to be very one-sided, confined to those sociologists to whom 'ideology' in relation to government had become synonymous with 'reactionary capitalist-imperialist-monopolist ideology'. This will not do, and we have to show the future planner the evolution of the ideas with which he works, over a long period of time, and in more than one country, to enable him to distinguish between what, in his activity, his transitory, a passing cloud, a recent innovation- what is insular and parochial; and what, on the other hand, are the common characteristics of the attempt to intervene in the free-market determination of land use patterns and environmental evolution (14.47).

The second permanent element should probably be some knowledge of one or other of the systematic, quasi-scientific approaches to the planning problem, or perhaps even more than one, on the strict understanding that such techniques are always explained with all their limitations; that their relative failure as tools of urban management, at least so far, is not only admitted but analyzed, and that the future planner learns the difference between an abstraction and a prescriptive structure. What this involves by way of educating the planning educators, has still to be thought out, since in practice all too often planning teachers are themselves naive consumers of other people's ideas, which they regurgitate uncritically because that is the easiest thing to do. The ideal exposition of the academic, model-making, analytical approach to planning would be almost wholly critical, allowing the student to read the books recommended, and then pointing out why, in practice, what he has just read is, at best, an aid to analytical thinking, and at worst simply misleading.

Thirdly, by way of making the transition from the ideal, or totally abstract world to the world in which we live and work, a much stronger element of 'social science' is required. One uses this portmanteau word in the full knowledge that much of what passes as social science is in fact woolly-minded, quite unscientific, ideologically strongly biased, and potentially as useless, if not dangerous, as the planning science approach already outlined.

Thus most of the outlines of 'urban sociology' courses are not about urban sociology at all, but about the iniquity of capitalist society; or, to take the other extreme, merely statistical expositions of social structure; or histories of modern society. But it is not necessary to choose to be so one-sided, and again the main component of social science teaching must be the critical exposition of a few of the larger number of varieties of urban sociologies (14.48) which are now available; point out how they contradict and attack each other, and leaving the intending planner not with a fixed idea of *a* modern industrial society, or *an* urban system in an under-developed antheap, but with the fact that the analyses of human interactions within the urban situation is possible with a variety of approaches, ranging from quite abstract models again to the use of 'hard' social indicators.

The same can be said of urban economics (though this subject is in much less disarray than urban sociology) and, as we have pointed out, political science: the indispensable understanding of the power structures of our modern urban societies, the forces at work which mould and change this society; the institutions which control us (or fail to do so), the processes whereby change comes about (14.49).

Perhaps one should mention, under this heading, the development, and now perhaps the incipient demise, of the science of cost-benefit analysis, one of those blind alleys (for planners) which were devised to be a useful auxiliary tool in rational decision making processes, but which, in the hands of zealots turned into something with a life of its own, unrelated to the original objective. In Britain, as we have pointed out before, it fell into disrepute in the days of the Roskill Commission, but in the hands of people like Beesley and Foster (14.50) who investigated the Victoria Line and the M1 motorway, it undoubtedly had its uses; the possibility of using it in a not strictly quantified way was shown to effect by Nathaniel Lichfield (14.51) and in the most recent period, highly sophisticated but nevertheless policy-relevant attempts have been made to apply cost benefit analysis to larger questions of the environment, notably by David Pearce, Alan Williams and Alan Walters (14.52). Some of these techniques, with the usual caveats, ought to be known to every planner though at present the literature is still very highly specialized and often not easily accessible.

Another special variant, still under the heading of economics, though strictly speaking a field claimed by natural scientists, is EIA (Environmental Impact Analysis), a special form of cost-benefit analysis based on measurement of matters like pollution, noise, erosion, landscape evaluation, resource depletion, etc. by now highly developed, especially in the United States, but again, like CBA and Social Indicators, well on the way to taking off into the higher reaches of self-contained lunacy where the relevance to the planner's education is quite marginal (14.53).

The fourth permanent element in any planning course must be something we can only call 'the state of the art'—and this needs annual revision. Starting from wherever the historical account left off (one suspects with the 1968 legislation, at least from a 1976 standpoint), one must teach aspiring planners how far the law has changed, what is in the pipeline, what further changes are contemplated, what important institutional changes are, at the time of teaching, likely to make most difference to the way planning is carried out. Thus, one would have imagined that in a course lasting from 1974-76, the 1972 and 1974 Housing Acts, the 1975 Community Land Act, and the implementation of local government reform, against a background of economic and demographic stagnation, would have been the backbone of a course to prepare the planner for the world in which he finds himself—with the caveat that, five years hence, his pre-occupations may be quite different ones.

The fifth element which one imagines as a permanent component of the planner's education, is education for management. This involves not only a knowledge of structures and the personal relationships within them, but also every aspect of communication, upwards, downwards and especially sideways. It might be called 'making the planner effective'. It should not, in its essentials, differ from the sort of instruction that is given to aspiring industrial managers, senior teachers, middle rank civil servants, or officers in the armed forces. The fact that planning need not be organized in hierarchies appropriate to these other branches of activity, is irrelevant: what is important is that the question of *effectiveness* must somehow be brought into the centre of the stage. Effectiveness does not mean the completion on time of a six-level interchange in the middle of a conservation area: it means rather that, once the goals have been set, objectives identified, and agreed, there are better and worse ways, slower and quicker processes of implementing environmental change—or even ensuring standstill. It is the planner as the effective manager—despised, ignored, held up to public ridicule, which distinguishes him, say, from the accountant who makes the budget of a local authority balance: he is an effective manager if, at the end of the year, he has kept his expenditure within the limits he was set. This is a different question from that whether the limits were right, the cuts justly distributed, or indeed the objectives adequate: what matters is the attainment of the goal, however limited. All too often the planner sees the multi-coloured, two dimensional plan, or the three dimensional balsawood model, as his end product. It is not. This is an activity behind closed doors. Effective management implies the securing of a desired change on the ground, but, as we shall point out, failure to do so is not always a sign of ineffectiveness.

To these five core elements one could add many options, alternatives, modifications. There is, indeed, in these suggestions, no *a priori* thought of standardization, because only after the core streams can the real education of the planner begin. And at this stage we abandon textbooks, lectures, visual aids, models, computers and indeed the idea of teacher and taught. The next stage consists of making future planners aware, sensitive, receptive, without totally losing their orientation, a consciousness of their role, or the courage to play that role. Here we deal with skills which, time and again, one sees blinkered academics trying to teach students by means of pre-conceived notions, textbook paradigms, and again the familiar flow diagrams. In fact the only effective way of learning the basic skill of being part of the community is to go out into it, to perform a task, however dirty, within that community, and then bring the experience of the real world back to the education process. There are, of course, all sorts of obstacles. The NUT might now allow a student planner to take a few hours of classroom time to try to bring environmental or ecological education into the curriculum. Social service departments are reluctant to take in planners as volunteer casework aides. So the only way open to those students who actually feel the need to dirty their hands as an antidote to the clinical neatness of their university courses, is to become activists, as they call it. Their activities will range from assisting squatters to leading protests against demolitions and closures, from being advocacy planners to barricade erectors (14.54). The pity of it is that this sort of activity, instead of being a normal and welcome part of the education of the planner, is in fact frowned upon, and disowned, by the heads of most planning schools. One can see their point of view: after all, they do not wish to be branded as producers merely of anti-planners. But this only occurs because the young planner is fobbed off with something usually, but misleadingly, called a 'project', in other words, a quite abstract exercise in which a few harmless survey questions at street corners are the nearest the student comes to an awareness of conflicts within his society. It is no wonder then that he breaks out, lends a ready ear to revolutionary theories, and in fact nullifies almost everything else he has learned or become interested in. It is the haphazard, grapevine, accidental introduction of the scandals of real life that makes a student planner so often disbelieve what he has been taught—because he knows one particular aspect to be untrue, or irrelevant, he tends to reject everything that has been presented to him. This is understandable. For the purpose of designing the education of planners, it is immaterial whether they discover in their first county planning jobs that the 1975 model structure plan already bears no resemblance whatever to the legislation of 1968 (14.55), or whether he finds that a high proportion of those rehoused by public housing departments express acute dissatisfaction with what they have got, whether through vandalism, demands for transfer, or rent strikes.

Planning education must be so organized, in fact, that the antithesis between textbook theory and later experience is never allowed to develop in the first place—that right from the start he knows that planning is often associated with failure. This is not to recommend a 'conflict theory of planning', merely to suggest that the non-attainment of at least a large part of one's paper ambitions is part of the iterative process of learning how to plan. This picks up again the theme of effective management: a planner can still be effective if his goal is the re-development of an area where at the end of the period 50% of those who wanted to stay are still in the area, 75% of those who have left are lodged in what the Americans call 'standard housing', and 90% of the dwellings in the block are, at the end of the period, in fit condition and ready to occupy if not actually filled. Because textbook planning pretends it can teach people 100% effectiveness, that management becomes ineffective, and disillusioning, and disbelief sets in. Probably the only way to build failure, non-attainment, the need for a new start, and the ability to withstand constant obloquy, into the planner's consciousness, is to expose him to this phenomenon from the start.

Our leading theorists are all agreed that uncertainty and surprise are the essence of planning (14.56). But having said this, the warning is immediately forgotten. It needs to be ever-present. All planning is surprise, a confrontation with the unexpected, resistance from precisely the quarter one had least thought would produce dissent. The aim of planning education should not be the elimination of this surprise element, but building it into the planner's consciousness: awareness must include the expectation that what one heard the day before yesterday, incorporated into a plan today, will turn out to have been wrong tomorrow, and that this does not constitute an invalidation of the planning process, only a judgment on how planners are educated.

It has long puzzled outside observers why, in the last 10 years, with all the availability of new approaches to planning education, with all the awful warnings available both in books and on the ground, our educational system still produces wide-eyed innocents—or else urban bureaucratic guerillas, bent on destroying the system they are paid to uphold. The answer may well be, once again, in the teachers themselves, because in the end they will so often go back on the uncertainty principle, as it were, and peddle their nostrums, after all, as if they could be made into cure-alls, sure shields against surprise and change.

"Thus all demands which would simultaneously deal with the ideas of systems, complexity, adaptability, learning, probabilism, positive and negative feedback, hierarchial structure, information, communication, conflict resolution, forecasting and learning *may be satisfied by recourse to cybernetic models of urban systems and urban planning processes.*" (my italics) (14.57).

Such a statement consists essentially of a series of double negatives. The planning dog has not only bitten its own tail, he has swallowed it, and thus he is condemned to be turned in on himself, to seek solutions within himself, or his skills, which belong to others in his world.

That this, in the end, cannot be taught in textbooks, and that the great majority of planning teachers are incapable of going beyond the banalities of mere acceptance of obvious generalizations, or at best, the higher mathematics of the more complex computer models, is the great failure of modern British planning education.

What has been said here could of course, with some justice, be said of the education of other practitioners as well. But somehow it matters less in dentists, electrical engineers, or accountants. Competence, success, and managerial skills (if any) are easily assessed. Those who cannot deliver the goods—sound teeth, bridges that stand up, books that balance, are incompetent and go out. The planners are much more in the case of, say social workers, remedial teachers, psychiatrists or even philosophers. Success and failure are subjective terms; social indicators to evaluate good performance have not been evolved; norms, fashions, received wisdoms, change constantly. So perhaps the constant return to the internal principle is not to be wondered at: no one likes to think they are quite so insecure that they are dependent for recognition purely on some external criteria invented by a bureaucratic machine, which is just as

THE EDUCATION OF PLANNERS

likely to reward inaction, or avoidance of commitment, as achievement.

This, to some extent, has always been so, but we must be aware that the circumstances of the world in which we live have vastly aggravated the problem. Somewhere, no doubt, in Cambridge, there is a small group of planners who can take some of the credit, and more of the brickbats, for the changes which that historic city's shopping centre is now under-going, and the traffic system which happened to be in force on 31 December 1975. But for every one such planner, there are hundreds who have worked hard at plans which were rejected, traffic schemes which were abandoned, regional shopping models that nobody wants.

It should come as no surprise to learn that the planner's prognoses are more often wrong than right; that what he produces on the ground, when he is allowed to perform at all, is reviled the moment it is taken into use; and that, having received his instructions in 1965, and carried them out in 1975, he must expect to be recalled as the most incompetent man of his age by a coming generation. On the other hand, the man whose plans never see the light of day, and more especially the academic theorist who cannot be proved right or wrong (except perhaps on the mathematics of an equation), and the teacher of planning in the university—all these are safe, and in due course, will receive their medals.

Planning education then is largely a question of learning about social processes rather than technical matters. But these social processes must not be forced into the absurd straight jackets of systems and diagrams learned by heart. They must remain in the mind of the student as living, adapting, notions, as volatile as the world itself. To be sure, values need not change in the individual's mind: nobody expects his conscience to behave like a chameleon. Nor need the politically desired ultimate goals vary: a juster distribution of wealth and income, a reduction of class barriers and social bitterness. What needs to change are the methods of attaining these goals. The whole point of this Chapter has been to point out that the nature of tactics to be pursued, and the current changes in social and economic climates, will affect even the abstractions of the theorists: the sequences of operation will not be the same, let alone the principles of implementation. To be aware of the permanence of change itself, and the ability to cope with it, should be the aim of planning education. Instead, both the Royal Town Planning Institute, and the theorists of planning, or rather their lesser interpreters, seem to be heading in the opposite direction, and this to ensure, from the start, the type of failure which leads to bitterness and disillusion, if not open rebellion, instead of a constructive recognition of a natural process.

The author is indebted to Mary Moody for undertaking the referencing of this chapter.

References

14.1   EDDISON, P.A. and EARWICKER, J., *The Demand for Planners*, Report to the Planning Committee of the S.S.R.C., 1976.

14.2   BELL, C. and BELL, R., *City Fathers: the Early History of Town Planning in Britain*, Penguin, 1972.

>   CHERRY, G. E., *Urban Change and Planning: a History of Urban Development in Britain since 1750*, G. T. Foulis, 1972.

14.3   KAYE, B., *The Development of the Architectural Profession in Great Britain; a Sociological Study*, Allen and Unwin, 1960.

14.4   MILLERSON, G., *The Qualifying Associations: a Study in Professionalisation*, Routledge & Kegan Paul, 1964.

14.5   CHERRY, G. E., *The Evolution of British Town Planning*, Leonard Hill, 1974.

14.6   EVERSLEY, D., *The Planner in Society: the Changing Role of a Profession*, Faber & Faber, 1973.

14.7   DIAMOND, D. and McLOUGHLIN, J. B., (Eds.), *Education for Planning: the Development of Knowledge and Capability for Urban Governance*, Report of a Working Group at the Centre for Environmental Studies, Pergamon, 1973.

>   'Education Policy: Guidelines for Planning School', *The Planner*, **60**, 7, July/August 1974, pp. 802-808.

>   GODSCHALK, D. E., (Ed.), *Planning in America: Learning from Turbulence*, American Institute of Planners, 1974.

>   OXFORD POLYTECHNIC, Oxford Working Papers in Planning Education and Research, e.g. No. 12, FALUDI, A., *The Specialist versus Generalist Conflict*, No. 4, FALUDI, A., *Sociology in Planning Education*.

14.8   DAVIES, J.G., *The Evangelistic Bureaucrat: Study of a Planning exercise in Newcastle-upon-Tyne*, Tavistock, 1972.

>   FRANKS, M., 'Liverpool: Resurrection or Decline', *Built Environment*, March, 1975, pp. 134-145.

14.9   My main debt is to the writings of J. B. McLoughlin and the Working Group at the Centre for Environmental Studies which produced *'Education for Planning'*, Pergamon, 1973.

14.10   EDDISON, P.A. and EARWICKER, J., *op. cit.*

14.11   EVERSLEY, D., *Planning without Growth*, Fabian Research Series 321, Fabian Society, 1975.

14.12   EDDISON, P.A. and EARWICKER, J., *op. cit.*

14.13 MURIE, A., *Household Movement and Housing Choice*, Centre for Urban and Regional Studies, Occ. Paper No. 28, University of Birmingham, 1974.

WATSON, C.J., *Household Movement in West Central Scotland*, Centre for Urban and Regional Studies, University of Birmingham, Occ. Paper No. 26, 1973.

14.14 LOMAS, G., *The Inner City*, A preliminary investigation of the dynamics of current labour and housing markets with special reference to minority groups in inner London, July, 1974, London Council of Social Service, April, 1975.

14.15 MINISTRY OF HOUSING AND LOCAL GOVERNMENT, *People and Planning*, Report of the Committee on public participation in planning, (Skeffington Report), HMSO, 1969.

14.16 REDPATH, R.U. and CHILVERS, D.J., 'Swinbrook: a Community Study Applied', *Greater London Intelligence Quarterly*, 26, Mar, 1974. pp. 5-17.

14.17 DEPARTMENT OF THE ENVIRONMENT, *Structure Plans. The Examination in Public*, DoE, 1973.

14.18 COMMUNITY ACTION, *Investigators Handbook, a Guide for Tenants, Workers and Action Groups on How to Investigate Companies, Organisations and Individuals*, 1975.

BROMHEAD, P., *The Great White Elephant of Maplin Sands*, Elek, 1973.

McKIE, D., *A Sadly Mismanaged Affair: a Political History of the Third London Airport*, Croom Helm, 1973.

14.19 DONNISON, D., 'Equality', *New Society*, 20 November 1975, pp. 422-424.

14.20 ADAMS, B., and others, *Gypsies and Government Policy in England*, Heinemann for C.E.S., 1975.

CHILD POVERTY ACTION GROUP, Guides to the Rights of Low Income Groups, e.g. *A Social Contract for Families*, No. 19, 1975.

HOLTERMANN, S., *Census Indicators of Urban Deprivation*, Working Note No. 6, ECUR Division, DOE, 1975.

14.21 LANCHESTER POLYTECHNIC, *Handbook*, 1975.

14.22 COCKBURN, C., *The Provision of Planning Education*, Information Paper 15, Centre for Environmental Studies, 1970.

REGIONAL STUDIES ASSOCIATION, *The New Planning Courses*, RSA, 1969.

14.23 McLOUGHLIN, J.B., *Urban and Regional Planning: a Systems Approach*, Faber & Faber, 1969.

CHADWICK, G., *A Systems View of Planning: Towards a Theory of the Urban and Regional Planning Process*, Pergamon, 1971.

FRIEND, J.K. and JESSOP, W.N., *Local Government and Strategic Choice*, Tavistock, 1969.

14.24 DEPARTMENT OF THE ENVIRONMENT, *New Local Authorities: Management and Structure*, (Bains Report), HMSO, 1972.

DEPARTMENT OF THE ENVIRONMENT, *Committee on the Management of Local Government Report*, 5 Vols., (Maud Report), HMSO, 1967.

COMMITTEE ON THE STAFFING OF LOCAL GOVERNMENT, *Staffing of Local Government*, (Mallaby Report), HMSO, 1967.

14.25 FRIEND, J.K., POWER, J.M. and YEWLETT, C.J.L., *Public Planning: the Intercorporate Dimension*, Tavistock, 1974.

14.26 MINISTRY OF TRANSPORT, *Transport Planning: the Men for the Job*, (Sharp Report), HMSO, 1970.

BRISTOL UNIVERSITY, School of Advanced Urban Studies, *Annual Report*, 1975.

14.27 DIAMOND, D. and McLOUGHLIN, J.B., (Eds.), *op. cit.*, p.35.

14.28 ROBINSON, J., *Economics of Imperfect Competition*, 2nd Ed., Macmillan, 1969.

14.29 DIAMOND, and McLOUGHLIN, J. (Eds.). *op. cit.*, pp. 53-54.

14.30 OFFICE OF POPULATION CENSUSES AND SURVEYS, *Variant Population Projections 1974-2011*, HMSO, 1975.

14.31 FORRESTER, J.W., *Urban Dynamics*, MIT Press, 1969.

14.32 MEADOWS, D.H. and others, *The Limits to Growth: a Report for the Club of Rome's Project on the Predicament of Mankind*, Earth Island, 1972.

14.33 BROADY, M., *Planning for People: Essays on the Social Context of Planning*, National Council of Social Service, 1968.

    MINISTRY OF HOUSING AND LOCAL GOVERNMENT, *People and Planning, op. cit.*

    DENNIS, N., *People and Planning: the Sociology of Housing in Sunderland*, Faber & Faber, 1970.

14.34 YOUNG, M. and WILLMOTT, P., *Family and Kinship in East London*, Pelican, 1957.

14.35 YOUNG, M. and WILLMOTT, P., *The Symmetrical Family: a Study of Work and Leisure in the London Region.*, Routledge & Kegan Paul, 1973.

    WILLMOTT, P., *The Evolution of a Community: Dagenham after Forty Years*, Routledge & Kegan Paul, 1963.

14.36 OWEN, R., *New View of Society, and Report to the County of Lanark*, edited by V.A.C. Gatrell, Penguin, 1970. Originally published 1821.

14.37 BELL, D., *End of Ideology*, Free Press, 1965.

14.38 HAYEK, F.A. and others, *Verdict on Rent Control*, Essays on the economic consequences of political action to restrict rents in five countries, Institute of Economic Affairs, 1972.

14.39 OLSON, M. and LANDSBERG, H.H., *The No-growth Society*, Woburn Press, 1975.

14.40 SUTCLIFFE, A., *Case Studies in Modern British Planning History: the Birmingham Inner Ring Road*, Paper submitted for discussion., History of Planning Group Meeting, 18 October 1975. Birmingham.

14.41 MITCHELL, E.B., *The Plan that Pleased*, Town and Country Planning Association, 1967.

14.42 'Education Policy: Guidelines for Planning Schools', *The Planner*, **60**, 7, July/August, 1974. p. 803.

14.43 *ibid.*, p. 805.

14.44 *Report of the Committee on Qualifications of Planners*, Cmd 8059, (Schuster Report), HMSO, 1950.

14.45 ALONSO, W., 'Beyond the Inter-disciplinary Approach to Planning', *Journal of the American Institute of Planners*, **37**, May, 1971, pp. 169-173.

14.46 SIMMIE, J., *Citizens in Conflict: the Sociology of Town Planning*, Hutchinson, 1974.

    BELL, C. and BELL, R., *op. cit.*

    CHERRY, G.E. *Urban Change and Planning: a History of Urban Development in Britain since 1750, op. cit.*

14.47 EVERSLEY, D., *The Planner in Society: the Changing Role of a Profession, op. cit.*

14.48 e.g. CAREY, L. and MAPES, R., *Sociology of Planning*, Batsford, 1972.

    MANN, P.H., *Approach to Urban Sociology*, Routledge & Kegan Paul, 1970.

    PAHL, R.E., *Whose City? And Other Essays on Sociology and Planning*, Longman, 1970.

14.49 ROSE, R., (Ed.) *The Management of Urban Change in Britain and Germany*, Sage, 1974.

14.50 BEESLEY, M.E. and FOSTER, C.D., 'The Victoria Line: Social Benefit and Finance'; *Journal of the Royal Statistical Society*, Series A, **128**, 1967, pp. 67-68.

14.51 LICHFIELD, N., 'Cost Benefit Analysis in Urban Expansion, a Case Study: Peterborough, *Regional Studies*. **3**, 2, Sept., 1969. pp. 123-155.

14.52 WALTERS, A., *Noise and Prices*, Oxford University Press, 1975.

PEARCE, D.W. and PETTMAN, B.O., *Research in Environment Economics in the UK 1974*, MCB Publications, 1975.

14.53 O'RIORDAN, T., *Report on the Seminar on Environmental Impact Assessment*, 15-16 November 1975, University of East Anglia.

14.54 The need for the dissatisfied young planner to present his dissident view point has given rise to a whole range of informal planning journals and newsletters ranging from an 'underground' format to a mere expansion of a radical standpoint.

Cf. *Planning*, published by Ambit Publications Ltd.; *Community Action, Architectural Association Newsletter; Forma* (based on the Oxford Polytechnic); *Social Audit* (supported by a Rowntree Trust); *Counter Information Service*.

14.55 THORBURN, A., 'The Annual Up-dating Method of Structure Planning', *Town and Country Planning*, April, 1975, pp. 219-221.

14.56 McLOUGHLIN, J.B., *Control and Urban Planning*, Faber & Faber, 1973, p. 146.

14.57 *ibid.*, p. 184.

Index

ARTISTS
LM